THE BALTIMORE SUN

baltimoresun.com

All images are available for reprinting and licensing on
http://baltimoresunstore.com/photos
by searching each image's street name.

MAN IN THE STREET

From Dirt Roads to Blacktop: A History of Baltimore Street Names

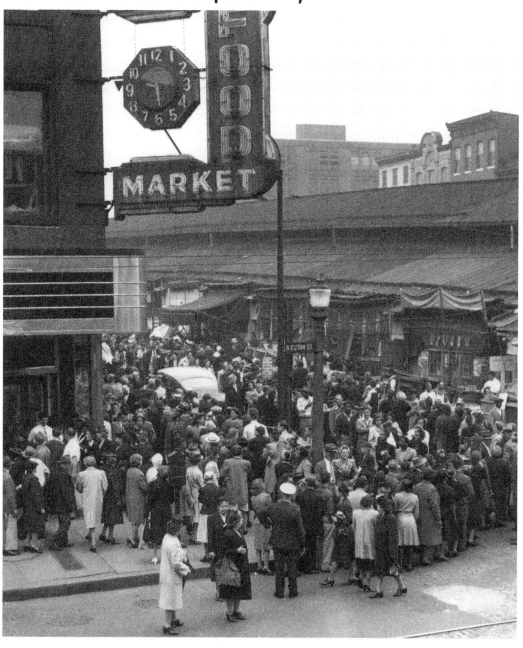

Man in the Street:
From Dirt Roads to Blacktop: A History of Baltimore Street Names
Copyright © 2014 The Baltimore Sun

All Rights Reserved. No part of this book may be used or reproduced
in any manner whatsoever without the written permission of the
Publisher. For information about reprints or licensing please address
the Baltimore Sun Store, 501 N. Calvert Street, Baltimore, Maryland
21278 or contact sunstore@baltsun.com.

Published by Lightning Source Inc.,
1246 Heil Quaker Boulevard
La Vergne, TN 37086

Library of Congress Control Number: 2014944613

ISBN-13: 978-1-893116-28-3

Cover photo: Redwood Street – 1948

Previous page photo: Eutaw Street – 1946

Opposite page photo: Charles Street – early 1900s

Hillen Road – 1941

FOREWORD

By Chris Kaltenbach ı The Baltimore Sun

Here's betting you thought Pratt Street was named for Enoch Pratt (just like the library was), that Redwood Street honors a bunch of tall trees and that Gay Street is a nod to the LGBT community.

Sorry, you're wrong on all counts. And how do we know that? Because of the invaluable — and under-appreciated — work of former Baltimore Sun reporter William Stump. From 1949 to 1954, he was the man primarily responsible for a series of semi-regular columns in The Sunday Sun, which are reprinted here, that unlocked one of Baltimore's most pervasive mysteries:

"Who are all these streets named after?"

Surely, that has been a puzzlement to young and old for decades, if not centuries. For unlike some more information-friendly cities — like Berlin, Germany, where street signs honoring individuals sometimes include thumbnail descriptions of who they were — Baltimore is apt to let fame speak for itself. And fame, as the cliché rightly notes, is fleeting.

Thus, while people may have little trouble realizing where the name Baltimore Street came from, and can probably figure that Fort Avenue is named for the national monument at its eastern end (the one that inspired "The Star-Spangled Banner"), do they know who the Erdmans were, or from where the name "Mondawmin" arose? Most people with at least a passing knowledge of Maryland history know the historical antecedent for names like "Calvert" (the family that founded the state), "Hopkins" (merchant and philanthropist Johns Hopkins) and possibly even "Latrobe" (a seven-term mayor of Baltimore in the last quarter of the 19th century). But quick: Who does Sisson Street honor?

And so we say, thank goodness for William Stump. A native of Orange, N.J., who was raised in Harford County, he was the son of a ship's physician and grandson of the founder of the Standard & Poor's financial ratings. A 1942 graduate of the St. James School in Hagerstown and an ambulance driver during World War II, Stump began writing for The Sun in 1949, after stints writing and editing in New York.

Local history was one of his favorite subjects, as one might surmise from this "Man in the Street" collection. He began it in 1949 with an article about John Potee, a two-term Baltimore sheriff; he appears to have ended the run in August 1954, with some facts on the name "Druid Hill."

(And don't be fooled by some of the other bylines that appear in this volume: Both James C. Bertram and Henry C. Rauch were simply pen names for Stump, who apparently didn't want to seem as prolific as he was. Other reporters such as Elizabeth H. Moberly and Ralph Reppert also helped write the columns.)

Readers will meet some fascinating characters while traveling the streets of Baltimore with William Stump as their tour guide. They'll meet Robert Oliver, whose estate would later become the site of Green Mount Cemetery; Lawrence B. McCabe, an engineer whose works include the rail tunnel under Howard Street (and whose son was a Kentucky Derby-winning jockey); businessman Henry Payson, who helped raise money to fortify Baltimore during the War of 1812; and Richard Caton, son-in-law of Charles Carroll of Carrollton and the man behind Catonsville.

We'll also wager there's plenty a bar bet to be won based on studying the fruits of William Stump's labors. Which Revolutionary War hero, for instance, has streets named for each of his three names? (That would be John Eager Howard.) What was Redwood Street's name before it was changed in 1918? (German Street, changed out of an abundance of patriotic fervor during World War I.) And just who is Pratt Street named for? (That would be not Enoch, but Charles Pratt, Earl of Camden, a British nobleman who fought for repeal of the Colonial-era Stamp Act.)

William Stump enjoyed a long career in journalism, most of it here in Charm City. After leaving The Baltimore Sun in the late 1950s, he was named editor of Gardens, Houses and People, a monthly publication focused on Baltimore's northern suburbs. From 1964 to 1968, he was editor of Baltimore magazine, then published by the Chamber of Commerce. He later went to work for the News American, where he remained until the paper closed in 1986.

William Stump died on Oct. 23, 2013, at age 90. His name may not live on in the names of any local thoroughfares, but thanks to the history he chronicled, he's remembered for the stories of the streets themselves.

Oh, and by the way: Redwood Street is named for 1st Lt. George Buchanan Redwood, the first Baltimore officer killed in France during World War I, while Gay Street bears the name of Nicholas Ruxton Gay, a surveyor in the early days of what was then known as Baltimore Town.

Abell family's estate — Guilford – Date unknown

A

August 17, 1952

Abell

By William Stump

Back in 1837, Baltimore had six daily newspapers — yet an out-of-towner named Arunah Shepherdson Abell figured there was room for one more.

For one thing, the existing papers each cost 6 cents, a price that the 31-year-old Abell was certain he could cut to a penny. More important, none of the papers printed local news; they functioned as mouthpieces for their owners' opinions, and their reporting, slanted outrageously to particular points of view, dealt usually with matters far removed from the interests of the majority of Baltimoreans.

Abell was more than theorizing when he concluded that a penny paper which aimed only to present impartial news would be a success. The Philadelphia Public Ledger, which he had founded a year earlier with William M. Swain and Azariah H. Simmons, had caught on and was doing very well indeed. It cost a penny and it printed local news — and like his partners, Abell was a professional newspaper man.

He was born in East Providence, R. I., in 1806, the son of Robert Abell, who had been a quartermaster officer in the War of 1812. As a boy he worked briefly in a store and then became a printer's apprentice on the Provincetown Patriot. As a journeyman, he went to Boston, where he was soon made foreman of a large print shop. From there he jumped to New York; it was in that city, after observing the success of the New York Sun, that he became interested in publishing a politically neutral, newsworthy and inexpensive journal.

The Ledger was the result. But to Abell, it was not enough. So he came to Baltimore, set up a press at 21 Light Street, and on May 17, 1837, delivered to every Baltimore household a copy of his new paper — which is still called The Sun.

The Sun alone has survived, of all the papers published in that day. But Baltimoreans, reading the first issue, were not particularly impressed, even though the lead story concerned the doings of their own city council. For brand-new newspapers were no novelty in the growing town; since the turn of the century, a dozen of them had been born and had died.

Baltimoreans soon took to the new paper nevertheless. By the end of its first year, the circulation was an amazing 12,000, a figure which Abell increased not only by concentrating on presenting the news but by getting the news first. He early saw the advantages to news-gathering of the telegraph, and that, used in combination with a pony express system of his own devising, turned weeks into days.

When, for example, the Mexicans were defeated at Vera Cruz, The Sun's system enabled it to be the first to inform the president of the United States — and to get a nationwide scoop.

As the years went on, the paper prospered, and its success, coupled with his magic touch with real estate, made Arunah Abell a wealthy man. He had a fine home at the northwest corner of Madison and Charles streets — and a splendid country estate of almost 200 acres.

This was Guilford — named in 1822 by its creator, Gen. William McDonald, who had fought at Guilford Court House during the Revolution. Abell bought the estate, complete with a 52-room Victorian mansion, in the late 1860s, paying $425,000 for it. He lived there until 1888, when he died at the age of 82.

The Abell family held the estate until 1907, when it was sold for $1,000,000 to the Guilford Park Company, which later sold it to the Roland Park Company, developers of the suburb of Guilford.

It was inevitable that homes would be built on the land. For earlier in the century the land to the south and southeast of the immense estate was gradually built up. It was then that the city named Abell Avenue — which today extends from West 30th Street to University Parkway in the Waverly area — for the publisher. The naming is done in a city ordinance passed in 1902.

Also in Baltimore is an Arunah Avenue; located in West Baltimore, it extends west from Kirby Lane to Rosedale Street. But whether or not it was named for the founder of the Sunpapers is speculative; no evidence is discoverable to indicate one way or another.

March 21, 1948

Aisquith

By Elizabeth H. Moberly

Most Baltimoreans can tell you with a fine appreciation of the past that Aisquith Street is one of the oldest streets in the city, but they are not so certain how it got its name.

Even those who live there aren't sure. A number confess they don't know, while others guess the street was probably named for the British Lord Asquith.

Tradition says the street was named for Capt. Edward "Ned" Aisquith, whose company of sharpshooters shot the British commander, Gen. Robert Ross, during the Battle of North Point. Actually, though, it was named 10 years before that battle was fought in 1814.

It was only a short street at first, by modern standards, running between Bridge Street (now Gay) and Pitt Street (now Fayette), where the Aisquiths lived. By 1807, however, an extension was made toward Harford Road and in 1813 its residents petitioned Baltimore County officials to pave it and fix its boundaries.

If the street was not named for Captain Aisquith it was not because he did not deserve the honor. He was a dashing figure and crammed a great deal of activity into his 35 years. However, the street name was more likely derived from his father, William Aisquith, a merchant.

Little is known about the elder Aisquith except that he arrived in Baltimore shortly before the Revolution and went into trade. He must have prospered, for he resided comfortably at No. 11 Pitt Street and in the city directory for 1803 was listed as a "gentleman." Edward studied law and at 28 was a Baltimore County delegate to the Maryland Assembly.

Like other young men of his day, Edward Aisquith was with the local militia when the British threatened, and with his company of riflemen marched to Bladensburg to engage them there, only to return to Baltimore without ever seeing action. Dan Wells and Henry McComas, the young militiamen credited with shooting the British general, were said to be members of Aisquith's company and the monument to them stands, appropriately, at the intersection of Gay and Aisquith streets.

Aisquith died in 1815 when thrown from a horse.

Running now beyond Gay Street to Harford Avenue and into northeast Baltimore, Aisquith Street has weathered many changes, including an unintentional effort to alter its name. In 1945, when new street signs ordered by the city arrived, it was discovered that the first "I" in Aisquith had been dropped.

B

Barney

By Elizabeth H. Moberly

A street running east and west about eight blocks on the approaches to Fort McHenry is perhaps Baltimore's most tangible memorial to one of its most colorful heroes.

Set among such streets as Wells and McComas and Winder (all named for the band of men who fought off the British in 1814), Barney Street takes its name from Commodore Joshua Barney, another of their group.

The seventh of a family of 14, Joshua Barney decided early that the sea would be his career, and by the time he was 12 he had persuaded his father to apprentice him to a Baltimore river pilot.

Barney Street – 1948

Barney's first real service afloat began in 1775, when he was 15 and sailed as an apprentice aboard a small brig carrying a cargo of wheat to Nice. Shortly after the vessel had left port the captain died, and Barney, who was his brother-in-law, took command. There was no other officer on board.

The boy decided to continue to voyage instead of turning back to port, and sailed the brig to Gibraltar where he sold the cargo for a profit. On the way back to America, Barney saw an opportunity to make some additional money for the owners and chartered the vessel as a transport aid in the evacuation of Spanish troops defeated by the pirates at Algiers.

When he reached Baltimore in October 1775, he found his country at war with England. He was appointed sailing master aboard the sloop Hornet, one of the ships in the squadron under Commodore Ezek Hopkins. As a result of his service with Hopkins, Barney was commissioned lieutenant in the fledgling United States Navy — he was 17.

The end of the Revolutionary War in 1783 brought with it a disbanding of the Navy, and Barney settled back to a life of comparative inactivity.

He was an ardent Federalist and, the story goes, when Maryland ratified the new Constitution in 1788, he rigged up a 15-foot boat and called it the Federalist. Until he sailed the craft to Mount Vernon, to be presented to George Washington, the boat rested at the site of the present Federal Hill.

In 1794, Congress authorized the construction of six frigates (one of them, the Constellation, was built in Baltimore) to be used to fight the Barbary pirates who were raiding American commerce in the Mediterranean. Barney was selected to command one of the new vessels and given the rank of captain.

However, feeling that he was unjustly ranked below one of the other appointees, Barney refused the commission and turned again to the merchant service.

Going to France as the captain of a merchant ship, he remained to become a commodore in the French navy until retired by the French Republic in 1802.

Barney never actually returned to duty with the regular Navy, even during the War of 1812, but as captain of a privateer out of Baltimore is credited with capturing or destroying $1,500,000 worth of shipping.

Because of his experience in sea warfare, Barney was consulted and asked to organize a flotilla to defend the river approaches of the capital against the advances of the British.

In August 1814, Barney, with 500 of his sailors and Marines, marched to Bladensburg to join the Army under General Winder. They formed a hardy band of fighters, with Barney himself directing the artillery, and when the rest of the Army fled the field, the group under Barney continued to fight until killed or captured. Barney was wounded and taken prisoner.

Following the war, Barney traveled in Kentucky, Maryland and Pennsylvania, and in 1818 he died while in Pittsburgh. He is buried there.

July 3, 1949

Barre & Conway

By Henry C. Rauch

Zachariah Hood was hanged in effigy in Annapolis. He was hanged in effigy in Baltimore. Also in Frederick, in Elkridge and in other towns in Maryland in 1765. Then, as that failed to disturb him perceptibly, a mob gathered in his hometown of Annapolis, attacked his house and tore it to the ground. That did disturb him; he fled the colony.

It was no crime he had committed that had suddenly changed Hood's status from that of respected merchant to that of fugitive. To the complete contrary, it was his undertaking to carry out a law — he had accepted appointment as tax-stamp distributor for Maryland. And the Stamp Act just passed by Parliament had infuriated all the colonies; even Maryland's reaction was mild, compared to the violence in some places.

All this despite the fact that the act was designed to raise money for the colonies' own protection.

By 1763, British and colonial fighters had taken Canada from the French, but this extension of the empire brought problems with it. The French, although conquered, were still hostile. So were the Indians, and in that year of 1763 they made a fierce attack upon frontier settlements.

The need for garrisons along the borders of the colonies was thus made plain. To the British Government it also seemed plain, however, that border defense could not be left to the separate colonies, with their conflicting interests. On the other hand, it meant a heavy expense that could not all be saddled on British taxpayers, either.

It was decided to call upon the colonies to share the cost of the American Army. The question of method then arose. Experience had shown that the colonies were lax about raising funds. So, although Parliament had never before taxed them for revenue purposes, it was now asked to impose a stamp tax for defense.

When they protested, the colonies were given a year to suggest an alternative. Then, as they proposed nothing other than the old, discredited method, Parliament in 1765 passed the Stamp Act.

Parliamentary taxation for revenue, however, threatened the very foundation of colonial self-government, and outraged the people's right to be taxed only by their consent. And so a terrific storm now broke out on this side of the Atlantic. Legislatures passed resolutions of protest. Citizens took direct action against supporters of the act — as in the case of Zachariah Hood.

And notwithstanding that Parliament had agreed to the tax, the colonies' position had defenders in England. One of the most effective of these was Col. Isaac Barre, a member of Commons who had fought at Quebec — he had, indeed, been beside General Wolfe when he fell, and appears in Benjamin West's painting of the general's death.

Another powerful man who took the colonies' side was Henry Seymour Conway, Secretary of State and leader of the House of Commons. And in 1766 Conway succeeded in getting Parliament to repeal the hated act.

Their stands made Barre and Conway tremendous heroes in America. Resolutions of thanks were passed by legislatures, including Maryland's. Towns were named for them in various colonies. And in Baltimore, two streets in the southern part of town were given their names and bear them still today.

Bayard

By William Stump

From where he was sitting, in the autumn of 1814, it seemed to James Asheton Bayard that there was little hope for America.

Together with such illustrious countrymen as John Quincy Adams, Henry Clay and Albert Gàllatin, he was sitting at a conference table in Ghent, Belgium — seeking an end to the War of 1812 with representatives of the British Government.

All the advantages lay with the British. News had just come that their army had routed the Americans at Bladensburg, and had captured Washington, burned the White House and put President Madison to flight. And in faraway Ghent there was little reason to think that the tide of the war would turn.

The cocky British had foreseen some great victories. Months before, in August, they had presented an ultimatum to the American negotiators. It had demanded some terrible things — that the Americans cease protesting the seizure of their ships and sailors. That they disarm and stay disarmed. That they give up northern Maine and much territory along the Canadian border. That they agree to share ownership of the Mississippi with the English forever.

And more than that. The ultimatum called for the creation of a so-called independent Indian state north of the Ohio River, a state that would act as a buffer and cut off thousands of Americans from their homeland.

The alternative offered was the continuation of the war which, Bayard later wrote, implied subjugation. When the Americans rejected the ultimatum, the enemy countered shortly with the notice that it would keep all that it won. No wonder that the news of Bladensburg and Washington, coming soon afterward, robbed Bayard and his colleagues of hope.

But soon some more news came — that a British army had been whipped at Baltimore, its general killed and hundreds of its men wounded. Moreover, the Americans had won a naval battle off Plattsburg. And as a result of that, the American negotiators pressed for a treaty which, in effect, spelled victory for the United States.

James Bayard's role in the treaty negotiations may be one thing that later led Baltimore to name a street for him; the street is in the southwestern part of the city. But then, Bayard played an important role throughout the war. And that, at first glance, is something of a paradox. For Bayard was a Federalist, and that party had for years been against a break with Britain.

Bayard, who was born in Philadelphia in 1763 — his father and his grandfather were born at Bohemia Manor in Cecil County — was educated at Princeton. Then he studied law and went into practice in Philadelphia, turning his interest to politics. He was successful from the start.

In 1796, he went to Congress and quickly made a name for himself by managing the case against a senator who had sold out to the British. In 1800, his behind-the-scenes manipulations enabled Thomas Jefferson to beat out Aaron Burr for the presidency in the election that had been thrown into the House of Representatives.

Elected to the Senate in 1804, Bayard worked to keep relations with the English smooth. But unlike most Federalists, he placed his country first. When England became obstinate, he urged the arming of our nation's merchant vessels, originated acts to strengthen the Army and Navy and, when the war finally came, went so far as to build fortifications with his own hands. More important than that, however, he rallied the Federalists on the government's side.

President Madison appointed him to serve as a representative at Ghent. And in that trying job, the statesman gave his life. For six days after he returned to America, James Bayard, sick and tired, passed away.

Bellona Avenue

By James C. Bertram

That James Beatty was a man with a whimsical nature can be seen from the name he gave to a local thoroughfare.

Bellona Avenue, a city street that turns into a country road, is that thoroughfare. James Beatty named it for the mythical Roman goddess of war — because it led to the mill where he manufactured gunpowder for the nation's cannons.

That was about the time of the War of 1812. Then, Beatty, who was a partner of Gen. John Stricker, was the largest manufacturer of gunpowder in a state that produced one-fifth of the American supply. The size of his operation is probably the reason he built his mill in a safe unpopulated place.

It was located on what is now the south bank of Lake Roland; indeed, fragments of its foundation can still be found there, near the rusty tracks of the old Valley railroad and not far from the point where Bellona Avenue, which begins at the 5500 block of York Road and winds through the suburbs across Charles Street, passes the lake on its journey to Ruxton, Riderwood and, finally, Lutherville.

But the original road that led to the mill is no more; it probably went under the water when the three branches of the Jones Falls were dammed to create Lake Roland in 1861.

When it actually came into being is a mystery; perhaps that was in the 18th century, for some accounts say the mill was in operation then. One tradition has it that James Beatty named it in 1815, shortly after Baltimoreans — including his partner — defeated the English at North Point. Another tradition says he named it after June 18, 1815 — the date of the battle of Waterloo, and the date that a daughter was born.

Bellona Avenue – 1924

So the actual circumstances of Beatty's naming his road are obscure. But one thing is certain, Beatty had a good knowledge of classic mythology. For Bellona is one of mythology's more obscure goddesses.

Classicists disagree on whether she was the wife of Mars, the daughter of Mars or a servant of Mars. She drove the chariot of the war god — Shakespeare called her the "fire ey'd maid of smoky war" — and she guarded his person. For that reason a temple was built to her in ancient Rome, where wars were declared, where heroes were welcomed home and where her priests, in fanatical rites, lacerated their arms and thighs and sprinkled the blood over their spectators.

September 16, 1951

Benson

By James C. Bertram

Down in Halethorpe, it is widely believed that Oregon Avenue was named for the Western state. This is not true — it was named for a man who was named for the state.

He was Oregon Randolph Benson, who was born in 1847, less than a year after the United States established title over the Oregon territory. Exactly why that historic event was important to his parents has been forgotten. But it was, as the son's name shows.

When Oregon Benson was born, there was no Halethorpe but only 150 acres of farmland which the Bensons — who lived at Windcrest, a brick mansion still standing — bought when they settled in the area in the early 1800s. The town of Halethorpe was born in the 1890s when Oregon Benson retired from politics, got into the real estate business and developed, along with other land, part of the family farm.

Benson Avenue, which is behind the St. Agnes Hospital grounds, was created during that period. But Oregon Avenue did not come into existence until 1925, two years after its namesake's death. It was cut through in a further development of the land by his son, Carville Dickinson Benson — whose name is preserved on a parallel street called Carville Avenue.

From 1906 until his death in 1929, Carville Benson was one of Maryland's best-known political figures. Born on the family estate in 1872, he was educated as a lawyer. At 21, he found his way into politics, and a few years later was a member of the House of Delegates.

In 1906, he was Speaker of the House; around 1910, he introduced the bill which established the State Roads Commission. In 1912, he was elected State Senator, and after the World War he served two terms in Congress.

Later, he was appointed state insurance commissioner by Governor Ritchie, his boyhood friend, and spent the remainder of his life at that job.

In addition to his political activities, Mr. Benson found time to conduct a law practice and the real estate company with which he further developed Halethorpe.

"And even with all that," a member of the family recalls, "there was time for a hundred other things. He loved baseball, and he loved horses, especially trotters. When he was a boy, he liked to say, one of his favorite pastimes was bicycle riding. He made much of the fact that he could ride up to Frederick and back on the same day."

February 20, 1949

Bentalou

By Henry C. Rauch

A French cavalryman who came to America with Lafayette in 1776 to help the Colonies in the Revolution is the man whose name is borne by Bentalou Street, which runs across West Baltimore from Western High School to the railroad below Wilkens Avenue — except for a short stretch where another railroad crosses it.

Paul Bentalou was one of a number of Frenchmen who accompanied Lafayette on the latter's privately chartered ship, the Victory. In a pamphlet published later, he wrote:

Bentalou Street – 1956

"I embarked at Bordeaux for America in November, 1776, landed in Philadelphia and proceeded to headquarters at Morristown, N.J., where I tendered my letters of recommendation to General Washington, and asked for a commission in the horse."

All cavalry posts were filled, but Bentalou was not to be denied a hand in the fighting.

"I said that rather than be disappointed I would serve as a volunteer in the infantry. On this the General granted me a lieutenancy in the German Battalion ... and I immediately joined the corps. ...

"The German Battalion was assigned to Muhlenberg's brigade of General Green's division, and therefore, I was both at the battle of Brandywine and that of Germantown."

Later, Bentalou became a captain in Count Pulaski's famous legion. He and Pulaski were wounded — Bentalou not very seriously — in the same cavalry charge at Savannah, Ga., in 1779, and both were taken aboard the same American war vessel. There Pulaski died the same day — in Bentalou's arms, it is said. Bentalou then became the legion's chief officer.

After the war, Bentalou settled in Baltimore and became a successful shipping merchant.

In 1789, when Washington passed through the city on his way to New York to be inaugurated as president, Bentalou was one of 11 signers of a congratulatory address. He seems to have been well regarded by Washington, for in 1794, he was appointed United States marshal for Maryland, and he retained this office until his death.

Despite his varied interests, Bentalou maintained an interest in the Army. In 1798, when international complications resulting from the French Revolution caused alarm in this country, he organized a Baltimore company of cavalry for service if needed. During the War of 1812, he served as quartermaster general of the Baltimore district.

In 1824, he published the pamphlet that has been mentioned, in vindication of his old leader, Pulaski, whose record in the Revolution had been attacked. In the same year he had the pleasure of a reunion with Lafayette, for he was one of the official welcomers when the general visited Baltimore.

His life after the war appears to have been a quiet one. The one colorful incident occurred in France, during a visit he made in 1806 with his Maryland-born wife. At Napoleon's order he was placed under arrest for a time, reputedly because of some part he had played in the marriage of Jerome Bonaparte and Betsy Patterson.

The manner of his death was anti-climax to such a career. He was fatally injured in a fall through a warehouse trapdoor.

December 4, 1949

Bessemer

By William Stump

There's a street in Baltimore named for the Englishman who made it possible for America and the world to mass-produce steel.

This is Bessemer Avenue, which extends east and west of Dundalk Avenue, a little to the northeast of Camp Holabird. It bears the name of Sir Henry Bessemer, who, around 1855, converted iron into steel so inexpensively that it was a major factor of the industrial revolution.

Today, the Bessemer converter has been replaced largely by the open-hearth furnace. But steel men everywhere — including those who live on Bessemer Avenue — can thank it for building their industry.

The man who invented the converter was born in Hertfordshire in 1813. As a child he played in his father's type foundry. He asked questions and he made things and, while in his 20s, invented a device that simplified the stamping of government records — which the government quickly adopted but did not thank him for until it knighted him 50 years later.

That invention was just the beginning. Bessemer made a gold paint, a machine for manufacturing velvet and a machine for casting type. When the Crimean War came along, he developed an artillery shell that was so advanced that there were no cannon sturdy enough to fire it.

In those days cannon were made of iron. If they were made of steel, Bessemer figured, they would be many times more effective. But the manufacture of steel in large enough quantities to turn out cannon was commercially impossible; the types of furnaces in existence could produce only wrought iron, and steel was refined in small quantities by very slow methods.

This problem aroused Bessemer's interest in steel making, and after many setbacks and disappointments resulted in the Bessemer converter.

A typical converter is a huge drumlike affair which needs a three or four story shed to accommodate it. The drum is filled with tons of molten pig iron, through which hot air is blasted to remove the carbon and some of the other elements that are found in iron. When this is done, certain alloys are added; the result is steel.

Bessemer's process made him a wealthy and world-famous man, and he kept right on working with new things until his death, in 1898. He worked to perfect the telephone, for example. He invented the process by which graphite is compressed to make the "lead" for lead pencils.

Bessemer Avenue came into being in 1916 as part of the Graceland Park development. A. Herman Siskind, who was connected with the syndicate that laid out the area, recalls that it was decided to name as many of the streets as possible for steel towns and steel men.

Bethlehem, Gary, Duluth and Youngstown avenues were named for steel towns. Graceland Park and Graceland Avenue were named for Eugene G. Grace, then president of Maryland Steel and now chairman of the board of Bethlehem Steel. And the part of Dundalk Avenue which now passes the development was originally called Carnegie Avenue in honor of Andrew Carnegie, of Pittsburgh.

If it had not been for Henry Bessemer, though, these streets might never have been named, for without the converter the growth of the steel industry might have been another story. Bethlehem, Duluth and Youngstown might well be villages instead of the industrial cities they are today, and Gary, Ind., founded as a steel town, probably would never have been built. And certainly the five American communities named Bessemer wouldn't have that name.

April 15, 1951

Biddle

By Karen Richards

When Catherine Biddle married George Lux in 1779, she left Philadelphia to live in one of Maryland's finest houses.

The house was Chatsworth. It stood near the intersection of what are now George Street and Pennsylvania Avenue. John Adams, who, like Washington and Lafayette, visited there when the Continental Congress met in Baltimore in 1777, wrote in his diary that the house had a "large yard, enclosed with stone and lime, and before the yard two fine rows of cherry trees that led to the public road."

As for the Lux family, Adams said its members lived like princes.

The Lux estate contained 950 acres when Catherine Biddle married George Lux and came to live there. A few years later, though, George sold off many acres. In the process a road which may have existed as a lane, or which George Lux may have created to divide his property, was named Biddle Street.

The Duchess of Windsor once lived at 212 East Biddle Street; she was then Wallis Warfield.

That the street was named for George Lux's wife is almost certain, said William N. Marye, who was a Baltimore historian and genealogist. "It is logical because of Catherine Biddle's connection with the area. Besides, there were no other Biddles in the area."

Relatively little is known of Catherine Biddle Lux. She was the daughter of Edward Biddle, Pennsylvania congressman who had homes in Reading and Philadelphia. The chances are she met wealthy George Lux when he was an officer in the Continental Army. She had no children, and was evidently sickly; when she died at Chatsworth in 1790, an obituary said she had been suffering from a "lingering disease."

Her husband was only 44 when he died in 1797. The most important thing he did, it seems, was to advocate resistance to the British and to prepare and rouse his fellow Baltimoreans for the Revolution. He sat on committees aimed at protesting British taxation and influence. In 1774, he helped organize the Independent Cadets to train Baltimoreans for war.

William Lux, his father, was also active before the Revolution: when the Revolution came, he helped, through his business and shipping interests, to obtain arms for the patriots. He was known as one of Baltimore's strongest partisans of the Revolutionary cause — one reason that Washington, Lafayette and Adams came to his house.

Chatsworth, which stood until the 1870s, came into the Lux family when William Lux married the daughter of Dr. George Walker, a well-to-do man who helped to start Baltimore — a town in which the Luxes were among the first settlers.

William's father, Capt. Darby Lux, an Englishman and a sea captain, came here in 1733; in a few years he was a town commissioner and the owner of a good deal of property on a street along the waterfront. Eventually this street was named Light Street — by someone who whimsically translated the captain's Latin-looking name into English.

Biddle Street – 1951

October 17, 1948

Bonaparte

By Karen Richards

Bonaparte Avenue, cutting diagonally across Northeast Baltimore between Loch Raven Boulevard and Harford Road, bears the name of the Baltimore Bonapartes, whom Napoleon for many years refused to recognize.

Though the street lies in a part of the city that is a relatively new development, the Bonapartes figured in the early history of Baltimore.

The first Bonaparte to come to Baltimore was Jerome, the younger brother of Napoleon. On a visit to his friend, Commodore Joshua Barney, in 1803, Jerome met and married Betsy Patterson, the daughter of one of the city's wealthiest merchants. Napoleon ordered the wedding annulled — his plans for Jerome were something different. Betsy was refused admission to France, and Jerome married again and became the King of Westphalia.

Mme. Bonaparte became a wealthy woman, and her son, Jerome, born in England, was accepted by his grandmother and his aunt, the mother and sister of Napoleon, although his uncle was never reconciled to the marriage. The son, Jerome, traveled through Europe with his mother, but returned home to marry a Baltimore girl, much to the chagrin of Betsy Patterson Bonaparte, who had hoped he would marry royalty.

In his town house, which was located at Park Avenue and Centre Street, Jerome lived a life of quiet ease. He had two sons. The elder, also named Jerome, graduated from West Point and chose a military career. He sought to ally himself with his cousin, Napoleon III, and the Second French Empire and rose to high rank in the French army, winning honors in the Crimean War. He was granted the title of "Prince Napoleon," but it was empty recognition. He died in 1893.

Charles J. Bonaparte, the younger son, turned his back on his royal connections abroad and took pride in being a Marylander and an American. Born in 1850, he knew the Bonaparte story first-hand — his grandmother lived till 1875 —

and had nothing to do with Europe.

He became a lawyer and close friend of Theodore Roosevelt, serving in his Cabinet as Attorney General and Secretary of the Navy. In the latter post he aroused ire of the historically minded by suggesting that the old frigate Constitution be used as a target ship.

He died in 1921, the last of the Bonapartes in Baltimore, though a nephew survived till 1945, the last of the family line.

April 25, 1948

Bond

By Karen Richards

Down on Fells Point there are three streets that serve as reminders of one of the families which first settled there and helped to develop what became Baltimore's "Sailortown."

It was John Bond, "Gentleman," a Quaker, who moved to the Point shortly after William Fell, and whose family gave their names to Aliceanna, Bond and Ann streets. On the Point, where most streets have names of British origin, these are among the few named for Americans.

In the earliest records of Baltimore, Aliceanna is written just as often as "Alesanne," which is quite in keeping with its times, for the street dates from the pre-Revolutionary period when phonetic spelling was the practice.

It is one of the few streets in the city that is named for an actual woman; in this case, Aliceanna Webster Bond, the wife of John Bond. Ann Street was probably named for their daughter, who married Col. Edward Fell. Crossing Aliceanna Street is Bond Street, which also takes its name from this family.

Very little is known of Mrs. Bond save that she was a devout Quaker who was evi-

Bond Street – 1948

dently held in high esteem by the community, for at the time of her death a rather lengthy tribute was published in the Maryland Gazette.

"Died, October 13, 1767, in Baltimore County, in the fifty-second year of her age, Alesanna Bond, wife of John Bond, at Fell's Point, one of the People called Quakers, to whom she was married thirty-three years; and on the 18th was interred in the Quaker's Burying Ground, on Bond's Forest."

"She was the youngest daughter of John Webster, senior, deceased; endowed with many good qualities, skilled in Medicine and Midwifery, which she administered with Freedom and Benevolence. She left ten children."

The Bonds were substantial citizens of Baltimore, with a country home at Bond's Forest, a section of woodland in Baltimore and Harford counties, as well as the home at Fells Point. John Bond, in addition to being a large landowner, was a merchant and built up a sizable fortune shipping tobacco from Joppa and Baltimore to England.

There was always a close connection between the Bonds and the sea, and one of the Bonds' daughters, named Alice Anne for her mother, was married to Capt. Thomas Kell, of Baltimore, who commanded the privateers Dolphin and Little Davy during the Revolutionary War.

Bond was a member of the Bush River Company, which he had helped organize, and through its efforts the first iron furnace in the colonies was erected. The venture proved unsuccessful financially, and when the company was sold in 1773, Bond owed more than £3,000.

It was the same John Bond who presented to the Quakers the land at Fallston which was the site of the burying ground where Aliceanna Bond was interred.

John Bond credited his wife with keeping him true to the Quaker traditions, for in the years following her death he was dealt with by the Gunpowder Meeting of Quakers because he took the oath of office as a magistrate, contrary to the Friends' precepts.

Bond was not the only "unruly" Quaker in the family, according to the evidence. One of his daughters was disowned by the meeting for "going to places of diversion and dancing." And others of the Bonds were disciplined for "joining the militia," "marrying out of meeting," "playing cards," "playing the fiddle" and "lending a man a gun."

It is likely that the Quaker meeting was also somewhat perturbed when John Bond, Gentleman, imported a coach from England, with the family arms emblazoned on the door.

July 29, 1951

Bouldin, Poppleton

By William Stump

Most of Baltimore's older streets were named in one great christening — sometime between 1816 and 1822.

It all started in the state's General Assembly when that body, realizing Baltimore was growing fast, determined to keep that growth orderly. To that end, it established a commission made up of the city's prominent men, which it directed to draw up a map, complete with new streets, that could serve as a master plan to be followed as the city grew.

John Eager Howard, William Gibson, John Hillen, Henry Thompson, James Mosher, Solomon Etting, William Lorman, Owen Dorsey, William McMechen, William Patterson, Joseph Townsend and George Warner were the commissioners. They set to work in 1816, by inserting an ad in a Baltimore paper calling upon local surveyors to bid on the map-making job.

Bouldin Street – 1967

The logical man for such a task was Jehu Bouldin, who, in addition to running a firm that had been synonymous with local surveying ever since his forebears determined the boundaries of Baltimore County in 1657, was employed as the city's official surveyor. But for all his stature, Bouldin did not win the contract — his bid was too high.

The winner was an Englishman named Thomas H. Poppleton; it is recorded that he accepted the job on the provision that he could use a surveying instrument called the theodolite, which he considered far more accurate than an ordinary compass. It is also recorded that the commissioners supplied him with an assistant who turned out to be none other than Jehu Bouldin.

The men did their job well. Their map, a beautiful affair which indeed served as a "blueprint" for Baltimore's growth, shows that they laid out their streets with a great deal of skill and logic. Perhaps that is why the commissioners, when they named the streets — for military, political and business leaders, and one for each of themselves, too — created a Poppleton Street and a Bouldin Street.

Details of Poppleton's life are few; one report, unauthenticated, says that he moved on to Bombay and worked there as a

Poppleton Street – 1973

surveyor. Details of Bouldin's life are not plentiful, either; about all that is known of him is that he married a Mary Askew in 1795, that he served as a captain in the Independent Light Dragoons during the War of 1812, that he was a colonel after the war, that he was city surveyor for 20 years, and that he died on May 7, 1830, in his 70th year.

Today Bouldin Street, which is located in the eastern part of the city, begins at Toone Street and extends north to Leverton, where it dead-ends. However, it takes up again at the Pulaski Highway, a few blocks to the north, and extends to Monument Street. Poppleton, in West Baltimore, extends from Washington Boulevard north to Franklin Street.

November 13, 1949

Brehm

By William Stump

How dear to my heart is the old George Brehm Brewery
With its vaults filled with nectar we all loved so well...
When our day's work is over, or when we feel lonely
Or jaded, or tired, or akin to despair
We drink of its nectar, the sweet "One Grade Only,"
And throw to the winds every thought of dull care.

Sung to the tune of "The Old Oaken Bucket," these words were well known in the latter years of the 19th century. The workers at Brehm's Brewery in Northeast Baltimore sang them with college-like spirit. So did the customers in Baltimore saloons; so did the Baltimore Germans who came to the brewery on warm Sunday afternoons to drink "One Grade Only" and eat liverwurst sandwiches beneath the thick shade tree.

The song and the product that inspired it are gone. Gone, too, is Brehm's Brewery. But Brehms Lane, which originally extended from the Belair Road out to Herring Run, survives in part. It now begins at Erdman Avenue and extends southeast and then northeast through Herring Run Park to Parkside Drive.

Members of the Brehm family believe that it came to be called Brehms Lane because it was used and owned by the brewery that George Brehm ran from 1866 until his death, at the age of 72, in 1904.

George Brehm was practically born a brewer, in Adelsdorf, Bavaria. His father was a member of an old brewing family there, and it was only logical that George should work with malt and hops soon after the family emigrated to Baltimore. He worked at Seeger's and at the Old Engel. Then he went with Neisendorfer's; he was foreman there when George Neisendorfer died. He married his late employer's widow, became the brewery's owner, and changed its name.

In those days the brewery was a small one, due to the difficulties in manufacturing beer. Water, for example, had to be piped from Clifton Park to a storage cistern. Ice, which is necessary, was made by flooding a neighborhood field. Under these conditions, Mr. Brehm could turn out only 3,000 barrels a year.

But these barrels were eagerly drained. "One Grade Only" became a household slogan. All one had to do to get a huge 5 cent stein of the light lager was to say "O.G.O." to his bartender. There was even an O.G.O. bowling league, which met every Sunday afternoon in a special building on the brewery grounds.

In 1899, Henry H. Brehm — who died in 1945 at the age of 78 — was taken into the business by his father. When George Brehm died, the son took over the family mansion and the plant. He installed electricity, built ice machines, put in modern bottling devices and bought Baltimore's first beer truck.

The production was increased to 40,000 barrels a year and sold to the thirsty with the advice that it was "not only a delicious and palatable beverage but a food, containing nourishing extracts for the prolongment of life."

People kept drinking "One Grade Only" until Prohibition. Then Henry Brehm changed the name of the brewery to the Brehm Beverage Company and sadly began making near-beer and soda pop.

But that way things weren't the same, and in 1923 the brewery was sold.

C

The Calverts

By William Stump

Every Baltimorean learns this in school — that the city and two of its major streets bear the names of the family that founded Maryland and virtually owned it for 139 years.

They learn that the streets, Baltimore and Calvert, are the oldest in the city. But do they learn that Baltimore Street was originally called Long Street and that although it was given its present name about 1745 most citizens referred to it as Market Street until well into the next century?

The reason for this would appear to be obvious: the little town's market stalls were situated on a corner of Gay Street, and Baltimore Street led to the spot. Indeed, the eastern portion of today's main stem was once officially called Market Street.

But there may be another reason why citizens did not use the street's proper name. And that is because in the early years of the town, the Lords Baltimore enjoyed little respect.

Charles Calvert, fifth Lord Baltimore, was the proprietor of the colony when Baltimore Street was named. Although he is said to have been good-natured, he was in the habit of sending mean and nagging letters to his governors. Although he is said to have been honest, he consorted with rakes and shady characters and led a life of wastefulness. And although he made much of loving literature and the arts, he was not very bright.

This, perhaps, annoyed Marylanders more than all else. For the fifth lord, during negotiations about the colony's north boundary, let himself be hoodwinked by the Penns, with the result that Maryland lost a great deal of its territory.

But Charles was a paragon of all the virtues compared to the son who succeeded him in 1751. That was Frederick Calvert, sixth and last Lord Baltimore, whose only interest in Maryland lay in the money he could get out of it. A man of foul character, he spent his life in scandalous pursuits, which culminated in his being obliged to leave England after an assault upon a woman. His only heir was an illegitimate son, John Harford — whose claim to the title was cut short by the Revolution.

How different were the earlier Lords of Baltimore! The first was George Calvert — who was given his title for long, wise and valuable service to the English crown. For that, too, he was given the colony, which he envisaged as a place where men could live in peace and worship in any way they chose.

But George Calvert did not actually found Maryland. He died before the royal charter, granting him and his heirs the colony for all time, was signed. It is to his son Cecilius that the bulk of the credit must go, although, like his father, he did not once see the lands along the Chesapeake.

Leonard Calvert, Cecilius' brother, led the first settlers to Maryland aboard the Ark and the Dove. Cecilius himself had to stay home and defend his charter against attacks from the Virginias. But for 41 years the wisdom and liberality of the second lord guided the formative era of the colony; in that time, such documents as the Acts of Tolerance came into being.

The third Lord Baltimore, also a Charles, was the first of the proprietors to set foot on Maryland soil. He came as governor in 1661, and 14 years later succeeded his father Cecilius to the title.

He did not have the mind or the personality of his ancestors. Nevertheless, he made up for the lack by hard work — and by obstinacy. The most American of the Calverts, he was also the hardest-boiled.

When the Penns tried to steal the upper part of the bay, he talked back. When James II tried to change the charter, he bluntly told the king he was wrong. When the Assembly gave him trouble, he bawled it out in person. But he was

Calvert Street – 1957

always fair, and once, the story goes, he refused the Assembly's gift of 100,000 pounds of tobacco on the grounds that it would hurt the taxpayers.

Upon his death in 1714 he was succeeded by Benedict Calvert, fourth Lord Baltimore. But he played no role at all in Maryland history. For, two months after his succession, he himself died, his title falling to the second Charles, then only 16.

November 1, 1953

Charles Calvert

By William Stump

Whom was Charles Street named for?

And, one should ask at the same time, when was it named? For the second question is important to the first.

The street is one of the city's oldest. It appears on the original plat of Baltimore Town in 1729 — but without a name. The act authorizing the founding of the town indicates that it lay on "Part of the Tract of Land, whereon a certain John Fleming now lives, and suppos'd to be the Right of the Heirs of Charles Carroll, Esq., deceas'd."

Some historians speculate that the street before that had been Susquehannock Indian Trail and later a farm road leading to Fleming's house, which supposedly stood on what would now be the east side of Charles, just south of Lombard; no facts, however, exist to back up the speculation. Nor does anyone know why in its childhood the street came to be known as Forest or Forrest.

Charles Street – Early 1900s

No records appear to exist stating why the name was changed to Charles — so the historians speculate some more. Some have considered Charles Calvert, fifth Lord Baltimore; others chose Charles Carroll of Carrollton, grandson of the aforementioned Charles. None seems to have considered that a clue to the name might lie in the time of the change — and none seems to have attempted to trace the name back to its earliest use.

But look at early land deeds on file in Baltimore's Courthouse. The name Charles Street first appears in 1761, when Daniel Barnet, who old newspapers show was later to build a tavern, bought "ground on Charles Street" from one Jacob Meyer.

And that, it would seem, rules out Charles Carroll of Carrollton — who in 1761 was 21 years old and who, moreover, had been a student in Europe for some years. That his grandfather had been dead many years when the town was laid out and that his father lived in Annapolis would tend to rule them out of the naming; besides, it is logical to assume that the last name of the Carrolls would have been used.

So there is a good chance that the historians who guess or deduce that the street was named for Charles Calvert, fifth Lord Baltimore, are right. For Charles was the proprietor of the colony of Maryland when Baltimore was founded and proprietor until his death in 1751. Besides, two more streets begin to pop up in the old deeds about the same time as Charles — and those streets are Baltimore and Calvert.

The fifth Lord Baltimore was far from being the most able or most attractive of his illustrious clan. On the credit side, he is reputed to have been good-natured and honest and to have loved literature and the arts. But he was not very bright; during some negotiations about his colony's northern boundary he was outsmarted by the Penns, and Maryland lost a good deal of territory. And of his character, it is said that he lived only for pleasure, consorting with rakes and ne'er-do-wells.

That, very probably, is the man for whom Charles Street, 10½ miles long and the city's pride and joy, was named. And if some see irony in it, it is understandable.

Caroline

By William Stump

Frederick Calvert, sixth and last Lord Baltimore, was no credit to his illustrious clan.

Maryland historians, giving him what seems like purposely vague attention, say that he was a rake, that he lived a wasteful life of dissipation, corruption and extravagance, and that he was finally forced to flee England after he narrowly escaped a court conviction for an assault upon a woman.

The fact that he was Lord Proprietor of distant Maryland apparently meant only one thing to him — the £13,000 of personal revenue he extracted from the colony each year.

Yet, amazingly, the colony was well handled when he was its proprietor — about as well handled, at least, as could be expected in a day when the prestige of the crown was on the decline throughout America. And the reason for this was the colony's governor, Sir Robert Eden, Calvert's personal appointee.

That appointment was due to the fact that Eden had married his sister, Caroline.

Caroline Street – 1956

Little is known about Caroline; the place and date of her birth are not to be found, and there is no existing portrait of her. She married Sir Robert Eden, a young officer of the Coldstream Guards, in 1765, and three years later, with their two young sons, sailed for Annapolis.

It is to be wondered how Caroline fared in the city described as "the Athens of America." For her husband, who was only 28 when he got his enviable job, had an eye for the ladies, and a fondness for the race track, theater and salon.

But with all that, he proved himself to be a hard-working and able man, a man who served as effective moderator between the Tories and the seekers of independence, and there is no indication that the colonists held him and his family in anything but the highest esteem. Indeed, they publicly mourned his return to England in 1776.

After the Revolution, Sir Robert returned to Annapolis to make claims for his property, and while on the visit he died.

His sons, Sir Frederick Morton Eden and William Thomas Eden, went on to important careers as an economist and a soldier, respectively.

What happened to Lady Caroline Calvert Eden, history seems not to have cared. Her name, nevertheless, is mentioned daily by the residents of Caroline County and by those Baltimoreans who come into contact with the 200-year-old Caroline Street in Fells Point.

Barrister Carroll

By James C. Bertram

Even though there is no record of his ever having practiced law, it is little wonder that a prominent 18th-century Baltimorean named Charles Carroll insisted that people refer to him as Charles Carroll, Barrister.

For in the 18th century there were four Charles Carrolls — and all of them were prominent. There was wealthy Charles Carroll and his famous son, Charles Carroll of Carrollton, signer of the Declaration of Independence and later the richest

Carroll estate — Mount Clare – 1941

man in America. There was Dr. Charles Carroll, a distant cousin, and then there was his son, who affixed the word barrister to his name.

He had the right to affix it. For although he did not practice — he did not have to — he was a lawyer, and a well-trained one, having received in England the best legal education to be had at the time.

Dr. Carroll had made that possible. He was an Irishman who had come to Maryland in 1715 and had gone into the practice of medicine. Then he had turned to the raising of tobacco; after that, he had made a fortune mining iron ore on the west side of Gwynn Falls.

Young Charles was born in 1723 at Annapolis. When he was 8 years old, his father set sail with him for England with the purpose of entering him in school. Bad weather, however, drove their ship to Portugal and, "the Child being much fatigued," the doctor placed him in the English college at Lisbon.

Eventually the boy moved on to England, entering Eton and later Cambridge. He did not excel as a scholar — one reason, perhaps, why his father, upon sending him money on one occasion, was moved to remark that "Women and Wine are the Bane of youth."

When he was 23, Carroll returned to Maryland. Five years later — what he did during those years is unrecorded — he returned to England and began reading law in the Middle Temple. Provided with plenty of money, he became a favorite of London society.

He returned in 1755 — and a few months later Dr. Carroll died, leaving the barrister great wealth and a brand-new house on the outskirts of Baltimore. This was Mount Clare, and Carroll made it one of the great homes of the state, even though he did not have a wife to share it. Not that eligible daughters didn't come to his attention. But he did not meet the right daughter — one reason being that he suffered for long periods from malaria, a curse in the colony.

Finally in 1763, the barrister took Margaret Tilghman as his bride and Mount Clare bloomed even more. Its rooms were filled with furniture which — along with the Carrolls' wine and clothes and horses and even servants — was imported practically by the boatload from England.

But as much as he enjoyed his life, Carroll was not content to retire from the world. As relations between England and the colonies became more and more strained, he became more and more active in Maryland affairs.

He presided over the convention which relieved the last royal governor of his office; it is said that he wrote the state's Declaration of Rights in 1776. He served on the Council of Safety, and was a prime mover in framing the construction that helped form a Maryland government. He served in Congress during the war and was appointed chief judge of the state's General Court, a post he refused, however.

The barrister died in 1783 at Mount Clare — which, restored, is in as fine condition now as it was in his day. Located in Carroll Park, it is but one memorial to the colonial gentleman. Another is Carroll Street, in Southwest Baltimore, close to the park which also preserves his name.

July 30, 1950

Carver

By William Stump

It is fortunate for America that Moses Carver, unlike a great many slave owners, valued human life above horseflesh. Otherwise, he might not have paid as ransom a favorite thoroughbred racehorse for the sickly, nameless black baby that roving bandits kidnapped from his southern Missouri plantation — and the baby might not have lived to become one of the nation's great scientists.

That scientist, christened by the plantation owner, was George Washington Carver, whose experiments and discoveries revolutionized Southern agriculture, added millions of dollars to Southern farm income and contributed hundreds of new products to American history.

Dr. Carver's accomplishments were many and diversified. He was the father of farm demonstration, a director of the government's agricultural research and extension divisions. He pioneered soil conservation and soil care in the South.

He wiped out hundreds of plant diseases. He weaned Southern agriculture away from a one-crop economy by persuading farmers to plant peanuts, sweet potatoes, soy beans and pecans in addition to their cotton — and made these crops vast moneymakers by finding hundreds of uses for their byproducts.

From the peanut, he derived over 300 products, ranging from peanut butter to axle grease to fertilizer. From the sweet potato, he perfected over 100, ranging from rubber to plastics to ink. He turned Alabama clay into paper, weeds and grass into nourishing foods.

When he died in 1943 at nearly 80 years old — he did not know the exact year of his birth, but calculated that it must have been around 1864 — he was mourned by scientists and farmers, rich men and poor men, citizens white and black. But he was mourned not only as a scientist who helped "liberate" the South; he was mourned as a man of rare character.

The people who knew George Washington Carver said that he did as much for human understanding as he did for science. A simple, deeply religious man, he wanted nothing for himself save his work — and that he shared freely with his fellow men. At Tuskegee Institute in Alabama, dirt farmers and industrialists and plantation owners knew he would solve problems for anyone and everyone who asked his aid.

Material wealth was nothing to him. Although he was never paid more than $1,500 a year during his 45 years at Tuskegee, he never thought of taking out patents on his discoveries; once, when Thomas Alva Edison offered him a position at $100,000 a year, he turned it down, saying he would rather remain in the South "to work among the trees and ferns and grass of God's green earth."

And while turning down money, he used his salary to help young people through school — a fact evidenced by the ragged clothes he wore and the humble way in which he lived.

Dr. Carver spent his early years on Moses Carver's plantation. But Moses could give him only a meager education, so, when he was in his teens, the boy hitched a ride West on a wagon.

Doing odd jobs, he worked himself through high school. Then he applied, by mail, for entrance into the University of Iowa, and was turned down when he presented himself in September. But he opened a laundry and saved enough money to enter Simpson College in Indianola, Iowa, and, after graduating from there, went to Iowa State, where he studied agriculture and science and taught until Booker T. Washington learned of him and took him to Tuskegee.

When he arrived there, the campus was barren and sandy; the "experimental farm" assigned him was eroded and ruined, as were farms for miles around. In a few months, though, the campus was grassy and rich in shrubbery, and the experimental farm was yielding rich crops. In a few years, so were the neighboring farms. In the course of the next 40 years, farms all over the South were benefiting from his wizardry.

In his laboratory, the original equipment of which was made from old bottles and odds and ends found on junk heaps, Dr. Carver spent most of his time.

He paused from his work only to make lecture tours, to meet people, and to paint delicate landscapes with pigments made from magnolia blossoms, banana skins and coffee grounds. He never married.

Save for Booker T. Washington, there is probably no black man more revered than George Washington Carver. So it was only logical that James H. Hunt, of the city's Bureau of Surveys, named a street for him when the Housing Authority of Baltimore started its development in Cherry Hill in 1944. Carver Road is the name of the street, and it runs from Cherry Hill Road on the north, three blocks to Roundview Road on the south.

July 20, 1952

Caton

By William Stump

Richard Caton married well — in more ways than one.

An Englishman of an honorable but decidedly not well-to-do family, he came to America shortly after the Revolution and settled in Baltimore. Soon he was deeply in love with the girl George Washington called the greatest beauty he had ever seen — Polly Carroll, daughter of Charles Carroll of Carrollton, signer of the Declaration of Independence and the wealthiest man in America.

The beautiful and spirited Miss Carroll, considered perhaps the finest catch in Baltimore if not in the young nation, reciprocated the love. But her father was not pleased. Caton was in debt and jobless, and besides he was a communicant of the Church of England, while the Carrolls were Roman Catholic.

Indeed the Signer — as the historians often refer to him — tried to interest his daughter in a distant cousin. When she would have none of him, Carroll asked a friend to beseech the girl to change her mind. The friend tried, by asking her who would get Richard Caton out of jail should he be sent there for debts unpaid. "These hands," she said proudly, "will take him out."

Touched, Carroll consented to the marriage, provided that Caton, described in biographies as a tall, handsome, dignified yet arrogant man, get himself out of debt and into business. He managed to do this, and in 1787 the young lovers were wed. Soon they were at home at Thunder Castle, a small mansion Carroll had built for them on a 2,000-acre tract, part of the over 30,000 acres he owned to the west of Baltimore.

Richard Caton, regarded by many of the Baltimore gentry as a foreign adventurer, built cotton mills at what later became Woodberry. They did not prosper, and he turned his attention to developing coal mines — a venture that failed so miserably that Carroll bailed him out and to be on the safe side, began paying Polly a regular allowance.

In 1810, probably determined to show his father-in-law that he could make his own way, the proud Caton went into real estate. The result was the village of Catonsville — which he laid out on the land surrounding Thunder Castle — not to mention Caton Avenue, which also preserves his name.

The venture by no means brought Caton out of bankruptcy, but, thanks to Carroll's endless bounty, the family was not exactly uncomfortable.

Few Baltimore clans enjoyed such social prestige or lived as well as the Catons; if Thunder Castle was fine, the new home that Charles Carroll built for them at the turn of the century was even finer. That was Brooklandwood, the manor house in the Green Spring Valley that was later owned by Capt. Isaac Emerson; much changed, it still stands today off the Falls Road, and is slated to become St. Paul's School.

There, the Caton daughters grew up — Marianne, Elizabeth, Emily and Louisa. Like their mother, they were women of exceptional beauty; to English society, in which they were just as much at home as in American, Marianne, Elizabeth and Louisa were the "Three Graces."

They married into that nobility. Marianne, the widow of Robert Patterson, became the wife of the Marquis of Wellesley, Governor-General of India and Lord Lieutenant of Ireland, and became, too, lady-in-waiting to Queen Adelaide, who ascended the British thrown with William IV in 1830.

Elizabeth married Baron Stafford; Louisa became the bride of Col. Sir Bathurst Harvey, aide de camp to the prince regent in the home of the Duke of Wellington, who gave her in marriage. Upon the death of her husband, she married the Marquis of Carmarthen, Duke of Leeds.

Emily, who remained in America, married well herself. Her husband was John Lovat Mactavish, British consul in Baltimore; the couple lived at Folly Quarter, a house built on part of Carroll's estate, Doughoregan. Her name is said by city authorities to be preserved by MacTavish Avenue — and her sisters' names by Wellesley Street, Stafford Street and Leeds Street, all of them in West Baltimore.

There was another daughter, named Anne, and there is a story concerning her. Some time around 1845, the year Richard Caton died, a child named Beulah Mary Dix was taken to Brooklandwood to visit her Cousin Mary, the once-beautiful Polly Carroll.

She wrote later that she found her Cousin Mary a tiny old lady with silver hair and, as she described it, lovely, dark eyes; she recalled the pride she felt when the old lady asked her to come along on walks through the gardens.

On one of these walks, the two passed a rustic seat. The old lady remarked that she sat there often with Anne on warm days. Puzzled, the child, who had heard only of the "Three Graces" and Emily, asked who Anne was; Cousin Mary, a little hurt, answered that Anne was yet another daughter.

The child thought nothing more of it until it came time to leave Brooklandwood. Then she remarked what a pity it was the old lady would have to stay there alone. She, in turn, said that it would be no pity at all, since Anne would stay, even though the others had gone.

Then Beulah "went out to say a silent goodbye to every corner of the place I had grown to love and might never see again." And in doing that, she discovered an overgrown cemetery she had not noticed in which, half hidden by vines, was a little headstone that read "Anne, daughter of Richard Caton and Marry Carroll, departed this life May 3, 1789, aged ten months and eleven days."

October 8, 1950

Chase

By William Stump

"Damned busy restless incendiary, ringleader of mobs, foul mouthed and inflaming son of discord!"

These words were spoken by the Mayor of Annapolis to describe Samuel Chase who, shortly before the Revolution, led the Sons of Liberty in a riot against the hated stamp tax — a riot in which the Annapolis tax collector was burned in effigy along with his stamps.

Later, when Chase became delegate to the Continental Congress, signer of the Declaration of Independence, delegate to the Constitutional Convention, chief judge of Maryland and justice of the United States Supreme Court, he heard many similar remarks directed against him. Indeed, his career, which was of great value to the young nation, was usually characterized by strong talk, hard in-fighting and raging controversy.

The most famous controversy occurred in 1805, when Thomas Jefferson sought to have him impeached from the Supreme Court. True, Justice Chase had shown typical high-handedness in certain of his decisions — but he certainly was not guilty of the "high crimes and misdemeanors" of the Constitution's Article 3 which the Senate attempted to convict him upon.

Historians indicate that Jeffersonians knew this too, and tried to interpret the phrase to cover "bad behavior"; they used it as a pretext to get rid of him because he stood actively in their way.

The trial, which stopped most of the government's activities and attracted national attention was held in the Senate chamber, lavishly decorated — and opened to the public — for the event. It lasted two months; Chase, who helped argue his own defense, was found not guilty.

About that time, Chase Street first appeared in the city records, although it did not come into actual existence until some years later. Many historians, without reason, state flatly in various books that the street was named for Samuel Chase. This may or may not be true. But it is nothing if not logical.

In Baltimore, Samuel Chase was one of the best known citizens — and probably would have been if he had not signed the Declaration and served on the high court. Over 6 feet tall and massive in build, he had snow white hair and ruddy features that earned him the nickname of "Bacon Face."

Every Baltimorean had seen his fine mansion at Eutaw and Lexington streets, every Baltimorean had heard about his exploits as judge of the city and the county; how for instance, when the sheriff quailed at arresting two prominent ruffians, he had stepped down from the bench, gone into the street and brought them in.

That act itself caused a controversy; a grand jury said that because Chase held the job of judge and policeman in the same court at the same time, the arrest was illegal. Judge Chase told the jury to stop bothering him. It did.

Samuel Chase was born in 1741 in Somerset County; his mother died when he was a child, and his father, a minister who had emigrated from England, educated him in the classics. At 21, he was a lawyer in Annapolis, and three years later, a member of the Assembly.

There, he baited the governor and vehemently cursed the British king. The riot against the stamp tax was only one active expression of his feelings; another was his vote to embarrass the governor by cutting the salaries of clergymen in half, including that of his own father. At the Continental Congress he urged a total embargo on British trade, arguing that it was the best way to bankrupt England. He was one of the first to urge federation of all the colonies, and he made a futile trip to Canada in an attempt to line up the king's subjects there.

After signing the Declaration, he remained in the Congress during the war, served on thirty committees at one time and worked successfully to stop those who sought to discredit Washington. During the war, too, he became involved in a furious battle when he tried to corner the flour market; due to the acid writings of Alexander Hamilton, his reputation suffered.

After Chase had served at the Constitutional Convention in opposition to the Federalist delegates, he voted against approving the Constitution, on the grounds that it was undemocratic, but later in life became a strong and voluble Federalist himself — and had made his mark as an able judge in Baltimore and Maryland. Washington remembered him and appointed him to the Supreme Court.

There he was known as a man of great wit, a jurist with an extraordinary grasp of legal problems. A popular man, even his fights and his near impeachment failed to hurt his reputation. In 1807, he became ill and attended fewer and fewer sessions. He died in Baltimore in 1811, and was buried in St. Paul's Cemetery.

December 28, 1952

Chatham

By William Stump

In 1765, the mere mention of the British Government was enough to anger the majority of Americans. The reason was the Stamp Act, which called for taxation of the colonists — without their consent.

But, for all the hatred Americans felt for the mother country, they found that some of the strongest opponents of the act were Englishmen — highly placed Englishmen like William Pitt, the eloquent former Prime Minister who later became the Earl of Chatham.

"I rejoice," said the great statesman in the heat of the fight, "that America has resisted."

The act passed and then, with the help of Pitt and his friends, it was repealed. Pitt was acclaimed in America. Charles Willson Peale painted an allegorical picture of him as Augustus, one version of which hangs in Annapolis. Marylanders attempted to erect a statue in his honor.

The attempt came to naught. But, in Baltimore, that section of Fayette between Charles and Calvert was named Chatham Street in his honor. About a half-century later, the name was shifted to a much less important street, which today runs a half-block south from the 1200 block of East Biddle.

As for Chatham Road in Ashburton and Forest Park, that came into existence much later, and the origin of its name is unknown.

Soon after the tax affair, Pitt lost his mind and retired to his home, shutting himself in an attic and refusing to see anyone. But he returned to Parliament in 1770 and made scathing attacks upon the government's American policy. If his health had not failed, the next few years might have well been different.

Yet, in 1778, he made a speech against granting American independence — and the effort of delivering that speech killed him.

June 3, 1951

Clay

By William Stump

Henry Clay, who ran for president three times and was defeated three times, was one of the most loved and hated men in American history.

Those who admired the tall Kentuckian during his half-century of public life regarded him as a brilliant and tireless statesman who, with his silver tongue and outspoken courage, fought for the nation's betterment.

Those who hated him regarded him as a ruthless politician whose every act was designed to get him in the White House, and whether or not those acts benefited the country was not considered.

Clay was a United States senator six times. The first time, he resigned to become a representative, and as such was speaker of the House for years. He had definite and loud opinions on everything that went on in the government, from the tariff to the question of slavery.

He fought duels with men who opposed him; he effected compromises, made decisions that pulled the nation out of some tough spots. He was the man credited with leading America into the War of 1812. He held off the split between the North and the South.

He had a personal charm that won friends by the thousands; he was never at a loss for words. As a debater and a speaker he was called great. His voice, one man wrote, "was like some superb instrument which could be pitched at will to majestic denunciation, withering scorn, light pleasantry, deep or tender emotion. It was the voice of an actor; the expressive face and emotional temperament of this man who could move others to tears belonged behind the footlights."

Opponents of the man who said "I would rather be right than president" held that his speech-making was a huge fraud, that there was nothing behind the words. They said he was so hungry for the presidency that he would say or do anything to win it.

There is much to back this up. Clay switched his opinions and allegiances frequently in his long career. When Monroe was president and John Quincy Adams secretary of state, he attacked them at every turn — and then, when Adams beat him for the presidency, became Adams' secretary of state in the hope of becoming president the next time.

Later, when he determined to run against Andrew Jackson and had no real issues to fight with, he supported the United States Bank (which Jackson was seeking to limit on the ground that it was a danger to the people) even though he had previously been against it.

Clay, a Virginian who moved to Kentucky and became a successful criminal lawyer before he went into national politics, was well known in Baltimore. In 1828, returning to Washington from Philadelphia, where he had consulted "medical gentlemen," he was tendered a dinner at the City Hotel, where he "cursed his detractors and deplored military rule" — a reference to Andrew Jackson, whom he hated.

In 1831, he won the presidential nomination at the Whig convention, held at the Athenaeum. In 1844, he won it again, in a convention held at the Universalist Church on Calvert Street. That convention set Baltimore wild; there was a huge, noisy parade along Baltimore Street, with flower-decorated arches at Calvert Street and at Hanover. Never before, says one historian, had Baltimore put on such an enthusiastic show.

Clay Street appears in the 1842 city directory; in 1851, a year before Clay died at the age of 77, it appears on maps. That the narrow downtown street, originally Waggen and later Barnett, was renamed for the politician seems certain since Baltimore was a strong Whig town and so his supporter.

January 22, 1950

Colegate

By William Stump

According to legend, there is buried treasure somewhere between South Canton and Bear Creek on the Patapsco neck.

The treasure might be under a barracks at Camp Holabird. Or in Canton, in land covered by factories and warehouses.

It could be near Dundalk. Then again, it might be near the body of water or the street which bear the name of the man who supposedly buried it.

The body of water is Colgate Creek, the street Colgate Avenue; both preserve the name — the misspelled name — of Col. Richard Colegate, a wealthy 17th- and 18th-century squire who owned most of the land which makes up Canton and the western part of Dundalk.

Colonel Colegate was one of the wealthiest Marylanders of his time — and one of the least known, evidently. Save on various land records, his name can be found in very few old documents. Perhaps what one historian calls "secretiveness" is responsible for this, and for the legend that Colegate buried most of his money on his vast estate.

Colgate Avenue – 1950

Richard Colegate was born in England in 1645. He may have been given his title of colonel there, for although there is nothing to prove that he served in his Majesty's army, his tombstone in Mount Carmel Cemetery is engraved with swords and guns and other military objects.

He came to Maryland in 1697, and added to his already considerable fortune by dealing in real estate in what are now Baltimore, Anne Arundel and Harford counties. In 1700, he married Rebecca Harcourt, who bore him four sons and three daughters named Prudence, Temperance and Patience.

In 1702, he served as county commissioner, and from 1708 until 1719, he was a delegate to the General Assembly. He died in 1722 and was buried near Old Homestead, his mansion near Colgate Creek. In 1870, his remains were removed to Mount Carmel, along with his ornate tombstone.

In connection with efforts to locate the treasure, Richard Colegate's name has come into the news from time to time over the years. And he was in the news in the 1890s when two New Yorkers, claiming to be his descendants, asked a court to award them the valuable land in Southeast Baltimore. Nothing came of the quest, and the New Yorkers went home empty-handed.

Colgate Avenue, according to city officials, derives its name from its proximity to Colgate Creek. It came into being as part of a real-estate development called Colgate Park in the early years of this century. Then, the street was located entirely in the county; now, it lies in both the county and the city.

April 5, 1953

Crittenton

By James C. Bertram

Up until 1882, Charles Nelson Crittenton had done nothing to ensure himself remembrance by posterity.

He was one of thousands of well-to-do 19th-century businessmen, and his success story was typical. Born on an upstate New York farm, he had attended a country school and had started his business career clerking in a country store. Then he had decided to go to the big city and make his fortune — which he did in a reasonable length of time, becoming the president of a large wholesale drug firm.

A typical story and, save for the inspiration that comes from most tales of success, a little dull. But then something happened which changed the entire course of Crittenton's life — and started him on a new career that has been of immeasurable benefit over the years.

The event was the death of Crittenton's 4-year-old daughter Florence, who was stricken with scarlet fever. To the businessman, it was a terrible shock. It caused him to examine himself. He became religious. Life was something he began to see in a new perspective.

Not long after the little girl's death a friend asked Crittenton to come along to a "rescue" mission in the Bowery's red-light area. There he heard a speaker exhorting a group of what were then fallen women to "go, and sin no more."

Florence Crittenton Home – 1961

But where, the businessman asked, could the women go? Who would help them? He answered the questions by opening a mission to aid them. It fulfilled a great need in the city of New York. And at the same time it helped the man forget a grief that had become unshakable.

So Crittenton gave up his business and plunged into rescue work. Soon he had developed another idea — homes where unwed mothers would be taken in, helped over their trying times and sent back into society with their self-respect restored. With evangelical zeal he began traveling the country in a special railroad car, organizing the homes in every major city.

The "Merchant Evangelist" — who died in 1909 at the age of 76 — visited Baltimore in 1896 and, soon afterward, a Florence Crittenton home was opened in the parsonage of the High Street Methodist Church.

In 1900, it was moved to 837 Hollins Street and in 1926 to its present location in Hampden, in the old Hooper mansion at West 32nd Street and Crittenton Place — that short street being named by the city soon after the move took place.

One of 57 Florence Crittenton Homes in the country today, the Baltimore House is a cheery place with a sunny nursery, and it is run on a common-sense basis. It is supported by private donation, and last year 97 young women, women of all circumstances and from all parts of the country, sought help there.

They were cared for, their children — some to be adopted, some to be kept — were born at downtown hospitals — and the young women went back into the world with hope and confidence and with the knowledge that now things were going to be all right.

June 18, 1950

Culver

By William Stump

When Helen Culver joined her cousin's Chicago real-estate firm in 1868, she found a business based upon a novel theory: If more poor people did not become homeowners, there was bound to be a revolution.

She found that her cousin, Charles Jerold Hull, who had been poor himself, was bent on making such a revolution impossible by buying up cheap land in a number of cities, building inexpensive houses on the land, and selling the houses, with no down payments, on an easy installment plan.

Charity, however, did not enter into the venture. For Hull, while he believed that land was a natural heritage and that even the poorest family should own a piece, hated charity.

He was convinced, he wrote, that "gifts demoralize and weaken the poor; their salvation is in working for themselves. Work and economy are their needs." Consequently, he proceeded on what he termed "sound business principles" — and made a fortune.

Hull, a natural altruist, spent his life in helping people gain self-respect. He worked in prisons. He found employment for criminals. He established homes for newsboys. He helped emancipated slaves acquire educations.

When he was building houses in Savannah, he and Miss Culver, whose approach to life was similar to his own, worked all day in their office, and at night turned that office into a school. Here, hundreds of emancipated slaves were taught to read and write under Miss Culver's instruction.

Sometimes, Hull put on old clothes and helped the former slaves paint the houses that he had sold them.

As partners, the cousins built hundreds of houses in Savannah. In 1871, with Miss Culver in charge of the Chicago office, Hull came to Baltimore and, characteristically, purchased tracts of land on the undeveloped edges of the city.

One of these tracts, located south and west of Gwynns Falls Park in the Irvington section, was the site of a development he called Whitehall; some of the houses he built there still stand — and the streets he cut through still bear the names he gave them.

One of the streets is Morley Street, doubtless named for a son who died of cholera. Another, running south from Hilton Street diagonally to the Old Frederick Road, is Culver Street.

Helen Culver, like her cousin and life-long friend, is still remembered in Chicago. And she probably will be for many years — for with part of the millions of dollars Hull left to her upon his death in 1889, she helped Jane Addams transform the Hull mansion into the Hull House Social Settlement, the first and long the foremost establishment of its kind in the country. And, over the years, she gave untold sums to help it in its work among the people of Chicago.

She also gave $1,000,000 to the University of Chicago for the four buildings that make up the Hull biological laboratories — and gave millions to hundreds of social, welfare, suffrage and educational organizations, including the black schools and colleges all over the country.

Helen Culver was born in Cattaraugus County, New York, in 1832, and spent her girlhood weaving and spinning and learning to read. In 1851, soon after her father's death, she moved to Illinois and founded a "select school for young ladies" near Chicago. At the age of 22, she became the principal of one of the city's seven public schools.

She was an abolitionist and a feminist. During the Civil War, she ran a Union Army hospital at Murfreesboro, Tenn., tending to the wounded with a like regard for both Yankee and Rebel. After the war, she returned to teaching. Then, when women in business were looked upon as freaks, she joined her cousin.

A few years after Hull's death, she turned the business over to a nephew and devoted her time to giving away the great fortune. Even though she lost her eyesight in the early years of the century, she remained active and interested in everything from Chicago political reform to new methods of education.

Even in 1925, Baltimore relatives recall, when she died at the age of 93, she could still recite long poems and entire plays, and tell clearly of the days when she and her cousin helped people get a little land of their own.

July 18, 1954

Cylburn Avenue

By William Stump

Much can be said about the grandeur and elegance that were Cylburn's in the years when the Bruce Cottens owned the estate. And much can be summed up, perhaps, by mentioning that the estate had its own railroad station.

The station was on the Northern Central line, just below Belvedere Avenue. The Cottens, their dozen servants and their legions of weekend guests reached it by a rustic road that began at the mid-Victorian stone mansion and stretched through acres of gardens and woodland.

Not a trace of the station remains. The once-famous formal gardens and the 32 acres of lawn are not as exquisitely cared for as there were in the days when Mrs. Cotten was Baltimore's social arbiter.

Now Cylburn is the property of the Park Department, which came into possession of it in 1942 and which, in 1944, loaned the house and grounds to the Welfare Department. That agency has been operating the place as a children's refuge since then; recently, however, the park authorities asked that the acreage be returned to them within two years so that it can be turned into a recreational area.

Occupying 180 acres, Cylburn is bounded on the east by the railroad tracks, on the north by Belvedere Avenue, and on the south by the woods of the section known as Melvale. On the west is a bit of Greenspring Avenue, the

Tyson-Cotten estate — Cylburn – 1954

location of the estate's big stone gateway. But most of the west boundary is made up by Cylburn Avenue, which, along with the children's shelter, preserves the name of this place.

Cylburn became an estate at the close of the Civil War when Jesse Tyson, who made a fortune mining chrome up the track at Bare Hills, began to build the house for his mother. She died before that was completed, and work was suspended for a number of years. But it was ready in 1889, when Tyson married Edyth Johns — a debutante many years younger who was considered one of the city's great beauties.

So great a beauty, indeed, that the late Alfred Jenkins Shriver stipulated that her portrait be displayed in the auditorium building that his will directed be built at the Johns Hopkins University and that is to be completed this July. The portrait will be one of a group of 10 likenesses of the Baltimore women Shriver called the most beautiful of his era.

The bride made Cylburn a showplace unique in Baltimore. Every summer she traveled to Europe to buy antique furnishings for its formal rooms. And the house soon became celebrated for the lavishness and elegance of its parties, and for the loveliness of its gardens.

Jesse Tyson died in 1906. Four years later his widow met a young lieutenant of artillery, a soldier who had fought in the Boxer Rebellion and the Philippines and had earned himself a commission. He was Bruce Cotten, a member of an old and respected North Carolina clan. When Mrs. Tyson went to England in the summer of 1910, the lieutenant, who was stationed at Fort McHenry, followed her. They were married in August.

In the years that followed, the Cottens made Cylburn even more of a showplace. In the Louis XV drawing room, with its furniture from a Rouen palace and its gold-embroidered satin damask draperies, Baltimore society gathered for musicales and receptions. In the summer, guests strolled the lawns lit with hundreds of Japanese lanterns.

A patron of music and the theater in Baltimore and chairman of the Matriarchs' Assembly for a quarter-century, Mrs. Cotten was renowned for an affable and democratic manner — one of the "greatest menaces is a snob," she said. It is said that servants who came to work for the family stayed for years; their faithfulness was reflected in the immaculateness of the house and the grounds.

Mrs. Cotten died in 1942, and Mr. Cotten sold the house to the city and moved to Hamilton Street. "Mrs. Cotten was anxious that the city and not some developer have it, and so was I," he explained. "I often told Howard Jackson that I would have given Cylburn to the city had not the city decided to purchase it.

"My friends thought I was making a mistake to get rid of Cylburn and move to Hamilton Street," said Mr. Cotten, who died April 1 at the age of 81. "But I knew I was right. I realized we were passing into new times, times in which there was no place for the kind of living that Mrs. Cotten and I had known for so many years."

D

April 16, 1950

Decatur

By William Stump

"Decatur — a man more unique, more highly endowed than any other I ever knew, to whom this country is indebted for the naval renown which is the admiration of the world."

Although these words spoken by a fellow naval officer in describing Stephen Decatur seem to be praiseworthy to an extreme, there is nothing unusual about them. Everyone who came in contact with the man, from president of the United States to ordinary seamen, was similarly enthusiastic. For Decatur's exploits, at a time when America's well-being was very much dependent on her Navy, made him one of the most celebrated heroes in the nation's history.

His popularity was especially great in Maryland. For one thing, he was a native of the state, having been born in 1779 at Sinepuxent in Worcester County. For another, he was a major figure in the War of 1812, a conflict which meant so much to the seafaring town of Baltimore. And he died in Maryland — as a result of wounds received in a violent duel at Bladensburg.

This duel occurred in 1820 about the time that a state commission was in the process of naming many proposed Baltimore streets for important Marylanders of the era. The commission, records show, named one for Stephen Decatur. The street is a few blocks from Fort McHenry.

Decatur spent very little time of his life in Maryland. His mother, the wife of a sea captain, moved to Sinepuxent when the British occupied Philadelphia during the Revolution. Decatur grew up in Philadelphia.

After his first voyage with his father, Decatur fell in love with the sea. He entered the Navy as a midshipman in 1798 and was commissioned a lieutenant only a year later.

Decatur became a national hero in 1804 when, at the age of 25, he took a small boatload of men into Tripoli harbor under the guns of the piratical Tripolitanians, boarded the captured ship Philadelphia, killed her pirate crew, set fire to the ship and, under heavy gun fire, escaped with all his men. For this adventure he was made a captain.

Soon afterward, Decatur played a conspicuous part in the attacks that ended the two-year war with Tripoli. He came home, married and served for a time on Chesapeake Bay.

When the War of 1812 came, he was commanding the United States, one of the Navy's mightiest frigates. He took her into action and was again nationally praised for defeating and capturing the British frigate Macedonian. Toward the end of the war, after being blockaded in New York, he took a ship into battle and ruined the British Endymion before he was forced to surrender to three more ships. After the war he led a successful expedition against the Dey of Algiers.

The popularity which Decatur enjoyed during his short life was based just as much upon his "private virtues" as upon his deeds in war. He always, one historian says, said the right thing at the right time. After his capture of the Macedonian, he told the defeated captain: "Sir, I cannot receive the sword of a man who has so bravely defended his ship, but will receive your hand."

And at Norfolk he said: "Our country! In her intercourse with foreign nations may she always be in the right; but our country, right or wrong!"

Dolfield

By Henry C. Rauch

Somewhat paradoxically, a man who during much of his life was particularly identified with East Baltimore affairs has left his name to a thoroughfare in Northwest Baltimore. The man was Alexander Y. Dolfield. The thoroughfare is Dolfield Avenue, which runs across Forest Park and Ashburton from Garrison Avenue to Hilton Road.

From the 1870s to the early 1900s, Mr. Dolfield was one of the city's most prominent bankers. He was the founder of the German-American Bank in East Baltimore, and of a series of German-American building associations that enabled thousands of homes to be bought in that area. He was one of the organizers of the East Baltimore Business Men's Association.

But his interests were not confined exclusively to the eastern part of the city. Around the late 1860s, he bought 65 acres adjoining the Gittings estate of Ashburton in the northwestern suburbs, and began its development by building five houses.

It is from this landholding that the street name springs. Into his property was cut a road that became known as Dolfield Road, and when in February 1923 — five years after Mr. Dolfield's death — this road was absorbed into a greater thoroughfare through the area, the name of the late owner was retained, in preference to a new one that had been proposed.

Alexander Yearly Dolfield was born in Baltimore on October 10, 1839. He attended the public grade schools and City College, graduating from the latter in 1857. He then taught mathematics at Trinity School, but the banking business attracted him and after something more than a year he gave up teaching to become a runner for the Franklin Bank. He advanced steadily during 12 years with that institution, and during six of these was paying teller.

In 1873, Mr. Dolfield organized the German-American Bank, on South Broadway, and became its cashier. Organization of the building associations followed, and meanwhile he had acquired the suburban land, as mentioned, and also a farm at Owings Mills. He was active until about 1906, when he went into retirement on the farm. He died in April 1918.

Frederick A. Dolfield, a son, has continued the family banking tradition. He is president of the Canton National Bank. From 1923 to 1927, he was city register (treasurer), and for a number of years he was treasurer of the Commission on Governmental Efficiency and Economy.

Druid Hill Avenue

From mansion, or costly or humble
We have come to these woodland homes
And for the park of the hill of the druid
We have left the far city's domes
And now, unto health and to pleasure
These forest-clad hills are devoted
By their old and ancestral name

The well-scrubbed schoolchildren on the lawn in front of the big house sang the song lustily, and parents and politicians and city officials beamed. It was a happy day, that day in October 1860. For after years of effort and wrangling, the estate called Druid Hill had become a park.

Indeed, of all the throng present for the dedicatory ceremonies, only one, it is said, felt any sadness. He was Lloyd Nicholas Rogers — whose clan had owned Druid Hill for a century and a half. He had almost angrily sold his 475 acres to the city, and the next day he was to move away forever. Perhaps, as he sat with his daughter on the porch of his mansion listening to the songs and speeches, he thought of that, and thought of the long history of his land.

Rogers was a proud man and a scholarly man, and he knew that long history. He knew that the land had originally been part of a tract assigned by Charles Calvert, Lord Baltimore, to one Thomas Richardson, who had sold 350 acres of it to Thomas Durbing.

Col. Nicholas Rogers' Mansion House – 1956

Durbing had named those acres, the heart of the present park, Hab Nab at a Venture — meaning, roughly, "hit or miss." Adjoining holdings were also whimsically named: Come by Chance, Haphazard, The Level, Happy Be Lucky, Fear. The park is made up of parts of all these.

Hab Nab changed hands a couple of times in the later 1600s; in 1716 most of it was purchased by Nicholas Rogers 2d, an inn-keeper, if old records are accurate, whose father owned all of what is now Baltimore east of Charles Street and south of Federal Hill.

Nicholas Rogers couldn't do much with his new land; he died in 1720. His daughter, Eleanor, came into ownership then. Five or six years later she met and married a young physician recently over from Scotland. His name was George Buchanan, and he had come to the colonies because, as the third son of a landed aristocrat, he had no possible chance of inheriting property or fortune.

His decision was a good one. He became involved in the affairs of the colony; in 1729, for example, he was chosen as one of the seven commissioners to organize and start up the town of Baltimore. He was a magistrate, too, and, besides, a practicing medical man and a real-estate operator of some ability.

Indeed, he added a good many acres to Hab Nab — which he renamed Auchentorolie after his family's land in Scotland. And he chose to live on the land, building a Colonial house which stood until 1860 or so.

Buchanan died in 1750; his son, Lloyd Buchanan, died in 1761, his only heir his 3-year-old daughter; when she reached young womanhood she married a dashing and prominent Baltimorean named Nicholas Rogers — a much younger brother of the Eleanor who had married George Buchanan half a century before.

Col. Nicholas Rogers was a Baltimore merchant. He was educated abroad. In the Revolution, he served as aide de camp to Baron de Kalb. He was an artistic man, and an architect of more than ordinary ability, and he designed the first house to be built on the site of what Baltimoreans today call the Mansion House.

That was a low, one-story affair built in the Federal style; in front of it stretched formal gardens of the colonel's design and a grove of trees that he planted so that they would form various patterns and color combinations when the leaves turned in the fall.

The house did not last long; in 1796 it burned down. Rogers designed another — which, so remodeled as to be unrecognizable from its original appearance, is the present Mansion House. Rogers named it Druid Hill, presumably for the ancient trees on the property.

After 1822, the year in which the colonel died, Druid Hill came into possession of Lloyd Nicholas Rogers, the man who sold it to the city. At the time he inherited the place he was a debonair and cultivated lawyer who made the property something of a showplace and who raised a large family there. But after the second of his wives died and his children married and moved away, Rogers became embittered with the world.

Much of his bitterness stemmed from the day that a turnpike company managed to get the state to condemn a portion of his land for a road. That is said to have made him eventually decide to sell Druid Hill to the city, which had been seeking a park. For a time, complicated politics held up the deal. But in 1860, the city bought his 475 acres for $1,000 per acre, and the park came into being.

For some 20 years, Baltimoreans reached the retreat aboard a railroad train called "the Dummy" which ran around the west side from North Avenue. But as the city grew, and the line discontinued, they came by streetcar up Druid Hill Avenue, which had been renamed for the park in the 1860s, debarking in woods where herds of deer roamed, or beside meadows where shepherds tended quiet flocks of sheep.

E

September 19, 1948

Eden

By Elizabeth H. Moberly

Eden Street, running through East Baltimore from the harbor to Lanvale Street, was 19th-century Baltimore's tribute to the last royal governor of Maryland.

Sir Robert Eden, whom contemporaries called "a hearty, rattling, wild young dog of an officer," arrived in 1769 to take over his royal office. Already there were rumblings of revolution, but Eden managed to win the friendship of the colonists though he remained completely loyal to the crown.

He was only 28 when Lord Baltimore named him to the governorship, and there were critics who felt that Eden's appointment was perhaps influenced by his marriage to Caroline Calvert, Baltimore's sister.

However, Robert Eden started early in his life to make a name for himself.

At the age of 16, he held a commission as lieutenant fire-worker in the Royal Regiment of Artillery, and by the time he was

Eden Street – 1938

21, when he gave up the army as a career, he was a captain.

He never lost his dashing qualities, even after he became governor, and in the colonial capital of Annapolis he patronized the theater, kept a racing stable, entertained a wide range of guests that included Indian chiefs and the Washingtons, and led the more sober-minded, like Charles Carroll, to look on him as something of a playboy.

At a time when his presence might be considered necessary to soothe the shortening tempers of the colonists, Eden returned to England to look after private affairs, and so missed the sudden violence and burning of the Peggy Stewart in Annapolis.

He returned to the capital a few months later, however, and resumed his popular place with the colonists. He laid the cornerstone of the State House — accompanied, it is said, by a terrific clap of thunder when he symbolically touched the stone with the trowel.

Perhaps to show there was nothing personal in their demands for liberty, the Marylanders named Caroline County for the governor's wife, and gave the name of Denton (shortened from Edenton) to the county seat.

His stay in America was to be brief; in 1772 it was deemed expedient that he leave once more. A British man-of-war anchored off Annapolis to take the governor and his family to England.

Eden, who during the years he was in England was made Baronet of Maryland, lost no time in returning to America at the conclusion of hostilities. Acting on behalf of Harry Harford, the last Lord Baltimore, he tried to obtain some payment for the lands and properties which had been confiscated.

He was stricken ill during his visit and died at the home of a friend in Annapolis. Legend has it that because of fear that latent anti-British feelings might be aroused by any ceremony, Sir Robert's body was moved across the Severn under cover of darkness and secretly interred at St. Margaret's Church.

The church was destroyed by fire in 1823 and the grave lost for over a century. Then it was located by searchers, and the body of Maryland's last royal governor was returned to his capital.

June 12, 1949

Edmondson

By Henry C. Rauch

Edmondson Avenue carries across West Baltimore, and on out into the country, the name of one of the city's earliest patrons of the fine arts, science and agriculture — Dr. Thomas Edmondson.

The street has not always borne his name. Once it was called Thompson. The name was changed about 1876, when the city dedicated as a park a tract presented by Dr. Edmondson's executor, which had been part of his country place, called Harlem.

The park then was named Harlem Park; the name of Adams Street, which bounded it on the north, was changed to Harlem Avenue, and Thompson Street was changed to Edmondson Avenue.

Dr. Edmondson was born in Baltimore in 1808, the son of Thomas Edmondson, a wealthy merchant who had come to the city about 10 years earlier. The son took an arts degree at St. Mary's College in 1831, then studied medicine at the University of Maryland and in 1834 gained a medical degree.

He never practiced medicine, however. Possibly one reason was that his own constitution was never very strong. A likelier one was the simple fact that he did not need to; from his father and a childless uncle he inherited a fortune that tradition says was about half a million dollars.

With such wealth, he was able to indulge his interest in the arts and sciences.

He patronized American painters; Calyo, Woodville and Fischer did portraits of him and his family — in 1845, he had married a Miss Mary Howell — and paintings of Harlem both inside and out. He also collected the works of other artists. A number of these paintings are now owned by his granddaughters, the Misses Hough, of Baltimore, and were exhibited several years ago at the Museum of Art.

Dr. Edmondson had a violin collection that included two Stradivarii and a Guarnerius. He amassed a large library. His interest in agriculture led to his serving for several years as president of the Horticultural Society, and to his establishment of one of Maryland's few orangeries. He propagated flowers and shrubs.

Dr. Edmondson died November 24, 1856, at the early age of 48. Eleven years later, John H. B. Latrobe, his executor, offered

Edmondson Avenue – 1954

the city as a park the tract of 9¾ acres that had been Harlem's "front yard." It was promptly accepted, but nine more years passed before the park was formally dedicated.

October 21, 1951

The Erdmans

By James C. Bertram

There is little doubt that Erdman Avenue came into being sometime between 1816 and 1840. There is little doubt that two brothers named Erdman cut it through. But the exact identity of those brothers is a point on which even the Erdmans disagree.

"My grandfather," says Miss Clara Erdman, "always told me that his father Adam Gottlieb Erdman, and Adam's brother Matthias were responsible for the street.

"The brothers came to America from Germany in 1816, Matthias settled on the Harford Road, somewhere near the northwest corner of what is now Clifton Park. In a few years, he was farming many acres, including a good bit of land between

Harford and Belair roads.

"Adam settled out on the Belair Road, on high land that came to be known as Erdman's Hill; he built a low stone house just across from the land now occupied by the Church of the Little Flower. He was a farmer, too, and grandfather said he owned most of what is now Herring Run Park, as well as land on both sides of the Belair Road down to Erdman Avenue.

"His farm was so big that 100 extra hands were needed at harvest time. My grandfather says that he used to go down and get German immigrants from the ships for that work. They were lodged in a big building on Erdman's Hill."

Erdman Avenue, according to Miss Erdman, was cut through from the Harford to the Belair Road by Adam and Matthias as a wagon road. Each gave a portion of the land for it. "It must have been before 1840," Miss Erdman says, "because an 1840 entry in the records of Jerusalem Church, for which great-grandfather Adam gave the land, mentions Erdman Avenue."

George Mumma, whose mother was an Erdman, agrees that one of the brothers who created the street was named Adam — but believes that the other was John.

"There may have been a number of brothers who came with Adam from Germany," he says, "and therefore a number may have owned land. But I've always heard that the farm adjoining Adam's property belonged to John. That's what my grandfather, Peter G. Erdman, told me — and John was his father."

Still another Erdman — the original Erdmans had many children, and today the clan is a vast one — recalls hearing that Erdman Avenue was cut through when Johns Hopkins owned Clifton. "The story goes," says C. E. Erdman, "that Hopkins wanted a road bordering the east side of his estate, which he was planning to turn into a park.

"As the Erdmans owned land to the east of that, Hopkins proposed that he give 25 feet for a road and the Erdmans also give 25 feet. The family agreed. But then Hopkins is supposed to have backed out, leaving the project in the hands of the Erdman family. This may be true or it may be legend."

Mr. Mumma recalls Erdman Avenue in the 1890s, just before the street and the surrounding area became a part of the city.

"You could hardly call it an avenue then," he says. "It would have been more appropriate to call it a mud hole. I remember going over it one Sunday morning to church, in a buggy with my family. That buggy bogged right down in that mud — and so did the horse."

Erdman Avenue has changed since then. Now it is one of the busiest streets in the city; every day, thousands of Baltimoreans drive over it to get to and from jobs at Sparrows Point, Middle River and Canton. It begins at Harford Road and extends many miles south of Belair Road, as a dual highway connecting with North Point Road at the city line.

Erdman Avenue – 1965

January 30, 1949

Etting

By Robert L. Weinberg

In Northwest Baltimore, a narrow street stretches for many blocks north from Hoffman Street almost to Druid Hill Park. It is named for the first Jew to hold a public office in Maryland, one of the prominent men of his day.

Solomon Etting came to Baltimore Town from York, Pa., in 1789 and opened a hardware store on Calvert Street at Lovely Lane (now Redwood Street).

Etting later moved up to Market Street (Baltimore Street) and his hardware store became a general shipping and commercial business, bringing him into contact with the important mercantile leaders of the town.

In 1792, he was appointed to a committee to protest to General Washington the terms of Jay's treaty with England; later he was made a director of the new Union Bank, and of the Baltimore Water Company. In 1814, his son, Samuel, served as a private with the Baltimore Fencibles when that gallant unit helped in the defense of Fort McHenry.

Solomon Etting had twice tried to have removed the political disabilities of the Jews, but it was not until 1825 when the struggle was taken up by Thomas Kennedy, General Winder and John V. L. McMahon, among others, that the bill was finally passed by the Legislature and Jews were permitted to hold public office.

The following year Etting was elected president of the First Branch of the City Council (it was a bicameral body), and soon afterward he was elected to the first board of directors of the newly formed Baltimore and Ohio Railroad — the project to stimulate commercial activity by providing a link between the harbor of Baltimore and the West beyond the mountains.

When Etting was laid to rest in 1847 not far from the street which bears his name, he had lived a life of accomplishment. His perseverance and the respect in which he was held had resulted in the political emancipation of the people of his faith in Maryland, and he had been a member of the farseeing group which organized the first railroad in the nation, an important event in the growth of Baltimore.

March 7, 1954

Eutaw Street

By William Stump

Col. John Eager Howard was "as good an officer as the world affords. He deserves a statue of gold, no less than the Roman and Grecian heroes."

That generous — even high-flown — tribute was paid the Maryland Revolutionary soldier by no less a figure than Gen. Nathaniel Greene. And Greene had good reason to pay it. For Howard and his men had served valiantly in one of the war's bloodiest battles.

Indeed Howard became so closely identified with the battle that people of Baltimore named Eutaw Street in commemoration.

The affair at Eutaw Springs occurred September 8, 1781. By that time Howard was an old soldier, the veteran of many a fierce fight. He had joined up the same month the Declaration of Independence was signed, accepting a captain's commission in the 2d Maryland Battalion.

Two days after his commissioning he raised a company and marched to join the Army in New York. That October he fought the British and Hessian regulars at White Plains. When the Army was reorganized in December, he was made a major in the Fourth Maryland and led it after its colonel was wounded at Germantown.

There, in advance of the Army, Howard and his men raced through the British tent lines, taking the camp by surprise.

In 1778, by this time the lieutenant colonel of the Fifth Maryland, Howard fought at the battle of Monmouth. A year later he was in action with the Second Maryland in the Southern campaign. At Camden, he ordered his men to use their bayonets to cover the American retreat.

Howard and his men of the Maryland Line used their bayonets again at Cowpens, used them to such advantage in a crucial charge that the day was won. "The Hero of Cowpens," they called Howard after that.

The campaigning in the Carolinas was hard; the fighting was frequent and furious. The British won the field at Guilford Court House and Hobkirk's Hill — but the victories were Pyrrhic and the enemy tottered. And that led to the battle of Eutaw Springs.

Greene sought that battle. Col. Alexander Stewart was encamped at Eutaw Springs; Greene and his militia and Continentals closed in. But the hoped-for surprise did not come off; British foragers warned the camp, and Greene had to draw up his men in line of battle.

The British regulars charged and smashed through the rag-tag militia and Carolina Continentals. Then Howard and the Marylanders counterattacked and ran into the Irish Buffs. The ensuing fight has been termed one of the bloodiest of the war. The Irishmen broke in full retreat.

The Americans lost the day when the British rallied, and in another bayonet attack Howard was badly wounded. The next day the British retreated — their energies spent in the South.

When he had partly recovered from his wounds Howard was invalided home. In later years he served as a Maryland congressman and as the state's governor. He lived out his life at Belvedere, his estate north of the city, and died in 1827 at the age of 75.

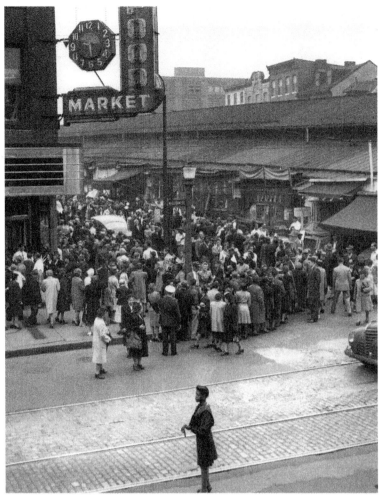

Eutaw Street – 1946

F

August 13, 1950

Fait

By William Stump

Thanks to William Fait, Baltimoreans of the 1890s enjoyed softshell crabs in the dead of winter and oyster stew in the heat of summer. So, for that matter, did the citizens of Chicago, Kansas City and Denver.

For William Fait sold the tasty produce of the Chesapeake Bay in cans — cans that were packed by special process, in his vast factory on the Canton shore. The oysters were carefully steamed in the shell, then shucked at long tables, then packed in a brine solution; the softshell crabs were gently sautéed in butter and put up in oval tins, four prime crabs to the tin.

"You could buy a dozen tins for two dollars," sighs Paul Johnson, who at the early age of 15 was William Fait's foreman. "And the crabs were actually more delicious than fresh ones. The oysters, because that brine acted upon them, made the finest stews imaginable. Mr. Fait really knew the canning business."

The canning factory was the largest in Maryland, in size, scope and production. Located at Boston Street and Patuxent Street — now Linwood Avenue — it took up an entire block. It included warehouses, a shucking shed, a processing plant, a canning and packing house, a can manufacturing works, an electric plant, artesian wells, stables and wharves.

In addition to the oysters, packed as the "Monkey" and "Rooster" brands, there were the crabs, gooseberries, blackberries, strawberries, plums, pears, peaches, peas, wax and lima beans, tomatoes and pineapples canned under the "Popular" brand label. The machinery in the plant was the most modern of the day. Six hundred people were employed; the weekly payroll was over $5,000.

Mr. Johnson recalls that the company did over $1,000,000 worth of business a year — good money in the '90s. "That wasn't surprising," he says. "The plant was busy most of the day and night. Why, I've seen oyster boats and vegetable schooners, loaded to the gunwales, standing off our wharves by the dozen. There would be so many of them that you couldn't see the water."

Fait, Mr. Johnson remembers, was a serious-looking, quiet-voiced man who, although he ran his business with a very firm hand, could be generous and jovial. "He was a hard worker," says Mr. Johnson. "He used to come down from his home on South Patterson Park Avenue at all hours. As a businessman, he had all the pluck in the world."

The cannery was just one of William Fait's interests. He was a bank director and an insurance executive; he was active in civic affairs and, as a politician, helped run the city jail.

Leo Fait, whose father was the canning company's treasurer and traveling salesman, believes it was William's business and political activities, together, that prompted the City Council to change the name of the eastern part of Lancaster Street to Fait Avenue. That was in 1894; now, a few blocks above the site the cannery occupied, Fait Avenue begins at Montford Avenue. Interrupted at a number of places by railroad yards, factories and a cemetery, it extends east to 51st Street.

William Fait was largely a self-made man. Born in Baltimore in 1855, of German parents who had immigrated a few years before, he went to school at Professor Knapp's Institute, situated on Holliday Street on the site of City Hall. At 14 he entered Professor Lozier's Business College, and at 15 went to work as an office boy in a cannery.

By the time he was 25, a biography written in the '90s reveals "his frugal methods of living had borne fruit and his bank account represented several thousand dollars." Soon he married Miss Louisa Hehl, and with the birth of a child — there were eventually two daughters and a son — decided to go into the canning business for himself. In 1882, the firm of Fait & Winebrenner, on Aliceanna Street, was founded. In 1892, the company was dissolved and replaced by Fait & Slagle. A year later, the panic of 1893 ruined the concern, but the 1896 Fait's factory was unequaled in the state.

The William Fait Company prospered into this century. Then, because the Eastern Shore canning industry was beginning to come into its own, Fait closed his doors — and turned to the motion-picture business.

Leo Fait recalls that his cousin operated two theaters in downtown Baltimore, the Red Moon and the Lubin. "He used to give me all the free passes I wanted," Mr. Fait remembers. "My prestige among my chums was something."

Later, William Fait entered the canning business in Charleston, but early in World War I retired and moved to Springfield, Ohio, where he died in the '20s.

September 24, 1950

Fleet Street

By William Stump

Baltimore's Fleet Street is long and wide and very busy; all day, rumbling trucks haul goods and materials to and from its factories and warehouses. In the evening, the people of its residential blocks sit on the white steps of their row houses to talk and watch the children at play.

The street, located in Southeast Baltimore, is old — one of the oldest in Baltimore, it is thought. Records show it to have been in existence before the Revolution, in the early days of Fells Point. But who named it and why are facts that are lost in history.

It may well be, however, that the name was chosen because George Calvert, the first Lord Baltimore, was buried at St. Dunstan's-in-the-West, a church on London's Fleet Street.

That, of course, was many years before the city that bears the name of his clan was founded. Indeed, London's Fleet Street was bustling when Indians were camping and fishing on the banks of the Patapsco.

Like many of London's principal thoroughfares, Fleet Street is rich in history and tradition. It took its name from the Fleet River, a large brook that once ran into the Thames at nearby Ludgate Circus. Now completely covered over, the brook is part of London's vast drainage system.

At its western end, Fleet Street joins the Strand at the Temple Bar, the old gate of the city of London. That gate disappeared

Fleet Street – 1950

many years ago, and was replaced by the ugly ornate Edwardian obelisk that stands there today. Even so, it is still tradition that the king, to "cross Temple Bar," must receive the permission of the Lord Mayor.

The street is often called the "Inky Way," for most British newspapers, and many foreign ones — including The Sun — have offices on or within a block or two of it. Most of them have locations with colorful pasts. The magazine Punch, for example, is situated at what once was known as Alsatia, the worst haunt of thieves and highwaymen in the city.

There is even a newspaper men's church, St. Bride's built by Wren; it was terribly damaged by German bombs at the height of the blitz.

Fleet Street has probably more literary associations than any other street in the world. Dr. Johnson lived just off it in tiny Gough Square; his famous "Sir, let us walk down Fleet Street" is to this day a well-loved and commonly used London phrase. He often took his meals at the Mitre Tavern, which was on the site of the building now occupied by the Manchester Guardian and The Sun's London bureau.

Johnson and his Boswell also spent a lot of time at the Cheshire Cheese. Tennyson, who knew and loved the street, mentions his favorite tavern, the Old Cock, in a poem. Izaak Walton was a vestryman at St. Dunstan's. Samuel Butler lived off the street at Clifford Inn. Dryden and Swift lived on Fetter Lane as did Swift's Captain Lemuel Gulliver when not on his legendary travels. Richard Lovelace, the cavalier poet, died in poverty in close-by Gunpowder Alley.

Early in the 17th century, Isaac Newton presided over the Royal Academy in Crane Court; in the same place, Coleridge delivered his famous lectures on Shakespeare. But the earliest known literary association of Fleet Street can be found on a tombstone at St. Bride's — the tombstone of Wynken de Worde, one of the pioneer printers who died in 1535.

June 4, 1950

Fremont

By William Stump

When the City Council named a street for him in 1846, John C. Fremont was a national hero. A year later, he was court-martialed for mutiny and insubordination.

Fremont's life was like that; one minute he was up, the next minute he was down. His genius for exploration — people called him the Pathfinder of the West — was matched by genius for getting himself into trouble.

To most of the country he was a romantic figure — the man who, in spite of his illegitimacy and his penniless youth, made friends in high places, eloped with the daughter of the rich and influential Senator Thomas Hart Benton, explored and opened up the wilderness and helped win California for the Union.

Fremont's exploits in California early in the Mexican War undoubtedly led to the naming of the West Baltimore street which runs from the foot of Eutaw Street diagonally north to Pennsylvania Avenue, a few blocks below North Avenue, but they also led to his court-martial.

This ill fortune was the result of a quarrel between Generals Stockton and Kearny, each of whom, due to garbled instructions from Washington, regarded himself as top man in California. Fremont backed Stockton, and was installed as governor. But the Army decided that Kearny was the man who had been in command all along.

Although Fremont was sent back to Washington in disgrace at Kearny's urging, and convicted of mutiny, President Polk pardoned him. Fremont headed back to California and had a change of luck — great quantities of gold had been discovered on land he owned. He could have stayed in the West, enjoying his wealth and reputation, but the political bug bit him, and after serving briefly as United States senator he decided that he would make a better president than James Buchanan.

In 1856, he won the Republican nomination. But Buchanan, after a vituperative campaign that harped on Fremont's illegitimate birth, defeated him. Once again, he returned to California and settled down. Then the Civil War came, and with it the promise of more adventure.

Again Fremont came in for bad luck; as military governor of the West, with the rank of major general, he made the mistake of freeing slaves in Missouri — an act which President Lincoln regarded as premature. This, plus two military defeats, cost him his job; but the following year he was back in the army as commanding officer in western Virginia. Still no success — Stonewall Jackson defeated him so badly that he retired from the army again.

Thereafter, says Allan Nevins, his principal biographer, "Fremont's history was one of adversity." He decided to run against Lincoln, but was persuaded to withdraw from the race. He went home to California, only to find that his fortune had been stolen. He speculated in railroads, and soon went bankrupt.

Characteristically, though, Fremont's fortunes took another swing to the good. His wife's writings — an author of note, she helped keep his early exploits alive — plus an appointment as territorial governor of Arizona kept him from poverty. Eventually, he even gained restoration of his army pay, but not until 1890, shortly before his death.

November 28, 1948

Furst

By Karen Richards

When Baltimore streets were renamed in the '20s to end some confusing duplications, First Street in Fairfield became Frankfurst Street, taking the name of a man who started out making $1 a week at his first job.

During his lifetime, Frank A. Furst was one of the state's leading political figures, although he never held a political office.

He was born in Baden, Germany, in 1845. In the wake of the revolutions that swept Germany in 1848, the family fled to America. They made the crossing in the steerage of an immigrant ship, and went first to the Flatbush section of Brooklyn in New York. The elder Furst had a brother who had gone to Baltimore and he brought his family south. They moved into a house on Shakespeare Street.

Furst's early years were spent in poverty, for his father died when Frank was very young and the family struggled along as well as it could.

Frank got his first job as a tobacco stripper, at $1 a week. At the age of 12, the eldest of the children, he was bound out as an apprentice to a shoemaker who, like a character out of Dickens, counted the number of pancakes the boy ate for breakfast — and stopped him at four.

The outbreak of the Civil War gave him an opportunity to leave the city, and in 1861 he went as a camp follower with the 14th Brooklyn Infantry, which passed Washington. He was with it at the first battle of Bull Run.

In the confusion of the Federal retreat from the battlefield, young Furst was run over by an army wagon and landed in a hospital for a while. He remained with the Army for three years in the engineers' corps and as a surgeon's assistant.

After Appomattox, he drifted to St. Louis, where he became a professional boxer. He managed to reach the rank of a local champion, but following his defeat in a long, bare-knuckle fight, he was satisfied to follow less strenuous pursuits and was employed in a grain elevator.

Mr. Furst stayed in St. Louis about a year, then returned to Baltimore — not to a job as a shoemaker but as manager of a floating grain elevator.

He later became manager of the Pennsylvania Railroad's grain elevators and by the time the 20th century had begun, he had acquired a fortune large enough to permit him to retire from active life to Drumquhazel, a home he had purchased on York Road.

Over the years he had developed an interest in politics, confined to his neighborhood at first, but extending to city and state. Though he never sought office for himself — he declined repeated proposals that he run for mayor or governor — his support was sought by all political factions and he was the senior, politically, of leaders like Mahon and Kelly. He was said to have greater influence with all branches of the party than any other man.

Both Mr. Furst and his wife felt isolated in the country and soon moved back into Baltimore. Then, at an age when most men seek rest, he returned to active business, at first to aid some friends who were in financial difficulties. He helped form the Baltimore Dredging and Contracting Company (part of his money already having been invested in similar concerns) and various companies grew out of this. Later they were consolidated into the Arundel Corporation.

Following the death of his wife in 1919, Mr. Furst went to Europe, making a trip they had planned to take together. He intended to visit his birthplace and convert the family's cottage into a home for the aged. Seeing a need for more immediate relief to the needy of his native country, he authorized the use of the money for that purpose.

He died in 1934.

G

April 3, 1949

Gable

By Henry C. Rauch

Shortly after the turn of the century, a Baltimore County road supervisor named Henry Gable had a half-mile road cut through a little area southwest of the city to a junction with Washington Boulevard. It came in at what is now the boulevard's 3000 block. On its way it crossed the Baltimore and Ohio's main line at a station called West Baltimore — this existed through 1940 — and so Mr. Gable named it West Baltimore Avenue.

There was, of course, already a West Baltimore Street in Baltimore City, but with the county area being served by the Lansdowne post office the similarity of names caused no trouble to Mr. Gable and the few other persons who lived on the avenue.

In 1919, however, the city annexed that area, and there was trouble. Mail and other deliveries intended for obscure West Baltimore Avenue began going to well-known West Baltimore Street. And as occasionally another family settled on the avenue — there are now eight houses — the problem grew.

Finally in 1942, one of the residents set out to end the confusion. He enlisted his neighbors' support for a change of name from West Baltimore to MacArthur Avenue. An ordinance to do this was introduced in the City Council, passed, and sent to the mayor. Then the councilmen took second thought; they decided that the general deserved a bigger street, and they recalled the ordinance and let it die.

That settled that; but it did not settle the problem of the avenue's residents. Their mail and parcels continued to go wrong, and recently they again decided that a change had to be made. What appropriate name could they get together on? Well, Henry Gable was still living on the avenue; he had cut it through, given it its old name, and lived to be its oldest resident; why not Gable Avenue?

It was agreed. A new ordinance was drafted. But now a new point arose. The city, it was discovered, did not have title to the street bed; this belonged to the various property owners abutting upon it. Therefore the street was not within the City Council's province, but within that of the Bureau of Plans and Surveys. All that was needed to change the name was this bureau's approval of a formal petition submitted by a majority of the property owners.

Such a petition was quickly circulated and submitted, and the bureau checked it and found it proper. Early in March the petitioners were informed that "Gable Avenue is satisfactory to this bureau"; if the petitioners would now ask the Bureau of Mechanical-Electrical Service to change the street signs the business would be complete.

And so West Baltimore Avenue passed away and Gable Avenue came into being.

Henry C. Gable Sr., for whom the street is thus named, was born in Baltimore City on March 11, 1865, a son of Warner Gable. When he was only 2 years old his family moved to the 55-acre estate that it still holds, built the house — now numbered 1325 — in which it still lives, and went into truck farming.

Henry followed his father's footsteps as a truck farmer, and in 1895 also became a Baltimore County road supervisor and held this position until his area was annexed by the city. Then he did farming alone; today at 84, he still putters about the place.

He married Miss Annie Davis of Baltimore, and there are five children: Mrs. Herman Langridge, Henry C. Gable Jr., Mrs. Vincent Hobbs, Mrs. Fred Beanfeld and Milton Gable. Mrs. Gable died in 1934.

August 21, 1949

Gay

By William Stump

Gay Street preserves the name of Nicholas Ruxton Gay, the surveyor who laid out the first part of it in the early days of Baltimore Town.

That original part — which ran north from the harbor for just a few blocks — once bordered a stretch of Jones Falls marshland that separated Baltimore Town from Jones Town to the east.

Baltimore had been laid out in 1729, on authorization of the Assembly, and Jones Town in 1732. In 1745, the legislators consolidated the two. Because of the marsh barrier, the move had little real meaning then, but it was shortly given meaning.

The marsh was spanned by a bridge, and over this was routed the Great Eastern Highway, then the principal artery of travel and commerce. Abruptly the land lying between the two parts of town gained value, the development of an 18-acre portion was authorized, and the records of the town commissioners for November 19, 1747, relate:

"The Commissioners met this day and employed Nicholas Ruxton Gay to Survey the Same and lay it out into Lotts and with convenient Streets and alleys which he accordingly did."

Gay Street is one of the thoroughfares that resulted, though whether it was at once given that name is not known. The name does appear in the city records as early as 1783.

Nicholas Gay laid out an addition to Jones Town in 1750, and in 1754 became a town commissioner himself.

Two other Baltimore streets seem to have been named for surveyors. These are Franklin Street and Poppleton Street, which runs north from Washington Boulevard to Lexington Street.

Gay Street, Engine House No. 6 – 1947

Although Benjamin Franklin is popularly believed to be the man honored, one delver into local history has said that Franklin Street's name "undoubtedly" derives from Thomas Franklin, who helped resurvey Baltimore in 1747 and who for 20 years was presiding justice of Baltimore. Yet little is known of Franklin.

Poppleton Street came into being — at least on paper — in 1822, when Thomas Poppleton made the famous map which projected many streets that were not created until years later, and which thus served as a "city plan."

But little is known of his life either. Records show that he surveyed the property of Samuel Chase at Eutaw and Lexington streets in 1812, and city directories list him as living on Exeter Street as late as 1840.

September 21, 1952

Gilman

By William Stump

In 1874, when the brand-new Johns Hopkins University was seeking a man to become its first president, three of the trustees, each independently of the other, asked Daniel Coit Gilman to take the job.

At the time, Gilman was president of the University of California. Even before he took that post, his achievements had been noteworthy. At Yale, he had conceived and helped organize the famous Sheffield Scientific School, and in it served as secretary, librarian and professor of his academic specialty, physical geography. There he had pioneered in scientific education — and, as a member of the New Haven School Board, in public education.

But it was Gilman's abilities as an organizer and administrator, and his concepts of education, that had made him famous.

"He was," wrote a colleague at California, "endowed with an extraordinarily sharp, quick and unerring discernment, first of measures and men, not merely as to things in themselves nor yet as to their latent values — he had all that and more. With it all was allied and the more fruitful sense of how to extract those values, and how, once extracted, to set them into active productiveness."

To Gilman, the freedom to think and teach and investigate in a university was of the greatest importance — more important indeed than mere instruction. And to the trustees, seeking a man who could and would fulfill Johns Hopkins' dream of a university where faculty and students would be unshackled, and would be encouraged to think and explore, Gilman was the logical choice.

As history shows, he did not disappoint them. He searched Europe and America for the best teachers, choosing men both famous and unknown. For the chair of physics, for example, he picked a 25-year-old scientist whose papers had been refused publication by American universities because he was considered too young. He was Henry A. Rowland, and his name became synonymous with physics; Ira Remsen's became synonymous with chemistry and Basil Gildersleeve's synonymous with classic languages.

But they might not have become great men had not Gilman nurtured the atmosphere which prevailed from the start. Historians say that the early days of the university made for a sort of intellectual paradise. "Exhilaration," one of his students wrote, "was in the very atmosphere." Such were the foundations that have made the university — and its medical school, which Gilman had so great a hand in building — an institution which today is world renowned.

Personally, Dr. Gilman was inclined to be reserved, a characteristic that commanded respect. But he was not a cold man.

He was a man of intense enthusiasm, and that quality remained with him even when he was well along in years. "I promise myself eternal youth," he once wrote. As a result, new ideas were not only entertained, they were put to work.

That enthusiasm was not confined to Hopkins. During his career, Gilman held many posts in education, civic affairs and government. When he retired from the university in 1901, he became president and helped organize the Carnegie Institution and was president of the National Service Reform League.

There are, of course, many monuments to Daniel Coit Gilman, who died at the age of 77 in 1908 at Norwich, Conn., the place of his birth. In addition to a Gilman School in Maine, there are Gilman School in Baltimore, Gilman Hall on the Homewood campus and, not far from that, on the western edge of Wyman Park, a street called Gilman Terrace, which city authorities say was named in 1920.

March 13, 1949

The Gilmors

By Henry C. Rauch

One sent to Russia in 1784 the first American merchant ship ever to call there.
One was one of America's earliest art collectors of importance.
One was a diplomatic attaché in France.
One was a famous Confederate cavalry raider.
One was a judge of the Supreme Branch of Baltimore.
All were members of the family from which Gilmor Street gets its name.

Robert Gilmor, the first, was born in Paisley, Scotland, in 1748. While still young he was taken into business there by his father. The American colonies attracted him, however, and in 1767 he made a voyage to Oxford, Md., with merchandise. In 1769, he again came to Maryland, and this time settled at Benedict, St. Mary's County, and there went into business and married.

In 1778, he moved to Baltimore, then in 1782 formed a partnership with some Philadelphians for trade with Holland and went to Amsterdam to handle its business. When a death broke up this firm in 1784, Gilmor formed a new one and made Baltimore its headquarters. It was now that he opened American trade with Russia. In 1799, he took his two sons into the

Gilmor Street – 1936

firm. He died in 1822, but for many more years the sons kept the Gilmor name prominent in the city's business life.

That Robert Gilmor was also prominent in other fields. In the first election after Baltimore was made a city in 1797, he was chosen for the Second Branch of the City Council, and held its presidency for several terms. In 1790, he helped form the Bank of Maryland. He was the first head of the Chamber of Commerce.

It was his son Robert, born in 1774, who was the art collector. This man took the occasion of his business trips abroad to indulge his love of paintings. In the early 1800s, he visited museums, dealers' rooms and studios in a number of countries and started his collection. He also encouraged American artists; it was for him that Gilbert Stuart painted the last replica of his Washington portrait. At the same time, he amassed a fine library.

Some of the paintings he acquired are scheduled for display at the Walters Art Gallery, and some of the books at the Peabody Library, in a joint exhibition opening March 19. These exhibits mark the bicentennial of the birth of the first Robert Gilmor and the centennial of the death of Robert Gilmor Jr.

A third Robert, son of William Gilmor, was the one who served several years as an attaché of the American Embassy in Paris. One of his sons, still another Robert, was for 15 years a member of the Supreme Bench.

The Confederate raider was a second son of that third Robert — Harry Gilmor, born in 1838. From 1862 until almost the end of the war, he served in the Shenandoah Valley in Maryland, with occasional stabs into Pennsylvania.

In one of his most famous raids, in February 1864, he cut the Baltimore and Ohio Railroad near Harpers Ferry. When Early made his dash on Washington in July 1864, Gilmor covered the army by raiding to the east. It was Gilmor who burned the town of Chambersburg, Pa.

After the war, Harry Gilmor engaged in business in Baltimore, and was police commissioner from 1874 to 1879. He died in 1883.

Gist

By Karen Richards

Gist Avenue in Northwest Baltimore bears a name which has figured in local history since the earliest days of Maryland.

The first of the family to settle in Maryland was Christopher Gist (sometimes spelled Guest), an English immigrant who made his home on the eastern bank of the Patapsco River long before the area was included in the bounds of Baltimore Town.

He did not live to see the settlement on the Patapsco become a real community, but his son, Richard, served as a surveyor of the Western Shore and in 1729 was one of the commissioners appointed for the laying out of Baltimore Town.

With the beginnings of the westward movement by colonists, Christopher Gist, Richard's son, went to Ohio and Kentucky and western Virginia as a scout and explorer. He is said to have preceded Daniel Boone in the Kentucky country by 18 years.

During the French and Indian War, Christopher went with George Washington on his trip to Fort Duquesne and is credited with saving Washington's life twice on the way. He was also with Washington at the surrender of Fort Necessity in 1754. This second Christopher Gist and two of his sons were with General Braddock on his fateful expedition. All three survived.

Perhaps the most famous of all the family was Gen. Mordecai Gist, of Baltimore. He trained for a shipping career, but with the approach of the American Revolution joined the Baltimore Independent Company, the first military outfit formed in Maryland for service with the American Army. By 1779, he had risen from captain in the volunteer group to a brigadier general in the Continental forces, commanding the 2d Maryland Brigade.

General Gist fought in the battles of Long Island, White Plains, Camden and Yorktown. At Camden, serving under Baron de Kalb, he took command of de Kalb's men when the Baron was fatally wounded.

Gist was given the thanks of Congress for his action at Camden in a resolution passed October 14, 1780. Although his men were forced to give ground before the British, he escaped capture and was present at Cornwallis' surrender at Yorktown.

He spent the last years of his life on a plantation near Charleston, S.C. He never outgrew his devotion to his country, which he put before his feelings for his family. Three times married, he named his two sons appropriately "Independent" and "States."

Gittings

By William Stump

When the body of Richard James Gittings was being borne to a city burial from Waveland — that was his summer home, and it still stands on the State Teachers College grounds, which he owned — every house along York Road was draped in black.

For Richard Gittings was well-known and well-loved in the city and the county. He was one of the prominent lawyers of his day, and he had the reputation of being one of the kindest men in the state. Besides, he had died suddenly when he was at the height of his powers.

That was in 1882; Gittings was 52 then. He was born at Roslin — a large mansion that still stands off Sunshine Avenue near Kingsville — the son of David Sterett Gittings, a medical man whose family was connected with a number of old Maryland clans.

As a youngster, Richard Gittings studied at a private academy in Pennsylvania and at a school at Sweet Air. Then he attended Princeton, graduating with honors in 1849. Having decided upon the law, he entered Harvard, winning his diploma in 1852.

Then he formed a partnership with Arthur Webster Machen; three years later he had acquired such a standing that he was elected state's attorney for Baltimore County and admitted to practice before the Court of Appeals and the United States Supreme Court. From that time on he and his firm — it became Machen, Gittings & McIntosh — ranked with the best in the state.

Gittings Avenue – 1959

Criminal cases were his specialty, and the public crowded the courtroom when he argued them, for he had a reputation for wit as well as for brilliance. Once during a tense moment in a murder trial a piece of plaster fell from the ceiling. Gittings jumped to his feet. "Your honors," he said with passion, "let justice be done though the heavens fall."

Gittings' practice made him a wealthy man. He owned the house at 521 North Charles where the Baltimore Symphony Orchestra's ticket office is located today. He owned the present W. W. Abell house in Washington Place, the summer retreat at Towson, and a large tract of land between Charles Street Avenue and York Road. The lane that bordered that tract is now Gittings Avenue, having been named in his honor about the time of his death.

Married in 1855 to Victoria Sellman, he was survived by six children, one of whom was the late D. Sterett Gittings, celebrated Maryland horseman. Two of his children are living today — Miss Mary and Miss Victoria Gittings, of 1428 Park Ave.

August 14, 1949

Gough

By Henry C. Rauch

There are two stories about the conversion of Harry Dorsey Gough from Episcopalianism to Methodism.

One of them is a very simple little story. Gough's wife, this one runs, was so impressed by the preaching of the early Methodist ministers in Maryland that he prevented her from attending their meetings. Nevertheless, she converted, and then under her influence he himself changed faith.

The other story has color. Gough, this one notes, was a tremendously wealthy man; in fact, the wealthiest in Baltimore in his time — which was the latter part of the 1700s. His fortune was put at $300,000; he had an imposing brick house and other property in the heart of town, and 12 miles out to the northeast a vast mansion named Perry Hall, the seat of an estate that consisted of thousands of acres and was worked by 300 slaves.

But despite his great wealth, Gough was not a happy man, this story says, and it implies that two of his chief sorrows were his wife's conversion to the new faith, and the necessity he felt for forbidding her to attend Methodist services. Drowning his sorrows with some gay companions one night, someone proposed that they further divert themselves by going to a Methodist meeting themselves.

They went to one at which Francis Asbury spoke. Afterward, on their way home, one of them exclaimed: "What nonsense we heard tonight!" To the group's surprise, Gough answered: "No; what we heard is the truth." And as he entered his home and met his wife he said to her: "I will never hinder you again from hearing the Methodists."

More, he switched to Methodism himself. He erected a chapel at Perry Hall, and had services there regularly; this chapel, incidentally, was the first Methodist place of worship in the United States to possess a bell. His mansion became a stopping place for every Methodist minister who passed near, including Bishops Asbury, Coke, Black and Vasey.

It was at Perry Hall, indeed, that the organization of the Methodist Episcopal Church in America was planned. There the religious leaders assembled in December 1784, and from there they rode by horseback to Lovely Lane Meeting House for the historic Christmas conference at which the church constitution and book of discipline were adopted.

When, a few days later, Francis Asbury was ordained the first bishop, Gough and his wife had prominent places at the ceremony, as this is depicted in a painting.

Today, only a remnant of the Perry Hall showplace survives; fire eventually destroyed the chapel and part of the mansion; the gradual selling off of farms decimated the acreage. But the estate's name draws continuing life from a community on Belair Road, and Gough's name is likewise perpetuated by a street that, except where Patterson Park interrupts, runs across East Baltimore all the way from Fawn Street to Haven.

Although nowadays it is for his part in the beginnings of Methodism that he is often remembered, Gough was active in other fields as well, as would be expected of a man of means. In 1769, it is recorded, he was one of those at a meeting of merchants and others called to pass judgment on some apparent violations of an agreement against importing European goods into Maryland.

In 1773, the Assembly appointed him as one of several trustees for the poor of Baltimore County, who were given the duty of erecting the first almshouse and workhouse. In 1793, he was similarly appointed to a board of commissioners named to establish a stock yard and market.

A few years earlier, he had been named the first president of a society formed to "encourage and improve agriculture and other branches of rural economy." His own farm was said to be among the most fertile and best cultivated in the state.

Gough was born January 28, 1745, the son of Thomas and Sophia Gough. His wife, whom he married May 2, 1771, had been Prudence Carnan. His death occurred May 8, 1808.

March 23, 1952

Govane

By James C. Bertram

A street that runs a broken course, and a small, neglected cemetery are the only things left to remind Govans residents of the man for whom their community is named.

The street is Govane Avenue, east of York Road. Local historians say it preserves the name of James Govane, whose small, battered tombstone can be seen within the low stone walls of the weed-choked cemetery, located just north of the city line between Walker Avenue and Winwood Road.

Despite the fact that a town is named for him, very little is known about James Govane. He was of Scotch ancestry; his grandfather, who was also James Govane, came to America early in the 18th century and became the high sheriff of Anne Arundel County.

That first James had a son named William who became a wealthy importer, a shipowner and a delegate from Baltimore County in the 1750s. His wealth or his political stature — or both — evidently made his position in Maryland a strong one, for in 1755 Frederick Calvert, sixth and last Lord Baltimore, granted him several hundred acres 5 miles north of the

James Govane's Grave – 1940

fledgling town of Baltimore.

William added to his grant by purchasing an estate called Friend's Discovery from one Job Evans. Then either he or his son James renamed the place Drumquhazel in memory of the town in Scotland from which the family had come.

James inherited the land upon his father's death in 1763. Twenty years later, he was dead himself — the last male of his family. In addition to 36 slaves, a microscope, a picture of General Washington and a map, he left the estate to a daughter, who had married a Howard from Anne Arundel County.

Three years after James died, York Road was laid out over the ridge that ran through his acres. Soon a tollgate was erected. Not long after that, a farmers tavern went up nearby and, on land bought from the Govane estate, a store or two. This was the nucleus of a town — Govane's Town, named with James Govane in mind.

By the end of the Civil War, its 500 residents were calling it Govanstown, the name that persisted through the years when the land around was taken up by vast estates.

Now, a residential community with home-lined streets like Govane Avenue — when the avenue was named is not known — most people call it simply Govans.

December 2, 1951

Grant

By William Stump

In Revolutionary times, there was no better hostelry in America than Daniel Grant's Fountain Inn.

The excellence of its kitchens, the pleasures of its bar and the comfortable accommodations for its guests — and for the guests' servants and horses as well — were famous from Boston to the Carolinas. Perhaps that is why George Washington spurned private invitations and stayed at the inn whenever he came to Baltimore.

It is not mere conjecture that he enjoyed himself during his numerous stays beneath Daniel Grant's roof. Once, while on his way to Yorktown to accept the British surrender, he and his party, which consisted of the Count de Rochambeau and six other French and American officers, drank £3 10s. worth of punch, £1 10s. worth of wine and 12 shillings worth of grog.

There were dinners for eight at one shilling sixpence — and on top of that, the seven servants in the party consumed a pound's worth of punch and wine and 10 shillings worth of food, and the horses ate two shillings of hay and one of oats.

The inn, located on the site of the Southern Hotel, was three stories high; in its center was a flowered courtyard, overlooked by balconies on each of the three floors. There were six parlors for "company to meet in," 24 bedrooms, eight garrets for servants, three kitchens, a laundry, extensive wine cellars, a springhouse, a larder and ice-house, a barbershop, four brick stables containing 84 stalls, a hostler's rooms and granaries.

It was an important place to Baltimoreans during and after the Revolution. This was not only because of the creature comforts to be obtained there, or even because personages like Washington, Lafayette, von Steuben, Greene and the members of the Continental Congress were guests; rather, it was because the inn, as a meeting place, played a major role in the city's political, civic and business life.

This was no accident. Grant, who was an extremely civic-minded man — or a man who was smart enough to see that what was good for Baltimore was good for business — made a point of throwing open the hotel for varied meetings and gatherings. During the Revolution, the committee of safety met there; after the war, for example, Baltimore's first bank was organized in one of the parlors.

After Grant's day, the inn's importance as a meeting place continued and grew; before the inn closed in the 1870s, the fate of many a presidential aspirant had been decided in its smoke-filled rooms.

Unfortunately, not much is known about Grant's appearance or personality; practically all the information about him comes from contemporary newspapers.

He came to the city in 1773, and soon took an advertisement in the Maryland Journal and Baltimore Advertiser, in which, referring to himself as having "lately kept Tavern at the Sign of the Buck, near Philadelphia," he advised that he was opening a new inn "at the Sign of the Fountain."

In 1778, the paper notes the marriage of his daughter Jenny; a son, Daniel Jr., married a few years later. In 1789, his wife Elizabeth died, and in 1795, he sold the inn to a James Bryden.

He lived on in Baltimore until 1816, when he died at 82.

Shortly after his death, sometime between 1816 and 1822, the narrow alley which ran behind the inn was renamed Grant Street — undoubtedly for the innkeeper.

Today, two blocks long, it runs from Lombard to Baltimore Street, a few feet east of Light.

October 10, 1948

Greene

By Karen Richards

Appropriately, Greene Street, in West Baltimore, starts at Camden Station and as it unrolls northward bisects Washington Boulevard and Lexington Market.

In the life of Gen. Nathanael Greene, for whom the street was named sometime before 1812, Washington and Lexington and Camden all played important parts.

Greene was born in Rhode Island in 1742 and was a major general while still in his 30s — yet he almost did not become a soldier. As a boy he had injured his knee, and though he helped organize a company of local militia at the first signs of the impending trouble with Great Britain, he was unable to become more than a private in the ranks.

But after word of the battle at Lexington arrived and the royal governor of Rhode Island tried to prevent the Colonial troops from joining the Revolution, Greene and some friends joined the Continental forces and Greene was made a brigadier.

His military career from that point on was marked by success. He became a brigadier general and one of George Washington's most trusted lieutenants.

Through the campaigns at Boston, New York and Trenton, Brandywine and Germantown, Greene played a major role. After the fateful winter at Valley Forge, Greene was made quartermaster general of the Continental Army. He resigned from the post as a result of the intrigues of the man he had replaced.

It was Greene, left in command of the forces in New York, who took over West Point after Benedict Arnold had attempted to betray it to the British, and when Gen. Horatio Gates was defeated at Camden, S. C., Greene was sent south to relieve him.

He managed to weld together the partisan troops who had been at odds with Gates, and harassed the British so badly in a well-planned campaign across the state that his Majesty's forces evacuated all of South Carolina except Charleston.

Greene, however, was conquered by the land he had liberated. After the Revolution, he made his home in Georgia on the plantation voted to him by the grateful people of the state. He returned only occasionally to his native Rhode Island, and at his death in 1786, he was buried in Savannah.

September 12, 1948

Gusryan Street

By Elizabeth H. Moberly

People who look at the signs labeled "Gusryan Street" can believe their eyes.

It's no new language with an exotic pronunciation, but a marker for one of the few streets in Baltimore bearing the complete name of the person it commemorates.

As Baltimore streets go, Gusryan is almost new, dating from July 1937, when the mayor and City Council ordered that the blocks of Gunter Street between Eastern Avenue and O'Donnell Street should be known henceforth as Gusryan Street. But then, Augustine J. Ryan, for whom it was named, is a man still remembered in many circles.

Mr. Ryan was a wholesale coal dealer who lived his entire life in the East Baltimore home of his family. A man of many parts, he was prominent in municipal circles, but never held a political job that had a salary attached to it. He was equally well known in art circles, and could hold his own as an amateur historian. But Gus Ryan was perhaps most famous for the midsummer parties he gave each year at his summer place on Back River. There you could meet lawyers, newspapermen, politicians, social leaders from the Green Spring Valley, struggling young art students and some of his neighbors from East Baltimore. They all called him "Gus."

Augustine Ryan was born in Baltimore in 1868 of Irish parents who had migrated here.

Gusryan Street – 1948

When he was growing up, there were many opportunities for a young man to find his place before settling down to a permanent career, and he tried his hand at them. He completed his education at Rock Hall College in Ellicott City, taking his bachelor of science degree in 1887. But instead of going into his father's business of manufacturing lime from oyster shells, he worked with a wholesale grocery firm for the next six years.

He was later associated with Daniel H. Burnham, who was then engaged in building the World's Fair in Chicago; Gus supervised the work which was done on the Arts Building. Returning to Baltimore after an absence of three years, he went to work as a newspaper reporter.

After more than a year in that field, he entered the wholesale coal business and established the company which he headed until his death in 1927.

He served on the board of directors of two banking and building associations. He was considered something of a national authority on archaeology.

He served the city as a member of the Park Board, the Charter Revision Commission and the Municipal Art Commission. During the heated controversy that raged in the '20s over the location of the Lafayette Statue at the foot of the Washington Monument, he favored a site where it would show to better advantage.

He was also vice president of the board of trustees of the Maryland Institute and a member of the executive council of the Archaeological Institute of America. He was a patron of many young art students.

Politicians considered Gus Ryan a hard worker for the Democratic Party, and sought his support. He himself ran for office only once; he entered one race for the nomination for representative from the Third Congressional district, but withdrew because of ill health.

He never married.

H

March 27, 1949

Hanlon

By Henry C. Rauch

Hanlon Avenue leads to a baseball diamond. From Mondawmin Avenue it runs east to the Longwood Street side of a park, the side on which the sports fields are located. The park is Hanlon Park.

All that is just as it should be. For Edward Hanlon, the man thus memorialized, was for twenty years a member of the Park Board, or its president. And before that, as manager of the famous old Orioles of the 1890s, he had gained the title "Father of Modern Baseball."

Hanlon was born in Montville, Conn., in 1857, and became interested in baseball in his early teens. He became a professional with the Providence (R.I.) club in 1875, in the next few years moved to other minor-league outfits, then in the early 1880s got a big-league berth with Detroit.

In 1885, he became Detroit's captain. The next year, Detroit finished a close second in its league, and the following year won the pennant. Then the team was sold. Hanlon went to Pittsburgh, and became manager.

During the winter of 1888-89, he took part in an "Around the World Baseball Tour." Two picked teams, which played at every stop they made, crossed the United States by easy stages, then went to Hawaii, Australia, Ceylon, Arabia, Egypt, continental Europe and Britain.

Upon returning to this country, Hanlon went back to Pittsburgh, then in 1892, after being injured in a game, came to Baltimore as manager of the Orioles. The Birds had just joined the twelve-club National League that year; they finished last. In 1893, they had come up only to eighth place. But then Hanlon started to work out new plays, and the result was three successive Oriole pennants.

Hanlon's revolutionizing of the game has been described like this:

"When 'Foxy Ned' began his professional baseball career back in 1875, the national game was a crude slugging match. Players had just one idea, and that was to hit the ball as hard as they could — and in their anxiety to 'kill' it, they were as likely to do a 'Casey' as to get to base. On the base it was a matter of being 'batted in' to score a run."

"Hanlon did some thinking. It occurred to him that a run gained by strategy counted as big as a run gained by slugging. Accordingly, he evolved an offensive technique that made baseball something of an art. He introduced bunting, sacrifice hits, base stealing and the hit-and-run tactics which have made baseball playing speedy and exciting.

"And he trained in the new cunning such men as John McGraw and Wilbert Robinson."

The new offensive game, of course, necessitated an improved defensive game. The consequence was greater emphasis upon skillful pitching and a constant cooperation of pitcher, catcher and infield in taking advantage of the batters' weaknesses and the situation on the bases. Infield playing became faster.

"It would be going too far to attribute all the present perfection of this form of play to Edward Hanlon. But it was he who started the new technique."

In 1897, Hanlon switched to management of the Brooklyn club, which thereupon took two pennants in a row. In 1900, he switched again, to Cincinnati, but after a year or two left there. His interest in baseball continued through ownership of the Orioles, until he sold to Jack Dunn.

Hanlon made Baltimore his home from the time he first came here to manage the Birds in 1892. He became a member of the Park Board in 1916, and was its president from 1931 until his death, April 14, 1937.

May 17, 1953

The Hanovers

By William Stump

Hanover Street, one of the oldest streets in the city, preserves the name of a family Baltimoreans came to loathe with a terrible intensity.

For the Hanovers were the family, or more correctly the dynasty, which produced George III, King of England before, during and after both the Revolution and the War of 1812. Americans, who pictured him as a gross and greedy tyrant, held him responsible for at least the Revolution. And well they might.

Hanover Street – 1948

But by the time of the Revolution, Hanover Street was close to 40 years old, having been created as Hanover Lane shortly after 1729, the year the city was founded.

At that time, the Hanovers were held in somewhat higher esteem — thanks, perhaps, to the fact that Baltimoreans, separated by the wide Atlantic, knew very little about the kings who bore the Hanover name.

The first of the dynasty to sit on the throne of England was George I. Even his country's historians deal severely with him. Son of the youngest daughter of James I, his father was a German aristocrat, and he was born and raised in the little duchy of Hanover.

As a young man he fought well with his troops with Marlborough at Blenheim, thereby making himself popular with Marlborough and the Whigs. When it developed that his elderly mother was legal heir to the throne, he went to England, and upon the death of Queen Anne was invited to take the crown.

The people of his new nation took an instant dislike to him. He could speak no English, which resulted in his being unable to do business with his ministers; it also resulted in long and frequent absences in his native land. Besides, Englishmen soon realized that the throne meant one thing to him — the acquisition of wealth for his wife and mistresses. Yet his reign was not entirely unsuccessful, for his prime minister was Sir Robert Walpole who, rather than the monarch, actually ran England.

The first George was a fractious man who hated his only son so much that he hesitated to make him Prince of Wales and, indeed, once arrested him over a petty quarrel. But the son became George II two years before Baltimore was founded — and, as king, almost made his father seem a paragon of virtue.

The trouble with the second George was that he was a mediocrity with the mind of an unsuccessful clerk. He was a man whose mind was incapable of rising over mere details — a man whose greatest pleasure came in actually counting his money piece by piece.

To any minister with a superior mind — and at least, he had the quality of recognizing men superior to himself — he always gave in. On a hit-or-miss basis, this occasionally worked out to the nation's benefit. But it also resulted in tremendous corruption.

And his people disliked him — mainly because he loved his ancestral Hanover better than he loved England. Time and again he jeopardized the nation to support the duchy with arms when there was no call for it. Yet, to his credit, he founded the University of Gottingen there, and through his patronage the great Handel came to live and work in England.

Like the first George, the second hated his own son. And there was good reason for this, for the son, Frederick, was a nincompoop who spent his life in an almost comic-opera defiance of his father. But Frederick did not become king; George II outlived him.

It was Frederick's son who succeeded George II. And he was George III. Though not above average intelligence, he at least became determined to work at being king, and he succeeded to such an extent that he actually ran the government. In this role he was the cause of many ills, including the hated Stamp Act and the Revolution — which, against advice, he insisted on prolonging. Finally Parliament was forced to check his increasing powers.

Unlike his ancestors, George III lived quietly, loyal to his wife and family. During much of his reign, he had the support and the love of his people.

But George III suffered fits of insanity — during which he was strapped up in a straitjacket. And although Americans hated him anew when the War of 1812 came along, the old man was hardly to blame. For from 1811 until his death in 1820, he knew absolutely nothing of what went on about him; the actual ruler during the war was his son, who acted as regent.

Upon the old king's death, that son became George IV. He was, it turned out, a complete wastrel who earned the disgust of his people by his loose living and his cruelty to his queen. In his reign, he accomplished nothing, and it was with relief that news of his death was greeted in 1830.

The next Hanover to occupy the throne was his brother, who became William IV. He was an amiable man and a naval hero, and the people regarded him highly. He was also well-meaning and hard-working — but so timid and wishy-washy that he nearly brought England to revolution. But his reign was short, his death occurring in 1837.

And then the name of Hanover came into its own. For William was succeeded by his niece. She was Victoria and she reigned for 70 years. When she died in 1901, the last of the Hanovers, the dynasty's name was as respected in the world as it had been disrespected in the agonizing days of the four Georges.

December 26, 1948

Harford

By Henry C. Rauch

An action that has been assailed as one of "low cunning" lies behind the name of one Baltimore street.

The action was the creation, in 1773, of a new Maryland county that would bear the name of Henry Harford, the illegitimate son who had recently inherited the province from Frederick Calvert, sixth and last Lord Baltimore.

The street is Harford Road, which acquired its name from that county to which it led.

The reason for an act of "low cunning" lay in the fact that Frederick Calvert's death had created a legal issue. This "selfish, dis-

Harford Road – 1948

reputable and dissolute degenerate," as one historian has summed him up, left at least five illegitimate children scattered over England, Ireland and Germany, but no legitimate ones anywhere. And when he bequeathed Maryland to his natural son he came into conflict with his own father's will.

For the fifth Lord Baltimore had provided that if Frederick died without a legitimate heir, the Proprietorship of Maryland should pass to Frederick's eldest sister, Louisa, the wife of John Browning. This provision Frederick tried vainly to break, then finally simply defied. Upon his death, late in 1771, therefore, Louisa at once filed suit against his executors to assert her rights.

The executors countered in their own way — which was to have Harford quickly recognized as Proprietor by the Maryland Assembly. This they were in a strategic position to do, for one of their number was no less a personage than Robert Eden, governor of the province and husband of Caroline Calvert, Frederick's younger sister.

A Hugh Hammersley, who was one of the executors in England, was later accused by Louisa's son of being the brains behind the scheme. "Hammersley," Browning wrote, "I did not know, but understood from my father he was a man that had little business, and that not very respectable, and was a shrewd, keen fellow, possessing a good deal of low cunning.

"He was quite prime minister in the whole business . . . and finding things were not likely to turn out so favorably as they [the executors] wished, he desired Governor Eden to get the acknowledgement of Henry Harford confirmed . . . by the

Assembly of Maryland as soon as possible. And to induce him to consider it would be as much for his interest as that of either Henry Harford, or his sister, proposed that two new counties should be laid out in the province, one to be called Harford, and the other Caroline, Mrs. Eden's Christian name."

Harford's recognition by Maryland was obtained, and in 1773 Harford County was created.

Although the Revolution quickly stripped the Proprietor of his possession, he did not give up without a struggle. As late as 1780 he paid to the Crown the two Indian arrows required as tribute from the province, and although this gave him no standing in America, it may have reinforced his claims in England for war-loss compensation.

Such claims Harford pressed on both sides of the ocean. In 1785, he even appeared personally before the Maryland Legislature to ask payment for, or restoration of, his confiscated property. He won neither, but in England he was awarded £90,000.

With this wealth, and the reputation of "an educated and courteous gentleman," he drops out of the Maryland picture.

March 5, 1949

Harrison

By Henry C. Rauch

Harrison Street, which runs from Baltimore Street to Gay just one block west of the Fallsway, preserves the name of a man who once owned all the land between the original settlements of Baltimore Town and Jones Town. The man was Thomas Harrison, a merchant who came here from England in 1742.

Harrison must have brought money with him, for he promptly built himself a house — near South and Water streets — bought up the lots nearest the water on both sides of South Street, and became a figure in the town. Already in 1745 he was a town commissioner.

His keen eye for real-estate investments is the principal thing that keeps Harrison's name in the records; however, some other bits of information about him have come down the years.

He was one of the subscribers toward the famous fence that for a few years around 1750 protected the finer part of Baltimore Town from the roving hogs and geese of the hinterland people.

He apparently never married, for from 1756 to 1762, when a tax was levied on bachelors, he paid it.

Presumably too old to fight — he died in 1782 "at an advanced age" — he filled various Revolutionary committee posts.

Harrison's biggest real-estate coup was made in 1747. Two years earlier, the Assembly had consolidated Baltimore Town and Jones Town, which lay on opposite banks of Jones Falls. The move was a paper one, with little meaning at the time, but shortly the construction of a bridge carried the Great Eastern Road directly through both parts of the town and gave value to the undeveloped land that lay between.

Probably foreseeing the annexation of that land, Harrison in 1747 bought all of it; there were 28 acres, including a great marsh thenceforth known as Harrison's Marsh. The very same year, the Assembly did annex 18 acres of the tract, and ordered streets laid out; Frederick, Harrison and parts of Water and Holliday resulted. In 1766, the marsh was ordered filled up, and streets were laid out in that area too.

Some important buildings of early Baltimore stood on Harrison land. One was a market house, which had "a large room in the second story, where public assemblies, dances, jugglery" and other affairs were conducted.

September 30, 1951

Heath

By James C. Bertram

History remembers little about Maj. Richard Key Heath — little, that is, except his bravery.

That bravery, which manifested itself throughout the Battle of North Point, was summed up in the report which Gen. John Stricker, the field commander, made to Gen. Samuel Smith after the battle had been won.

Stricker wrote that Major Heath, "who led on the advance party to bring on the action (i.e., to begin the battle), behaved as became an officer; the facts of his first horse being killed under him in the first skirmish, his second being badly wounded and himself receiving a severe contusion in the head, by a musket ball, during the general action, are ample proofs of his bravery and exposure in the discharge of his duty."

He did not tell that Heath and the men he led volunteered for that skirmish — although most of them were green, although their British enemy was skilled and tough.

He did not say that the action took place in woods so dense that a soldier had trouble seeing the man next to him. He did not tell that the action was confused and fierce — and that Heath's force, when it withdrew, withdrew in exhaustion, leaving Maj. Gen. Robert Ross, the British commander, dead on the field.

Heath's men were not without their casualties. Daniel Wells and Henry McComas, credited with having killed the British general, were themselves killed. So was Gregorius Andre, a lieutenant in the Union Yagers who, having tarried to get in a last shot at the enemy, was killed as he began to retreat.

In Southwest Baltimore, in an area where many streets preserve the names of War of 1812 figures, there are a Wells Street and a McComas Street — and an Andre Street and a Heath Street. All were named at the same time, about 1820, by a committee of prominent citizens.

Virtually nothing is known of Andre. All else that seems to be recorded about Heath is that he married a Mary Hall of Harford County in 1793, that he became a general after the war, that he lived on Howard Street — or on Cheapside, if he is the Richard K. Heath an 1815 city directory lists as a "tanner and currier" — and that he was "interred with highest civic and military honors" upon his death in 1821.

February 6, 1949

The Hillens

By Henry C. Rauch

A family that provided Baltimore with the youngest mayor it has ever had also provided it with a couple of its most familiar place names. The family is the Hillen family; its own name is perpetuated by Hillen Street and Hillen Road, and the name of its country estate is perpetuated by the various uses of Hillendale.

The mayor who was the city's youngest was Solomon Hillen Jr. — actually the third Solomon in a family that had settled in Baltimore County far back in colonial times. This Solomon was born in 1810 at the old homestead that served the family for more than 100 years and that at various times was known as Shoemaker's Hill, Mount Healthy and finally Hillendale.

Hillen Road – 1941

Solomon Jr. graduated from Georgetown College in 1827, and, handsome, accomplished and popular, soon became an important figure in the political and social life of Maryland. He was a lawyer, but abandoned practice because of ill health.

However, he became a member of the House of Delegates, then a member of Congress, and, in 1842 — when but 32 years old — he was elected to fill the short unexpired term of Mayor Samuel Brady, who had resigned. He was also re-elected for a term of his own, but then himself resigned near the end of 1843.

Solomon Jr. was for a time a captain of the well-known company of Independent Blues, and later became a colonel

Hillen Street – 1944

of the old 5th Regiment. He made his home at a place he inherited on the Hillen Road opposite Woodbourne Avenue; he called it Palmyra. His wife was Emily O'Donnell, daughter of Gen. Columbus O'Donnell.

Several other Hillens filled public roles of more or less importance in their times. The first Solomon was a constable of Back River Hundred in 1730.

Thomas Hillen, a son of the second Solomon, was in 1802 a justice of the peace in Baltimore County; in 1805, a member of the First Branch of the Baltimore City Council; and, in 1812, was made a magistrate and justice of the Tax Levy Court of Baltimore County.

Thomas, it is related, lived the life of a country gentleman of ample means. His hospitality was described as unbounded, and he is said to have made the old Hillendale mansion the scene of many brilliant entertainments.

John Hillen, another son of the second Solomon, also made a particular record. He had the distinction of fighting in two wars. He was born in 1761, and as a mere boy took part in the Revolution. Then in 1814, as a lieutenant in the 5th Maryland Militia, he fought in the Battle of North Point.

Between those times, John made himself a figure in Baltimore's mercantile life, and he, too, was for many years a member of the First Branch of the City Council.

January 28, 1951

Holliday

By William Stump

That Holliday Street was named for John Robert Holliday, high sheriff of Baltimore County in the years just preceding the Revolution, seems certain. But that it was named for him because of his office seems extremely doubtful, for as sheriff he won more censure than praise.

He was found guilty of what was possibly skullduggery in connection with the election of 1771, the year after he took

Holliday Street – 1951

office. A document in the archives of the Colonial Assembly indicates that he left several important names or facts off the election returns which, in his capacity as sheriff, he was supposed to send to the Assembly.

The document directed that he be "admonished for his Neglect of Duty in not making a proper election return, and that he be Discharged...."

For some unexplained reason he was not discharged, for it is known that he stayed in office until the middle of 1776.

Records of Baltimore Town indicate that Holliday Street got its name simply because John Robert Holliday (the name was often spelled Hollyday) owned land along it. Old tax records tell that he owned "Three Lotts"; the town records say that on September 11, 1783, "the commissioners open'd a street called Hollyday Street of eighty feet wide."

Later entries mention Capt. John R. Holliday in connection with the street, and, in fact, use the term "Holliday's Street" on one occasion.

Little is known about Holliday. Why he was called "captain" is a mystery.

An obituary notice says that he was born in 1747 and that he died in 1801.

Holliday Street has a lively history. Early in the 19th century, thanks to Rembrandt Peale's experiments, the city's first gas lamps were erected at Holliday and Baltimore streets.

In 1814, Rembrandt Peale opened "Peale's Museum and Gallery of Fine arts" on the street; in 1830, the museum became the City Hall, and it served as this until 1875, when the present City Hall was completed. In 1930, the old building became the Municipal Museum.

As much a landmark as the museum was the Holliday Street Theater, which stood on the site of the War Memorial Plaza. Originally built by public subscription in 1794, it burned in 1813 and in 1874 and was rebuilt each time. It lasted until 1917.

Around 1890, Holliday Street was the cause of a bitter row. The bed of the street, between Bath and Centre, at that time was owned by a large distillery, which simply let the public use it — until one day a large wagon crashed into a distillery building and broke a window. Then, because the owner of the wagon refused to pay damages, the distillery closed the street.

At that a howl went up, for Holliday Street was important to business. But the city found that the distillery was within its rights, and for a time irate citizens were kept off. After a while, though, the distillery officials reopened their part of Holliday Street. A few years later, it became city property.

Hollins Street, Hollins Market – 1957

August 21, 1949

Hollins

By William Stump

Those Baltimore historians who say Hollins Street was named for John Hollins are probably right — but probably wrong. Research suggests that they are thinking of the wrong John Hollins, or that the street was possibly named for two Johns.

John Smith Hollins, mayor of Baltimore from 1852 to 1854, is the man from whom the street name has been generally believed to derive. Possibly he is; at the time the street was named, in 1822, he was only 35 years old but he was an officer-veteran of the War of 1812.

A surveyor named Thomas Poppleton was the man who named the street — before it ever really existed. In 1822, he drew a map embodying plans for the future development of the city. On it, in areas which at the time were farmland and forest, he marked out streets that were one day to be cut through, and to these streets he gave the names of Baltimore's prominent citizens and heroes.

But if John Smith Hollins had earned a place on the map by his war service, his father — also named John — had earned one ahead of him, by prominence alike in the city's social, political and business life. Poppleton had reason to name a street after either of the men, or after both of them together.

John Hollins the elder was of English birth. He came to Baltimore in 1783 from Liverpool, where he had been a successful banker. Here he founded a marine insurance firm which also was very successful, and two years after his arrival he married Jane Smith, sister of Gen. Samuel Smith.

Eventually, Hollins built a large house on fashionable Washington Square, as Monument Square was called before the

Battle Monument was erected there in 1825. His interest in politics led to his election to the City Council; he served in the Second Branch from 1813 to 1820.

Whether he took any part in the War of 1812 — his English background plus the fact that his father-in-law commanded Baltimore's defenses pose interesting questions as to his sentiments — is not a matter of record. But his son, John Smith Hollins, served as an officer under General Smith.

The senior Hollins died in 1827; his widow in 1832. A few years later, Hollins Street, up to that time little more than a line of Poppleton's Plat, began to grow. Hollins Market, said to be the oldest in the city, was founded by a group of merchants in 1836; eleven years after that, the Donnell family gave a plot of land to the city for a park and named it Union Square.

John Smith Hollins, who grew up in the Monument Square house, on the site of which the courthouse stands today, became mayor in 1852 and served an uneventful two-year term. He died in 1856, at the age of 69.

There is another thoroughfare bearing the family name. This is Hollins Avenue, in the Lake Roland district. It led to the old Hollins Station, which was named in honor of Robert Smith Hollins, a railroad executive who, born in 1798, was another son of John and Jane Smith Hollins.

County officials believe that Hollins Avenue derived its name from its proximity to the station, probably in the 1870s or 1880s.

In the Westport area of South Baltimore there is a Hollins Ferry Road, which old maps indicate once led to a ferry that crossed Gwynns Falls. But as histories make no mention of John, John Smith or Robert Hollins in connection with the area, it is doubtful that the road is named for their family.

July 4, 1954

Hopkins

By William Stump

When men drank store-bought whisky in Maryland and Virginia and North Carolina in the 1820s, like as not they drank "Hopkins' Best." Even as far away as the wild Ohio country, hard-working and hard-drinking citizens gained comfort from the Baltimore-bottled elixir.

And so did Johns Hopkins — but in a far different way. For his whisky selling started a career that was to see him become the premier merchant, financier and philanthropist of his generation.

Ironically, it was the business depression of 1819 that made it possible for the Baltimorean to make a whisky fortune. A few years before that, in 1814, Hopkins left the Anne Arundel plantation where he was born and came to Baltimore to work with his uncle.

The uncle, Gerard Hopkins, operated a commission grocery business; in that, the bright young Hopkins was an instant success. But the 1819 depression came, and the country storekeepers who bought provisions from the house were unable to pay cash. Instead, they offered to pay in whisky.

Their offer seemed like a good one to Johns Hopkins. But not to Uncle Gerard — who stated flatly that he would "sell no souls to perdition." His feelings may have been colored by the fact that he was not getting along too well with his nephew, who had fallen in love with his daughter Elizabeth and wanted to marry her. Permission was refused because of the relationship.

Johns Hopkins Monument – 1935

The upshot was that Johns Hopkins, then 24, opened his own commission house, began to take whisky instead of cash, and bottle it and ship it.

Johns Hopkins, expelled from Meeting because of the whisky trade, began to branch out. He built warehouses, and he

Johns Hopkins' Clifton Park Mansion – 1938

went into banking. He succeeded, and the thing that made him succeed was his toughness, his nerve; he was, biographers say, always willing to take a chance.

When the young and struggling B.&O. Railroad seemed like the world's riskiest investment, Hopkins invested heavily, becoming a director of the road and later chairman of its finance committee. When the panic of 1857 came, his shares, the biggest block next to those of the state and city, saved the road. And he saved the city from financial ruin by putting up vast sums in 1863 and again in 1873, the year he died.

Steamship lines, banks, insurance companies, and a host of lesser businesses filled his coffers with money. Although a picture has come down of him as a gentle man, he was not popular in the business community. If, for example, a young and diligent man applied for a loan, Hopkins would make the loan and not charge a cent. But wealthy men who got themselves into financial difficulties were charged whopping sums for the same service.

The hardheaded merchant was a thinker, though. And the older he grew, the more he thought about his fortune. It was then that he decided to provide money for a hospital and a university — a new kind of university that would provide training in a variety of fields. To be sure, he did not plan out what he wanted the university to be exactly; indications are that his idea was a vague one, one that Daniel Coit Gilman translated into a reality.

But Hopkins did plan out one thing — he wanted the university to be located at Clifton, his summer home. And he wanted the university and the hospital to be joined together by a tree-lined boulevard.

That plan did not work out, of course. But Broadway, with its grass plots running down the middle, grew out of the idea. And Clifton Avenue was named for the estate that is now a city park; Hopkins Place, too, was named for its association with the merchant. But these, plus the few statues that commemorate the man, mean little when compared to his two great monuments, the university and the hospital.

John Street – 1956

January 2, 1949

Howard

By Henry C. Rauch

Just like the Redcoats during the Revolution, Baltimoreans today meet John Eager Howard coming and going.

John Street is named for him. Eager Street is named for him. Howard Street is named for him.

Eutaw Street is named for one of this battles, Camden Street for another.

Public School No. 61 is named for him, and the Sheraton Belvedere Hotel is named after his mansion, Belvedere.

An equestrian statue of him stands in Washington Place.

John Eager Howard was born in Baltimore County on June 4, 1752. Soldiering apparently was in his blood, for his grand-father, Joshua Howard — the first of the line to come to America — had fought under the Duke of York. At the very beginning of the Revolution, the committee of safety that was established in Baltimore offered Howard a commission as colonel.

Howard declined that, through distrust of his ability to perform such high duties, but in July 1776, he did accept a captaincy in the 2d Maryland Battalion of the Flying Camp commanded by Col. J. Carvel Hall. In two days he had recruited a company and was on his way to New York, where, on October 28, he fought in the battle of White Plains.

A few months later, the Army was reorganized and Howard made a major in the 4th Maryland Regiment, again under Colonel Hall, and in the battle of Germantown on October 4, 1777, he commanded the regiment after Hall was disabled. In this battle, he first saw a place that later had great significance of another kind for him — the home of Benjamin Chew. Soon

Eager Street – 1934

after the close of the war, Howard married Chew's eldest daughter, Margaret.

In March 1778, Howard was promoted to lieutenant colonel of the 5th Maryland Regiment, and with it took part in the battle on Monmouth. Then in October 1779, he was transferred to the 2d Maryland, with which he was destined to achieve his greatest renown.

When the retreating militia at the battle of Camden left the two Maryland brigades under Baron de Kalb to bear the whole British onset, aided by a few other gallant corps, the brigade that included Howard's men offered the fiercest resistance by bayonet fighting, and came near to reversing the tide.

Again in the battle of Cowpens, in January 1781, Howard distinguished himself, leading a charge at the critical moment that brought the American victory. Congress voted him a medal, and he became known as the "Hero of Cowpens."

In that same year, Howard materially aided General Greene in making his retreat at Guilford Court House, fought at Hobkirk Hill, and then at Eutaw Springs led another effective bayonet charge — in which he was severely wounded, so that he had to be furloughed.

"As good an officer as the world affords," General Greene wrote of him at this time. "My own obligations to him are great — the public's more so. He deserves a statue of gold."

At the conclusion of the war, Howard returned to Baltimore, and was honored with various offices. He was a delegate to the Continental Congress in 1787-1788, governor of Maryland from 1788 to 1791, and United States senator from 1796 to 1803. Two other posts, both offered by President Washington, he declined; that of secretary of war, and that of brigadier-general.

During the War of 1812, Howard contributed liberally to defense moves, and when Baltimore was threatened he organized a corps of veterans, which, however, was not called out.

He was a leader of the Federalists, and was their candidate for vice president in 1816.

Howard's landholdings extended from Jones Falls to what is now Eutaw Street, and from Pratt Street to the northern edge of the city. His mansion, Belvedere, stood at about Calvert and Eager streets.

Colonel Howard died on October 12, 1827. He is buried in Old St. Paul's Cemetery, on West Lombard Street.

Howard Street – Date Unknown

December 20, 1953

Hutton

By James C. Bertram

When Celeste Marguerite Winans Hutton died in 1925, one newspaperman wrote that an era had ended.

A cliché, yes. But the newspaperman could hardly have been more accurate. For in the minds of many a Baltimorean, Mrs. Hutton had been the most powerful symbol of a fabulous age — an age in which a man could build himself a couple of empires with seemingly little effort.

It could be said that the era began in 1827 when Mrs. Hutton's grandfather came to Baltimore. He was Ross Winans, and he was a horse trader from New Jersey. He had traveled to Baltimore as soon as he heard that a strange new company called the Baltimore and Ohio Railroad was planning to lay down a track to Ellicott's Mills over which freight and passenger vehicles would be pulled by horse teams.

No records exist to indicate whether or not Winans sold a horse to the new company. Indeed, he shortly made it impractical for the railroad to own horses at all. An engineer at heart, he pioneered the line's locomotives and invented many a piece of equipment that made the line a going concern. And in the next few hectic years he built all the company's locomotives, first as an employee and then on his own with the aid of his sons, William and Thomas.

At the same time, a new chapter in the Winans saga was being written thousands of miles away — in Russia. There Czar Nicholas I, intrigued by the new invention of the West, had ordered a line built between St. Petersburg and Moscow. The workers boondoggled, stalled and stole, telling the czar that the problems were insurmountable. The angry Nicholas took a map, placed a ruler between the two cities — and called upon Winans to finish the railroad on that line, and equip it.

Ross Winans would not leave Baltimore. Instead, he sent his sons. To say that they were successful is to understate. Both of them made millions. Moreover, Thomas met and married Celeste Revillon, a Russian of French and Italian descent. In a burst of pride he brought his millions and his wife back to Baltimore — and built a mansion that was beyond the comprehension of the populace.

That was Alexandroffsky, named for Czar Alexander. Located on a 3-acre tract bound by Hollins, Baltimore, Fremont and Callender streets, it was furnished with the best the world's craftsmen could produce.

It was there that Celeste Marguerite Winans, daughter of the empire builder and his Russian bride, grew up — there and at Crimea, the family's country mansion near Gwynn Falls. She made her debut at a gigantic party at Alexandroffsky, then she began the Grand Tour in the company of an aunt.

In England, she met an aristocratic American in the consultant service. He was Gaun M. Hutton. Not long after

Winans-Hutton estate — Crimea – 1949

that he was transferred to Russia; the Baltimore heiress met him again there and married him.

In the years after they had returned to America they lived variously at Shamrock Hill in Newport, at Alexandroffsky and at Crimea, all of which Mrs. Hutton had inherited from her father. Mrs. Hutton became known as one of the state's brilliant hostesses, a patron of the arts, a keystone of the sedate life.

Even during the changes brought about in the new century, the Huttons' life remained the same. When the automobile came in, for example, they would have no part of it, preferring to be seen in a carriage.

One change did occur, however. In 1896, the family sold off 80 acres of the Crimea estate to a developer; Windsor Hills was the result. But the property was so vast that it made little difference; indeed, most of Leakin Park was part of Crimea, as was the wooded area to the north. Through that, extending from Ridgetop to Wetheredsville Road, runs Hutton Avenue; moreover, another segment of the street is in the neighborhood of West Forest Park Avenue.

Gaun Hutton died in 1916. After that Mrs. Hutton became something of a recluse. But in 1923, to aid the South Baltimore General Hospital, she opened up Alexandroffsky for a card party and Baltimoreans at last got the opportunity to see the mansion.

Two years later, Mrs. Hutton was dead. Soon after that, Alexandroffsky was demolished. But Crimea will remain for generations to come, for five years ago it was designated the mansion house for Leakin Park.

K

Key

By William Stump

Surprisingly enough, Baltimore's city fathers didn't get around to naming a street for Francis Scott Key until 1913. But then, they can't be considered tardy — Congress didn't make "The Star-Spangled Banner" the national anthem until 1931.

Key Highway starts at Light Street and runs a crooked course southwest and south to McComas Street. When the City Council created it, the song that most Americans regarded as their national anthem, even though the government officially did not, was just about a century old.

The story of how Key came to write the words of the song has been told a thousand times — and in a thousand different ways. The following version, parts of it based on information unearthed in recent years, appears to be the one most widely accepted by historians.

It seems that a Dr. Beanes, of Upper Marlboro, was entertaining some friends in the summer of 1814, when some straggling British soldiers appeared at his door. They either made themselves obnoxious, or the doctor and his companions (one

Key Highway – 1949

account suggests that he was in his cups) took exception to the fact they were enemies; at any rate, the doctor had the soldiers marched off to the local jail. When the British heard about this, they sent some Marines around and arrested the doctor.

Key, a prominent Washington lawyer, was asked by the government to seek out the British and ask them to release the popular medical man. Key agreed to do so, and, with Col. John Stuart Skinner, government agent for the exchange of prisoners, boarded "one of Furguson's Norfolk packets" (before Louis H. Dielman turned up this information in an old newspaper account written by Colonel Skinner, the vessel was generally supposed to have been the cartel Analostan) in Baltimore and headed down the bay.

That was on September 5, 1814. Two days later, the men reached the British fleet, anchored at the mouth of the Potomac, and boarded the Tonnant, Admiral Cochrane's flagship. Key and Skinner were received graciously by the admiral who, nevertheless, took his time in agreeing to release the doctor.

Key and Skinner spent several days with the British. Treated like honored guests, they dined at the admiral's table, where plans for the bombardment and invasion of Fort McHenry and Baltimore were freely discussed. In light of that, according to Colonel Skinner's account of the adventure, the admiral told the Americans that they "could hardly expect us to let you go ashore ahead of us . . . you will have to remain with us until it is all over."

So Key and his companions, who were allowed to board their own vessel and compelled to accompany the invasion fleet, had grandstand seats for the bombardment. To them, it was a night of terrible anxiety and intense emotion. The British, who had bragged of victory, were pouring cannon balls and rockets into Fort McHenry and the city; there was hardly a lull in the furious, terrifying bombardment.

Early the next morning, the bombardment ceased. When Key saw that the flag still waved over the fort, when he learned that the British forces had been chased from the edge of Baltimore back to North Point, he was so moved that he composed his poem, on the back of an envelope.

According to Roger B. Taney, Chief Justice of the United States Supreme Court, and, as a young lawyer, Key's closest friend, the poem was rewritten in a Baltimore hotel. Shortly afterward, Key showed it to Judge Joseph Hopper Nicholson, who was married to his wife's sister; the judge was so enthusiastic that he had a printer run it off on a stack of handbills, which were distributed throughout the city.

The poem, titled "The Defense of Fort M'Henry," was eventually taken to Carr's music store on Baltimore Street, and set to the tune of "To Anacreon in Heaven," an English drinking song. No one seems to agree who, exactly, took the poem to Mr. Carr, or whose idea it was to use the British tune; there are many versions of how the poem became a song.

The man who wrote it was born in 1779 at Terra Rubra, his family's estate in Frederick, then Carroll County. He entered St. John's College at 10 and graduated at 17 to become, eventually, a lawyer.

Key was blue-eyed, friendly, intelligent and deeply religious — so religious that he almost gave up law to enter the ministry. As a lawyer he was first-rate, arguing and winning a case before the Supreme Court at the age of 27, and earning a fine reputation by the time he was 30.

Married in 1802 to an Annapolis girl, he was the father of 11 children. Before and after the War of 1812 (which he regarded as senseless), he wrote light verses that a biographer calls "respectable in meter but slight in consequence," and a number of hymns, but the anthem is the only work at all known.

His family, his law and his religion were his main interests. He died in 1843, at the age of 64, while visiting the Mount Vernon Place home of his daughter, Mrs. Charles Howard. For a time he was buried in St. Paul's Cemetery; now his body lies in Frederick, under an American flag that flies 24 hours a day.

January 9, 1949

Konig

By Henry C. Rauch

An East Baltimore man who inaugurated a tradition of political activity that kept the family name prominent for three-quarters of a century is the man who provided a name for Konig Street — that single block which stood quietly between Linden and Brookfield avenues, in Northwest Baltimore, until the Hiss-Chambers espionage case threw it into prominence.

The man was George Konig, the second of a straight succession of five George Konigs who have lived in or near East Baltimore, and the father of that section's beloved "man of blood and iron," Congressman "Koonicks" — as the name was often pronounced.

The first George Konig was a native to Germany who came to the United States around 1815 and settled in Maryland. His son, George, born in that same year, became a farmer at North Point, but upon marrying and acquiring a family found the farm an inadequate support, and in 1856 moved into Baltimore.

Here he "entered the industrial world," a move that does not seem to have solved his problems, since his son had to forgo school to help support the family. But he also entered politics, and in this field gained prominence in his section. About 1867 he was made keeper of the Block Street drawbridge across Jones Falls, and he held that post until his death November 20, 1892.

It was in acknowledgment of political help given in the Fells Point section, according to a family tradition, that Mayor Ferdinand C. Latrobe had Konig Street named after him.

The third George, who became the most famous bearer of the name, was born on the farm at North Point on January 26, 1856, just before the family moved to East Baltimore. As stated, he had no formal schooling; he had not yet learned to read or write when he had to go to work as an errand boy.

He proved to be determined, aggressive and fearless, however, and from his late teens on steadily advanced — and also educated — himself. His own background, perhaps, made him highly sympathetic with his struggling neighbors, and he, too, entered politics and fought for them and their section.

In 1903, he was elected to the First Branch of Council, then was re-elected until 1907, and then promoted to the Second Branch. In 1911, he was promoted again, to Congress. He had not yet completed his first term there when he died on May 31, 1913, a tremendous hero to his people, great numbers of whom he had helped with money and other aid.

The congressman's son George, born in 1886, in time followed in his footsteps by winning a City Council seat as his first elective position. He was representing the First District at the time of his death in 1913 — his son, the fifth George Konig, later held a city post for a time.

One of the congressman's daughters, incidentally, Mrs. Margaret Konig Mayhew, was also active politically for a number of years, and another daughter became the wife of William Curran, who had been the congressman's private secretary.

June 25, 1950

Kossuth

By William Stump

Few Baltimoreans know the story of Louis Kossuth, the Hungarian patriot who made a spectacular visit to their city a century ago in the cause of his country's freedom. But many are familiar with his name, thanks to a celebrated dessert and an old street.

The dessert is Kossuth cake — ice cream between two layers of sponge cake topped with frosted chocolate sauce — which has been popular in the city since 1851, when an enterprising baker introduced it in conjunction with the visit of the man people called "the George Washington of Hungary."

Kossuth Street, which extends southwest from North Hilton Street to Old Frederick Road, was created some 20 years later by a real-estate man who admired the Hungarian's passionate devotion to freedom.

Kossuth came to America in the autumn of 1851, having been forced to flee the leadership of his country by the armies of the Austrian Empire. Americans, who remembered that their freedom had been won under stress, received him with enthusiasm. He was the chief topic of conversation everywhere.

In the 1840s, Americans learned from their newspapers, Kossuth, a man of wealth, had demanded that Austria allow Hungary its own government. The Austrians threw Kossuth into prison. There he stayed for two years, occupying his time learning English and realizing that the sentence had won him great prestige.

Upon his release, indeed, Kossuth's popularity was so great that Austria granted self-government to Hungary. But in a matter of months, Austrian armies were crossing the Hungarian borders — and a few weeks later were driven back to Vienna by Kossuth's followers. Then Hungary was proclaimed a separate state, and Kossuth became its governor. The free nations of the world, especially America, rejoiced.

The new freedom did not last. Once again, aided by thousands of Cossacks loaned her by Czar Nicholas, Austria invaded. This time Kossuth was forced to flee. Finding refuge in Turkey, he caught the attention of the world with his pleas for

Hungarian freedom. America was so sympathetic — men like Horace Greeley said that Kossuth was democracy's last hope in Europe — that it sent the U. S. S. Mississippi to fetch him.

In America, Kossuth hoped that he could get government aid. When it became doubtful that he would, he decided to tour the country and raise money himself. His reception in Baltimore was typical of those he received in other large cities.

Wearing the colorful costume of the Magyars, and accompanied by a large number of imposing-looking followers, he was met at the station by Mayor Jerome and escorted, amid cheers and fireworks, up Broadway and Baltimore Street to the Eutaw House, the city's most fashionable hotel. That night he spoke to 6,000 citizens in the great hall of the Maryland Institute.

He spoke skillfully, too. He recalled Maryland's place in the history of religious toleration, likening Maryland's struggle to Hungary's. He pleaded that the United States speak sternly to Austria and Russia. He subtly suggested that any donations he received in Baltimore would eventually be used to buy Baltimore ships and Baltimore supplies.

But Baltimore, like the rest of America, was not lavish in the opening of its purses. A few months later when Kossuth left for Europe, he had netted only $90,000 — though it was suspected that he had acquired a lot more that had gone for his comfort and entertainment.

In one Washington hotel, for example, it was rumored, Kossuth and his friends spent $5,000 in 10 days, most of it for the finest of wines and foods. As a result, many Americans openly distrusted him, among them Senator Thomas G. Pratt, of Maryland, who arose in Congress and all but denounced him as a fraud.

Even so, Kossuth left for Europe with good wishes of many thousands of admirers. Among these was the real-estate man who (in the 1870s) created Kossuth Street as part of a housing development for small-wage earners.

At that time, although self-government had been granted to Hungary in 1867, Kossuth was just as energetically working for Hungary's full independence. He was still working when he died in 1894, at the age of 88.

L

July 22, 1951

Lafayette

By William Stump

Two streets and a park preserve the name of the man who received the biggest welcome ever given a visitor to Baltimore.

Fayette Street, Lafayette Avenue and Lafayette Square — all were named for Marquis de Lafayette, once considered by Americans as great a Revolutionary hero as Washington and as great a man as any who ever figured in American affairs.

In reality, the Frenchman who joined Washington's forces as a 19-year-old major-general was not an outstanding soldier or statesman by any stretch of the imagination. But the fact that he was a nobleman from a great foreign land who came enthusiastically and voluntarily to aid America in its dark hours gave him lofty stature in the eyes of the new nation.

That stature increased in the years after the Revolution; it reached its apex in 1824 when, upon President Monroe's invitation, Lafayette paid a return visit to America — a visit which historians have called epochal. Never before had Americans shown such enthusiasm for a man, either foreigner or native, as they showed for the Marquis on his year-long tour.

Lafayette Avenue – 1956

Lafayette came to Baltimore on October 7, 1824, arriving on the steamboat United States which, after being circled in the harbor by vessels festooned with flowers and flags, docked amid the booming cannon at Fort McHenry.

There, in a tent that George Washington had used during the Revolution, he was met by Gov. Samuel Stevens, John Eager Howard and Charles Carroll of Carrollton, whom he fondly embraced. Old newspapers tell that on seeing some of Washington's equipment that had been replaced in the tent, he whispered emotionally: "I remember." There was not a dry eye among the gathering.

After that, the undistinguished-looking, aging Marquis, with his son, George Washington Lafayette, was borne up Charles to Baltimore Street, where he passed beneath a magnificent floral arch. Then the party went to Fells Point and eventually returned to town to the Fountain Inn.

Ten thousand soldiers and 100,000 civilians — an amazing number, considering that Baltimore's population was just under 65,000 — watched the procession, cheering madly and waving flags and handkerchiefs.

For the next four days there were parades, receptions, balls and banquets. Business came to a standstill; Baltimore was like a carnival midway. Crowds followed Lafayette wherever he went in his green and cream barouche.

And wherever he went — to luncheon with John Eager Howard at Belvedere, to a banquet at James Buchanan's mansion on Monument Square, to the University of Maryland at Lombard and Greene streets to receive the university's first honorary degree — he complimented Baltimoreans for their patriotism, their industry and their beautiful women.

That visit, which ended as he departed for Washington in a blaze of glory, was not Lafayette's first visit to Baltimore. In 1781, while on his way south with his American troops, he camped on what are now the Cathedral grounds. Even then he was high in the hearts of Americans, and Baltimore went all out to stage a banquet for him.

During that banquet, Mrs. Davis Poe noticed that the young general was moody. She asked what was wrong; he replied that it was difficult to enjoy the festivities while his men were in rags. The next day, under Mrs. Poe's direction, the women of the city sewed hundreds of new uniforms from cloth donated by local merchants and, in spite of the hardship of wartime living, also supplied flour, pork and beef.

Lafayette came to the city again in 1784. Then he returned to Europe, where for the next 30 years he was in turn idolized, jailed and exiled for political activity. Restored to grace before the 1824 visit, he lived out his life with the aid of money donated by America. He died in 1834 at the age of 77.

Fayette Street first appears on a 1792 map; Baltimore histories say it was named for the Marquis. Lafayette Square was created in 1857, and Lafayette Avenue, which had theretofore been Townsend Street, was named in 1869.

Fayette Street – 1935

November 20, 1949

Lanier

By William Stump

If a musician had not interrupted his journey through Baltimore in 1873, there probably would be no Lanier Avenue in the city today.

For Sidney Lanier, the poet, musician and scholar whose name is high on the city's roster of famous men, accidently became a Baltimorean while on his way to New York in quest of a musical career. An accomplished flutist — his prowess on the instrument was a boon to the morale of his fellow Confederate prisoners during the Civil War — who looked upon his ability to write verse as a "mere tangent," he had stopped over in Baltimore to visit a friend.

The friend introduced him to Asger Hamerik, the director of the Peabody Conservatory of Music, who listened to him play and then invited him to join the Peabody Symphony Orchestra. Lanier jumped at the invitation — and lived in Baltimore for the rest of his life.

The street bearing his name lies in Pimlico, south from Oakley Avenue to Woodlawn Avenue. The name was chosen by the late William Whitney, a surveyor who "liked poets and poetry."

Mr. Whitney is also credited with having named Poe Avenue, located one block west of Lanier.

Both these streets, mere lines on maps for many years, are now beginning to come into their own, as a result of the postwar building boom.

Lanier was born in Macon, Ga., in 1842. Though a frail child, he played the usual childhood games, adding to them his own flair for the poetic. Once, for example, he organized his playmates into an "army," made them wear uniforms and plumed helmets, and marched them down the main street of the town.

Not many years later, Lanier was writing poetry — addressing many of his verses to the girls of Macon — and taking a delight in playing the flute. He had one ambition, he told his father, and that was to devote himself to music, literature and scholarship. He entered Oglethorpe College and was pursuing the ambition when the war came.

When the students and the faculty went off to fight the Yankees, Lanier went with them. He joined the Confederate Navy and served as a signal officer aboard a blockade runner until he was captured in 1864 and thrown into prison at Point Lookout.

The prison was so horrible that Lanier, whose health had never been good, was an easy victim of tuberculosis. Writing of his prison experiences, Lanier said he was "emaciated as a skeleton, downhearted for want of news from home, downheaded for weariness."

At the end of the war, Lanier's excitement at his release was too much for him. Aboard the ship carrying the ex-prisoners to freedom, he collapsed and for a time lay near death.

Lanier walked all the way back to Macon. He married and tried his hand at various occupations. But the arts, especially music, were uppermost in his mind, so in a few years, still suffering from tuberculosis, he began the trip that brought him to Baltimore.

His eight years in this city were the happiest of Lanier's life. Here he found expression for all his talents. He played the flute and studied music to his heart's content, wrote his best poetry, and lectured at the Johns Hopkins University.

He was poor much of the time, often discouraged and always sick. Yet the men who knew him write of him as having been exuberant, keen, stimulating and impressive looking.

Lanier was just beginning to win acclaim when he died, at the age of 39, in 1881. His early death may be one reason why literature accounts him a "minor poet." Scholars believe that had he lived longer, he might well have developed into a major one.

October 28, 1948

The Latrobes

By Elizabeth H. Moberly

Latrobe Street is only a few blocks long, running north and south between Oliver and Lanvale streets just east of Guilford Avenue, yet the family whose name it bears was one of the most notable in the history of Baltimore.

As if to equalize matters, however, there are also Latrobe Park and Latrobe Park Terrace in South Baltimore.

The first of the family to make his mark in Baltimore was Benjamin H. Latrobe, who designed Baltimore Cathedral and the old Custom House. Although Latrobe is best known for his architectural and engineering work, he began his career as a soldier in the Prussian army (though born in England) and after his period of service was over, he became the engineer of London.

Because of his political views, he came to the United States in 1795. His skill as a designer took him to Richmond, where he planned many public buildings, and led to his appointment by President Jefferson in 1803 as surveyor of public buildings in Washington, D. C.

Latrobe designed the restoration of the United States Capitol after it was burned by the British. He died in a yellow-fever epidemic in New Orleans, where he had gone to complete the installation of waterworks begun by his eldest son, who was also a victim of the fever.

Carrying on in the tradition of their father were Latrobe's two younger sons, John H. B. Latrobe, who invented the Latrobe stove, and Benjamin Jr., who designed the Baltimore and Ohio Railroad bridge at Relay and other railroad and canal projects.

John Latrobe was perhaps more closely associated with Baltimore than his brother. Appointed to West Point, he was forced to resign following the death of his father in 1820, and though he regretted giving up a professional military career, he served for several years as aide to the commander of the 3d Division of the Maryland militia and was at one time president of the board of visitors to West Point. He was known in his generation as a writer, lawyer and artist.

He helped found the organization that later became the Maryland Institute for the Promotion of the Mechanical Arts. The stove for which he is perhaps best known was to be found in nearly every home in the United States during the 19th century.

John died in 1891.

Next of the family to gain prominence in the city was Ferdinand C. Latrobe, the son of John H. B. Latrobe and seven times the mayor of Baltimore.

His career began in the office of his father, where he read law, and though the elder Latrobe declined to run for office, the son was elected to the Maryland Legislature, eventually serving as Speaker. While in the legislature, he helped reorganize the Maryland militia; for many years he was judge advocate general of the militia and was called General Latrobe.

He was first elected mayor in 1875, and re-elected in 1877, 1879, 1883, 1887, 1891 and 1893.

His administrations were marked by many reforms in the city government and by municipal improvements, such as the establishment of a board to improve the inner harbor of the city; the designing of the sunken gardens and terraces around Pennsylvania Station (then Union Station); the erection of several bridges across Jones Falls (these were designed by his cousin, Charles H. Latrobe, who had served with the Confederate engineers during the Civil War, and who later designed a 575-foot span in Peru); and the construction of Baltimore City College and Western High School.

Mayor Latrobe died in 1911.

May 1, 1949

Laurens

By Henry C. Rauch

In the words of George Washington, John Laurens was a young man of "intrepidity bordering upon rashness." He was a man whom Washington often used for secret missions during the Revolution, who at the age of 26 was made a special envoy to France and there recruited money and military supplies, and who fought at Yorktown and after the victory helped dictate the terms of Cornwallis' surrender.

In the words of Gen. Nathaniel Greene: "The love of military glory made him seek it upon occasions unworthy of his rank." And because of that, before he had quite reached the age of 28, Lt. Col. John Laurens died on an unimportant and nameless field of battle that he need never have entered.

It is for this Revolutionary zealot that Baltimore named Laurens Street, which starts at Park Avenue just below North and runs southwest to Fremont Avenue, then turns west for the rest of its length to Pulaski Street.

Laurens was born at Charleston, S.C., on October 28, 1754, the son of Henry Laurens, a merchant and planter of French descent who was an important Revolutionary statesman. The boy studied under tutors in Charleston, then was sent abroad; there was more tutoring in London, then schooling in Geneva, and then he returned to London and began studying law.

Although in October of 1776 he married an English girl, the Revolution quickly drew him home and the very next year he joined Washington's staff as a volunteer aide. Later he was commissioned a lieutenant colonel, and he fought at Brandywine, Monmouth and Germantown — he was wounded here — besides carrying out special missions.

At Valley Forge he kept his father, then president of the Continental Congress, informed of the movements of the conspirators in the Conway Cabal.

He showed his zeal in another way, too; near the end of the year 1778, angered by what he considered the "constant personal abuse" of Washington by Maj. Gen. Charles Lee, he challenged that officer to a duel, and wounded him.

In 1779, Laurens was elected to the South Carolina Assembly, but when that state was invaded he promptly returned to the Army and fought until Charleston capitulated the following year. That unfortunate event made him a prisoner, but before long he was paroled and exchanged, and that same year Congress dispatched him to France.

As special envoy, Laurens was not intended to supersede Benjamin Franklin, then American minister to the country, but it was thought that, as a soldier who "could speak knowingly of the Army," he could more easily obtain needed aid from the French Government.

Congress had picked the right man. Immediately upon his arrival in Paris, Laurens began negotiation with the foreign minister, and when progress seemed slow in that quarter he went directly to Louis XVI. At a reception, he presented a memorial directly to the king, and as a result was soon able to start four transports to America with money and supplies.

In achieving this, Laurens, "brusqu'd the Ministers too much," Franklin thought, yet was "thoroughly possess'd of my [Franklin's] esteem" that he then came home to report to Congress and rejoin the Army.

After Yorktown — which, it may be supposed, was a particular pleasure for him, since Cornwallis was constable of the Tower of London, in which the elder Laurens was at that time confined — the young patriot once more returned to South Carolina and its legislature.

There, however, that excess of fearlessness soon manifested itself again, and he recklessly engaged in the irregular warfare that still persisted in his home state. And there, on August 27, 1782, he died in the insignificant fighting that evoked General Greene's sad comment. His wife had died a year before, in France.

June 19, 1949

Lazear

By William Stump

In Havana one September day in 1900, Dr. Jesse William Lazear made his rounds in the yellow fever ward at Las Animas Hospital. Most of the patients were seriously ill; many of them, he knew, were going to die.

Dr. Lazear was a Baltimore man serving on the Army's Yellow Fever Commission. He was certain that mosquitoes were to blame for the disease, but he was still puzzled. Mosquitoes of what species?

Just then, "a common, ordinary brown mosquito," to use Dr. Lazear's words, settled on his arm. It probably wasn't dangerous, he thought — but, on the other hand, it might be a major transmitter of the fever. Knowing the chance he was taking, Dr. Lazear watched with interest as the mosquito bit him.

Five days later, Dr. Lazear was racked with yellow fever. Ten days later, he was dead.

"Thus ended," Dr. James Carroll, a colleague, said later in an address at Johns Hopkins Hospital, "a life of brilliant promise at the age of 34. Dr. Lazear died that his fellow men might live in comfort and happiness. It is no exaggeration to say that hundreds, nay, thousands in the Southern states owe their lives to the results of the work in which he was engaged, and for which his family has paid such a penalty."

The man who gave his life so quietly has not been forgotten in Baltimore. On a wall at the Johns Hopkins Hospital there is a plaque which his colleagues dedicated to his memory. For many years there was a Lazear battery of guns at Fort Howard. Today, in Gwynn Falls Park — he lived in that area with his family — there is a winding thoroughfare named Lazear Road. This byway, connecting Franklintown Road and Rokeby Road, was opened in the martyr's honor in 1930, when James Hunt, of the city's Bureau of Surveys, was renaming many streets.

Dr. Lazear's character and work are portrayed in Sidney Howard's famous play, "Yellow Jack," which, more fully then any official document, tells the story of the bravery of those scientists and soldiers who risked their lives to defeat the disease.

Jesse Lazear was born in Baltimore County in 1866, and received his early education at Trinity Hall, a private school in Pennsylvania. He then went to Washington and Jefferson College — the chemistry building there is named for him — before entering Hopkins University.

After graduating with honors from Hopkins, he studied medicine at Columbia and received his degree in 1892. Two years as an intern at Bellevue Hospital followed, and in this period he decided to make bacteriology his specialty.

He went to Europe, visited and worked in the major hospitals on the Continent, and spent many months at the

Pasteur Institute.

After two years, Dr. Lazear returned to Baltimore, got married and was appointed staff bacteriologist at the Johns Hopkins Hospital. Right away he resumed study of the mosquito, about which he had already made important discoveries while still an intern. He spent hours at his microscope; his research at Hopkins helped science better understand the malarial parasite which the mosquito carries.

It was only logical, then, that Dr. Walter Reed and Dr. Carlos Finlay, who had an idea that mosquitoes were responsible for spreading yellow jack, asked Dr. Lazear to join the special commission which was preparing to work in Cuba. The invitation was one which the young doctor could not refuse.

Not many months later, Dr. Lazear was dead. But the work he had accomplished, the discoveries he had made after days and nights of study and experiment, the notes and information which he had passed on to Dr. Carroll during his days of sickness, helped his colleagues stamp out a dread disease. Less than a year later the commission disbanded, its work done.

Now, yellow jack is almost forgotten — and Dr. Jesse William Lazear, who gave his life to make it so, is a hero of medical science.

June 24, 1951

Leakin

By William Stump

Although Captain Sheppard Church Leakin did nothing of importance during the British bombardment of Fort McHenry, he enjoyed the distinction of being the only man who had to be carried in for the defense of the bastion.

He should not have been there at all — he was supposed to be home in bed nursing the leg which had been terribly crushed by a falling tree while he was building fortifications on Loudenslager's hill, east of the city.

Indeed, the leg was so bad that doctors were all for amputating it. But Leakin, a 24-year-old officer in the 38th United States Infantry, talked them out of it.

When the guns of the fort boomed out to warn Baltimore that the British were coming, Leakin's sense of duty — or perhaps his newspaperman's instinct for a big event — moved him to insist that he join his men.

Reluctantly, his servant lifted him to a horse, and got on behind to keep his master from falling off. At the fort, his surprised troops carried him to a camp stool, where he happily sat out the fierce bombardment.

Leakin was born in Govanstown in 1790. As a youth, he learned the printing and newspaper business and, for a time, worked in Easton for the Gazette. After the war, he went into business on Fells Point and ran a print shop and book store.

Subsequently, he became a president of the Canton Company, a wealthy banker, a general of the state militia, the publisher, with Samuel Barnes, of the Baltimore Chronicle, and finally mayor.

In that office, which he held from 1838 to 1840, he had opportunity to draw upon his military background — when, in 1839, an angry mob attempted to storm the Carmelite convent on Aisquith Street on the grounds that the nuns were running a virtual prison.

It was one of the worst riots in the city's history, and at first it appeared that there would be serious trouble. But the mayor took a firm stand, and although the riot flared and reflared for almost two weeks, not one life was lost, nor a dollar's worth of property damage done.

Leakin Street (not to be confused with Leakin Park, which was named for his descendants) was named by the Canton Company in honor of its former president, and is located on land that once was owned by the company. Two blocks long, it extends northwest from Boston to Essex streets.

December 30, 1951

Lee

By William Stump

Resolved, that these United Colonies are, and of right ought to be, free and independent states; that they are absolved from all

Lee Street – 1940

allegiance to the British crown; and that all political connection between them and the State of Great Britain is, and ought to be, dissolved.

Those words, which let the world know formally and definitely that America was determined to tolerate the British yoke no longer, are perhaps the most important uttered in American history. True, they have become overshadowed by the Declaration of Independence; but the Declaration was a direct result of them.

The words were spoken before the Continental Congress on June 7, 1776. It was an exciting event for Americans — especially since they were spoken by Richard Henry Lee, whom historians sometimes call "The Father of Revolution."

The nickname is an apt one. For the Revolution did not just happen; it was no sudden, automatic thing. It was the culmination of years of work, work that included the very planting of the idea of independence in Colonial thinking, and after the planting, the cultivation of that idea. It was fortunate that there were men like Lee to do the work.

Lee was born in 1732, at Stratford, his family's seat in Westmoreland County, Virginia. This, says a biographer, automatically made him an aristocrat among aristocrats, for his clan — an aristocratic one for seven centuries — was one of the oldest in the colony and one of the most celebrated in America, even though its most famous member, Robert E. Lee, had not yet been born.

Little is known of Lee's early years. As a child, he was tutored at home; as a youth, he went to England to school, after the custom of his class. When school ended, he traveled for a year, returning home in 1752. Five years later, having presumably devoted his time to studying law, history, government and politics, he was a county justice of the peace. A year after that, he entered the House of Burgesses. Considering that his family had been members for a generation, this was not surprising.

At first, Lee did little but listen to older men — who were shocked when he raised his voice for the first time in support of legislation to check the growth of slavery. From that time on, it was apparent that his voice was a democratic one.

As the years went by, respect for him grew. But it was his clearheaded and articulate opposition of the Stamp Act of 1764 that gained him his reputation as a champion of Colonial rights. With Patrick Henry, he led Virginia's fight against the act and the unjust tax that it called for, and he won. From then on, when any English move seemed to threaten Colonial liberties, Lee raised his voice in protest. He acted, too; especially in setting up the intercolonial committees of correspondence that united the colonies in their opposition.

He called the English despotic. He referred to the king as the "Author of Our Miseries." He chided those who thought that conciliation and conservatism would stop the "dangerous and alarming" threat. While others spoke softly, he brought the word independence out into the open — and in doing so eventually won the cautious to his side. The result, in an aroused Continental Congress, was the resolution that led to the Declaration of Independence.

Lee quite naturally became a hero in the towns and cities of America; with the Adamses, Patrick Henry and Jefferson, he was toasted everywhere. One Maryland historian feels certain that Lee Street, in South Baltimore, was named in his honor — which is nothing if not logical, considering that it came into existence about the time of the Revolution.

The presenting of the resolution at the Continental Congress was the climax of Lee's career. After he signed the Declaration of Independence, he returned home and took part in the formation of a new state government. When the war was over, he served in Congress, and there he fought to improve the Constitution — which he had opposed on the grounds that it was not democratic enough.

His success is apparent. Most of the propositions he put forward are embodied in the first 10 amendments. Perhaps, when these became law, Lee considered his job done, for soon afterward he retired to his home in Westmoreland County, where he died in 1794.

December 11, 1949

Lombard Street

By Ralph Reppert

Outside of a six-century difference in age, 3,847 miles and the fact that most of its residents know how it came to be named, Lombard Street in London is quite similar to Lombard Street in Baltimore.

The London thoroughfare, one of the principal banking and financial centers of the city, assumed its name and its now well-known characteristics in the 13th century. That was the period in which merchants from Lombardy, becoming the chief money lenders in England, made the street their center.

From that point forward, the street has also been known as a street of interesting signs.

One of the most famous signs on the street, the "Cat-A-Fiddling" of the Commercial Bank of Scotland, was destroyed in an air-raid during the London Blitz. Another prominent sign of the street, the three golden balls taken from the Lombardy coat of arms and used by the money lenders, is perhaps more generally recognized today as the "shingle" of the pawnbroker.

Lombard Street – 1949

Baltimore's Lombard Street came into being some six centuries later. The first reference to it in the Bureau of Legislative Reference occurs in 1801. Why it was given the name of Lombard is a matter of speculation.

Baltimore's Lombard Street, in a manner of speaking, has also been a street of considerable international commerce. Until a few years ago, particularly on Thursdays and Fridays, East Lombard Street was the site of one of the busiest markets in Baltimore, a congested stretch of small shops, street stalls, pushcarts, hucksters and other "curbstone" business establishments, with most of its business done in every language but English.

Shoppers made their way there for fruits, vegetables, fish, clothing, dry goods, lace — practically anything that can be found in a large shopping center today.

Today Lombard Street is more of a cross-section of the times. It has a few cigar manufacturers, engravers, a tea company, some bookbinders, some silversmiths and a few other businesses which retain a slight flavor of the old days, but these are the exception.

The street now leans more to such types of businesses as radio distribution, printing and advertising, machine supplies, sound and recording equipment.

Like Lombard Street in London, Lombard Street in Baltimore has lost some of its quaint and distinctive signs. The one best remembered, probably, was the huge bottle of medicine which used to sit atop the tower building. It was removed in 1936, principally as an economy measure. It required the services of a crew of steeplejacks twice a year for cleaning and repainting.

January 8, 1950

Lorman

By William Stump

William Lorman was a Baltimore "merchant prince" — one of those immensely wealthy businessmen whose great energy, shrewd foresight and civic spirit helped transform Baltimore from a small town into a thriving city.

His fleet of clipper ships carried Baltimore products all over the world. His stagecoach lines extended north, south and west. He helped organize the Baltimore and Ohio Railroad and, with Rembrandt Peale, James Mosher and William Gwynn, founded the Baltimore Gas Light Company. He was the company's first president, and the president of a bank. He owned farms, wharves and city property.

There is a Lorman Street in Baltimore today. Located a few blocks south of North Avenue, it extends east from Monroe Street to Mount, then as Lorman Court to Gilmor Street. It came into being, at least on paper, in 1823 when Thomas Poppleton, a surveyor, completed his map of Baltimore's proposed development.

Indications are that the street was named for the merchant, for aside from his son Alexander, then a young man, he was the only male Lorman in the 1818 city directory. And the special state commission which in 1818 authorized the Poppleton map made a point of naming streets for Maryland statesmen, soldiers and businessmen.

William Lorman, "small in stature and dignified in bearing," was more than a prominent businessman and citizen; he was a man who thoroughly enjoyed life. With his son, who fought at North Point with the 1st Baltimore Hussars, he saw the world from the decks of his clippers, and galloped merrily down the streets of Baltimore in a handsome four-in-hand rig.

William Lorman town house — 1830 – 1889

The cellars of his mansion on the southeast corner of Charles and Lexington streets were filled with fine European wines which heightened the conviviality of his celebrated drawing room. There he conducted much of his business, and entertained such citizens as John Eager Howard. There he helped plan the defense of Baltimore during the War of 1812.

Upon William Lorman's death in 1842 (old records, which show that he came to Baltimore in 1783, give no birth date), his son Alexander inherited his fortune and his mansion. When his father was alive, Alexander was like him in his love of travel, fine horses and exclusive resorts. But when his father died, he became a recluse and seldom left the mansion. Alexander, a bachelor, died in 1872.

The mansion was converted into a bank in 1873. In 1890, it was torn down to make way for the building which occupies its site today. By that time the growth of Lorman Street, which Poppleton proposed to extend from the city's western boundary, now Pulaski Street, to Cove Avenue, now Fremont Avenue, was just beginning,

---

May 25, 1952

Luerssen

By James C. Bertram

It was time to close the grocery for the night, and Charles W. Luerssen, a young veteran of Pershing's American Expeditionary Forces, was beginning to count the day's receipts with his father when someone rattled the screen door.

The rattling was persistent; the veteran's father, Charles H. Luerssen, thought it was a neighbor playing a joke. With a smile, he unlatched the door — and a gun was jammed in his stomach.

Young Luerssen, who had been in some pretty tight spots as an artilleryman in France, instinctively grabbed a gun from a drawer and raised it to fire. But two more hoodlums came in a side door and shot him down.

Luerssen died almost immediately. The bandits escaped in a waiting automobile. Later, three men were arrested, but were acquitted for lack of evidence.

The shooting took place in June 1921. Almost seven years later, the murdered man's father was building some houses on part of a 10-acre homestead he owned off Moravia Avenue, west of Belair Road. In the process, he created and named Luerssen Avenue, which begins today at Moravia and extends to Southern.

"The city asked him to name the street," recalls Mrs. George Seyboth, a daughter. "But for whom he named it he would not say. I've often wondered whether it was for my brother Charley, the whole family, or for himself."

That will always be a mystery, for Mr. Luerssen died five years ago. But neighborhood people think of the street as named for Mr. Luerssen, who came to Baltimore from Germany as an immigrant in 1889.

He was 17 then. He had immigrated under the sponsorship of an uncle who owned a grocery at Fairmount and Dallas streets. He went to work there.

The boy learned the English language and the business rapidly; in two years, he had his own grocery across the street and was married to a German girl. They had seven children.

By 1908, things were going so well that Luerssen bought his land off Belair Road and moved his family there. He also moved his grocery to Patterson Park and Mura avenues; it was there that young Charles learned the business, and there that he met his death.

Charles H. Luerssen got out of the grocery business when his son returned from the war; he was only helping out in the store on the night of the murder. After the trial, he went into the construction business and stayed in it until his health failed him.

December 5, 1948

Lux

By Henry C. Rauch

A man who lived in Baltimore when this was, in part, the only "walled" town in the American colonies is the man to whom Light Street's name is attributed.

Light (Lux) Street – 1948

He was Capt. Darby Lux, a merchant sea captain, patriot and town official.

It was in 1730 that this street was first laid out, as a lane 1 perch wide. What name it bore for the next two decades has not been discovered. In 1750, however, Captain Lux built a brick house on the west side of it, somewhere near what is now Redwood Street, and it thereupon became known by his name.

Then, later — apparently during his lifetime — the Latin-looking word "Lux" was translated into its English equivalent of "Light."

Captain Lux appears in Baltimore annals as early as 1733, at which time he was commanding a ship in the London trade. By 1743, he had acquired lots in the young town, and two years later he was appointed one of the town commissioners.

In the years before the Revolution, and during that, the captain held important posts. He was vice chairman of a "committee of observation," and a member of another group appointed to superintend transactions in arms. His son William and a George Lux, who is believed to have been another son, were also active on these and other committees.

William and George followed in the captain's footsteps as important figures of their day. William was a ship owner, was one of the managers of a lottery organized to finance a public wharf, had the first ropewalk in Baltimore, was a trustee of the poor and a commissioner. George in 1785 contributed ground toward a potter's field.

The town "wall" was a thing of Captain Darby's day. A law of the time forbade the raising of pigs and geese within the town limits — but the law was insufficient to keep such animals from straying in from the outside.

In 1750, an effort was made to solve this problem by fencing the entire part of town in which Captain Lux and some others had built substantial homes. With funds obtained by a general subscription, the fence was built — "having a gateway for carriages on the north end of Gay Street, and another at the west end of Baltimore Street, with one smaller for foot passengers."

For three or four years, the fence did its job well. Then, however, its palings "became a prey to the wants of needy inhabitants." An attempt was made to prosecute some of these raiders, but the town commissioners found that the law was insufficient for this, too.

The fence "was discontinued."

M

September 17, 1950

Madison

By Ralph Reppert

Like the Baltimore street and avenue which carry the name of Madison, the career of the fourth United States president, James Madison, ran a long and successful, but changeable, course.

When he was a young man just out of Princeton, the Virginian passed through a period of melancholy. He became convinced he could not "expect a long or healthy life," and his attitude virtually retired him from the life around him.

An interest in politics brought him out of the depression and resulted eventually in his election to the Virginia convention, where he was a member of the committee which framed the Constitution and Declaration of Rights.

Madison was a member of the first Assembly under the new Constitution — and then he "retired" again. He was defeated

Madison Avenue, Druid Hill Gate – 1966

for re-election, legend has it, because he refused to canvass or treat for votes. However, the Assembly elected him to the governor's council in 1778, and in 1780 made him a delegate to the Continental Congress.

While in Congress, he almost had to "retire" again. "He served his state and country well," a historian writes. "His state requited his services by a chronic failure to pay his salary. He was continually in money difficulties and was often saved from serious embarrassment by a philanthropic money lender."

Madison withdrew once again from public life, returning to Virginia at the close of his term in Congress. A few months after his return, he was elected to the Virginia House of Delegates.

Madison again returned to Congress, but a few years after he married Dolley Payne Todd withdrew once again to devote his time to scientific farming.

The inauguration of his friend Thomas Jefferson, however, again brought him into prominence. He became secretary of state and the president's chief adviser. He was elected president in 1808, and re-elected in 1812.

Reviewing the War of 1812, a historian says: "Unfortunately, Madison, despite his admirable qualities, was not the man to lead the country through such an ordeal." Nevertheless, "Mr. Madison's war" was an American triumph.

Mr. Madison finally retired from the nation's service in 1817. A visitor in 1835 "found him weakened by rheumatism but mentally agile . . . given to gay conversation and anecdote."

The first part of the Baltimore street was given his name in the year 1833.

April 23, 1950

Malster

By Francis E. Old Jr.

There is a little secret one block long, near the west end of the North Avenue bridge, with a warehouse at one end and a firehouse at the other.

But small as it is, the thoroughfare is impressively labeled an avenue, the only remaining grandeur of an effort to honor a former mayor of Baltimore.

The mayor was, moreover, operator of one of the world's great shipyards, and the man who put into practical form the plans for the world's first feasible submarine.

William Talbot Malster, thirty-first Mayor of Baltimore, was born in Chesapeake City, Cecil County, on April 4, 1843.

He had no schooling as a youngster. He became a farmhand, then, successively, he was a grocer, confectioner, baker, painter, lumberman, blacksmith, carpenter. Finally he became a deckhand on a steamship, and from this slim toehold climbed rapidly. He studied hard, worked hard, read voluminously.

Before he was 30 he was consulting engineer to a steamship line.

In 1871, in a shop at the foot of Caroline Street, he began manufacturing marine engines. Subsequent expansions brought him, by 1880, to a 13-acre plant on Locust Point, adjacent to Fort McHenry.

Under the name of Columbian Iron Works and Dry Dock Company, Malster's firm grew to be the largest shipyard in Baltimore — one of the four or five greatest in the country.

This shipyard had at least two "firsts" to its credit. The giant oil tankers which today stream into Baltimore harbor had their prototype in the Maverick, the first tank steamship, built for the Standard Oil Company.

The submarines which a few years ago were sinking oil tankers may be said to have had their genesis in Baltimore too — at Mr. Malster's works.

There had been many earlier attempts to build a submersible, but in August 1897, the Argonaut lumbered from its ways at the Columbian Iron Works. It is generally acknowledged to be the first really practical submarine.

It was the brainchild of a young Baltimore machinist, Simon Lake. It was, too, a favored child of the shipyard — for many of the employees, and Malster himself, put money into it.

Ironically, on an adjacent way, they were also building the Plunger, another submersible. This had the backing of the government, but it failed and was junked.

Besides the street there are other Malster mementoes in Baltimore — memorials at least to the integrity of his work.

Many of the old iron bridges of Baltimore came from his works. The Calvert Street bridge, with its fabled iron-tailed stone lions, is one of his. Built in 1879, its sturdy bowstring trusses have withstood 71 years of traffic.

In 1878 the ice-breaker Ferdinand C. Latrobe was launched at Malster's yard. It is said to be as sound today as when built. The Malster yards were ultimately absorbed by the Bethlehem Steel Company's Shipbuilding Division.

Mr. Malster first tried for the mayoralty in 1893. His opponent was the redoubtable Ferdinand C. Latrobe, who in that year won the office for the seventh time before retiring permanently from competition.

On November 17, 1897, William T. Malster became mayor of Baltimore. He was the last to hold office for the two-year term of the old Charter. The great accomplishment of his administration was the framing and adoption of the famous "1898 Charter."

Mr. Malster lost the election of 1899 to Thomas G. Hayes. He died on March 2, 1907. Malster Avenue was named and dedicated on April 15, 1910.

June 21, 1953

Maynadier

By James C. Bertram

If Jeremiah Yellott Maynadier had been a stubborn man, Roland Park might be located in some other part of the city.

Maynadier owned a farm on the north side of Cold Spring Lane between Roland Avenue and the railroad tracks — and the men who were planning Roland Park in 1888 had to have it, for the suburb was to be centered around the farm's 17 acres.

Indeed, Edward H. Bouton, the father of Roland Park, told Maynadier that the development would have to be started elsewhere if he refused to sell.

But the farmer was only too pleased to oblige. The company gratefully paid him $20,000 for the property — and a few years later named a street in his honor. That is Maynadier Road; originally the lane that led into the old family home, it is now an unmarked, dead-end alley leading off Cold Spring between Hawthorn and Schenley roads. There is also a Woodlawn Avenue, named for the farm.

It was a wonderful farm, remembers Mrs. Anne Fendall Gwynn, a daughter of Jeremiah Maynadier. "It had been in possession of my mother's family, the Fendalls, almost since Colonial days. My mother, who met my father in Harford County when she went there to live during the Civil War, inherited it in the '70s, and the family moved in."

It was primarily a fruit farm, Mrs. Gwynn recalls. "There were nine varieties of cherry trees there; my father used to get boys up from the country village of Woodberry to do the picking. Most of the cherries were sold to canners, but some went to Valentine's, a Charles Street dealer in fancy fruit."

There were pear trees, too; Maynadier shipped pears all the way to Philadelphia.

And there was still another cash crop — iron ore. That came from the high bank along the Ma and Pa tracks, and was dug out profitably for five years or so.

The Maynadiers lived a quiet life. By tradition, they were a family of stay-at-homes. "Father had to go into a hospital once for a minor operation," says Mrs. John Donaldson Murray, who lives with her sister at 206 West Monument Street. "He complained about it, saying it was the first time he had spent a night away from home in 60 years."

Before creation of Roland Park, the area around the Maynadiers was characterized by large country homes. Amusements were few — the family's biggest affairs were picnics at Rock Springs on Falls Road. Mrs. Murray recalls walking through the dense woods that covered what is now the golf course of the Baltimore Country Club to get there.

"Our neighbors were the Caprons, who owned another place called Woodlawn," says Mrs. Murray, "and John McCormick, who owned the land of what is now St. Mary's Orphanage."

The family moved from Woodlawn in 1889, and eventually settled in Pikesville, where Mr. Maynadier died in 1917 at 83.

May 18, 1952

McCabe

By James C. Bertram

He built a large part of New York's subway system, the big railroad bridge over Jones Falls at North Avenue between John and Oak streets, the 7-mile-long Montebello water tunnel, part of the Belt Line tunnel under Howard Street, countless other tunnels and bridges, and mile after mile of railroad. Yet Col. Lawrence B. McCabe's name is preserved only by one short street.

That is McCabe Avenue in Govans. Extending today from York Road east to Midwood Avenue, it originally ran a block from York Road to the colonel's home. It became a public street when a part of his land was developed by a real estate concern around 1912.

The man for whom it was named — or who named it himself — was an extremely successful engineer and contractor; a biographer, writing before McCabe reached his peak, called him "one of the leading railroad, bridge and tunnel builders of his generation."

He was born in 1847 in Havre de Grace of Irish immigrant parents. As a child, he went to school in the small town on the Susquehanna, and later entered Lehigh as one of that university's first students. He graduated from there as a civil engineer and soon became associated with an uncle in the general railroad contracting business.

When the uncle died, his brother James — who had spent a few romantic years in the West surveying for the railroads and fighting Indians with Buffalo Bill — came into the business. It prospered; soon the men were laying track and building bridges throughout the East. It was around 1900 that they went to New York and worked on the new subway system, constructing, newspaper accounts say, a good many miles of it.

But McCabe always lived in Baltimore County. In 1877, he married Ellen Keabney. They had six children, one of whom, Lawrence B. McCabe Jr., became a well-known jockey and won the 1914 Kentucky Derby on Old Rosebud.

In the late '80s, the elder McCabe was appointed to the military staff of Governor Elihu Jackson, an appointment which resulted in his honorary rank. He also served a term in the Legislature. After his retirement from his business he lived quietly on McCabe Avenue, where he died in 1921 at the age of 74.

August 28, 1949

McCulloh Or McCulloch?

By Robert L. Weinberg

McCulloh Street, the once fashionable thoroughfare that runs north from Monument Street to Druid Hill Park, is a street of mystery — nobody knows for whom it was named. The earliest ordinance referring to it spells its name McCullough; because of this, some antiquarians have thought it honored John McCullough, a famous mid-19th-century actor. But the street had its name by 1831, and McCullough was not then yet born. An ordinance only slightly later uses the spelling McCulloch, and now for a long time the accepted form has been McCulloh. It seems likely, therefore, that the street was named for either James H. McCulloch or James W. McCulloh.

James W. McCulloh took part in two of the most significant legal actions in Maryland history, yet not as a lawyer but in both as a defendant against suits by the State of Maryland.

But even earlier in his career he took part in big events.

On the evening of May 16, 1812, a group of Baltimore citizens sat at the Fountain Inn, at Light Street and Lovely Lane, where the Southern Hotel now stands. These men constituted the General Committee of Baltimore, which was passing a resolution calling on President Madison to declare war on Britain for her continued insults on the seas. James W. McCulloh was there, as was James H. McCulloch.

When the war was raging in the Chesapeake Bay region, James W. McCulloh was a corporal with Baltimore United Volunteers; he fought in the Battle of Bladensburg. John P. Kennedy, later a famous author, relates an incident of that battle in his autobiography:

"I lost my musket in the melee while bearing off a comrade, James W. McCulloh, afterwards the cashier of the Branch Bank of the United States in Baltimore, whose leg was broken by a bullet."

Before he joined the United Volunteers, however, McCulloh had held a responsible post as acting deputy quartermaster general, having been appointed temporarily by Gen. Sam Smith.

McCulloh was appointed cashier of the bank on December 4, 1816. The bank was just being formed, with James A. Buchanan as president of the Baltimore office, and about $4,000,000 was subscribed in capital. Two years later, the State of Maryland passed a law requiring all notes issued by banks not operating by authority of the state to be printed on stamped paper, the tax for which depended on the amount of the banknote.

McCulloh Street – 1949

McCulloh and the bank directors knew that this was an effort to make the cost of operation so heavy that the bank would be forced out of existence; they therefore refused to pay the tax, and the state sued the cashier as the disbursing officer.

The case was finally decided by the Supreme Court. Chief Justice John Marshall wrote the opinion deciding that the power of the national government could not be abridged by the state taxing authority, and McCulloh was excused from paying the tax.

Although that case assumed great importance in American history because of the gravity of the political controversy it decided, the second case in which McCulloh was a party was probably of graver meaning to him.

In July 1819, criminal indictments were returned in Baltimore charging McCulloh and Buchanan with embezzling and conspiring to defraud the bank of $1,500,000. The case was prosecuted for the state by Attorney General Luther Martin, one of the great lawyers of his time.

The defendants were represented by General Winder, formerly McCulloh's commanding officer at Bladensburg, and by William Pinkney, another leader of the bar.

The case was removed to Harford County in order not to prejudice the defendants, and went from there to the Court of Appeals in Annapolis. It was there that a decision was rendered, establishing once and for all time the necessary elements to be proved in a conspiracy, and the case was returned to the lower court for further trial.

Both defendants were acquitted, and thus McCulloh was twice victor in battles with the State of Maryland.

James H. McCulloch is the subject of an amusing Revolutionary War story.

Joshua Barney, later the famous commodore and naval hero, was given command of a small ship out of Philadelphia called the Hyder Ally, mounting 16 six-pounder guns. During the ship's first cruise it met an enemy brig, and as it prepared to engage in combat, Barney saw a passenger roaming the deck and requested him to go below out of danger.

The man looked at Barney, then walked to an arms chest on deck and began examining the muskets. He put several of them to his shoulder one at a time to test their triggers and see that the flints were snapping properly. Finally he found one that suited him. Then he slung a cartridge box over his shoulder and tied a handkerchief around his head — and became the first man aboard to fire at the enemy ship.

He stood high in the most dangerous part of the ship, and sailors said he fired more often than any one of them and acted no more concerned than if he were sitting at his fireside.

That is our first glimpse of James H. McCulloch. Whether he was a Baltimorean then is not known, though he is said to have come to this city about the time of the Revolution.

By 1800, however, he definitely was living in Baltimore. In that year, he was elected a delegate to the State Assembly, and a few years later he was chosen for the State Senate. He resigned that post in 1808 to become Collector of the Port of Baltimore, an office he held until 1836.

When Baltimore was attacked by the British in 1814, this McCulloch volunteered. During the Battle of North Point, he was wounded and captured.

Coincidentally, his son, James H. McCulloch Jr., was dispatched to the same battlefield as an army surgeon. At that time, he arranged for the release of a number of American soldiers, among whom was his father.

In 1834, the elder McCulloch was given the honor of being one of the pallbearers in the funeral ceremonies held here to mark the death of Lafayette.

December 19, 1948

McDonogh

By Henry C. Rauch

Down in New Orleans, on October 24, 1850, the greatest land owner in the United States spent a dime to use an omnibus instead of walking on an errand.

Townspeople who saw him were astounded. When he tossed money around like that, they told each other, something was going to happen.

They were right. On October 26, the rich man died. And forthwith the people hurried to eat their sharp words; for his will disclosed that the "old miser" had divided his entire estate between their town and Baltimore for educational purposes.

That is how New Orleans got a co-ordinated public-school system.

It is how Baltimore got McDonogh School, and also a street named McDonogh. The "old miser" was John McDonogh. In 1872, just a year before the school here opened, a part of Regester Street in East Baltimore was rechristened in his honor.

McDonogh was born in South Baltimore on December 29, 1779. At 15, he went to work for a merchant who had 40 vessels in the trade between Europe, the West Indies and Spanish America.

In 1800, he became his employer's New Orleans representative, and managed his interest there with such success that he was soon headed for wealth.

He bought real estate. By 1806, his holdings had become so vast that he retired from the mercantile business. He acquired hundreds of thousands of acres in Louisiana, Florida, Mississippi and Texas.

During the War of 1812, he was a member of Beale's Rifles, a company recruited from men of property and influence. After the war, he became a director of the Louisiana Bank.

Then, abruptly, he became a recluse. A lady's slipper and a piece of ribbon found among his effects are regarded as the clues.

It is related that McDonogh fell in love with a Miss Johnson. His love was returned, but when he asked for her hand in marriage her father refused consent unless he changed from Presbyterian to Roman Catholic faith.

When McDonogh refused to make that change, his beloved entered a convent and he withdrew from society. Many years later, however, McDonogh is said to have called at the convent each New Year's Day to see her.

Although it is his posthumous gifts that preserve his memory, McDonogh was not, even during his lifetime, the complete miser his townsfolk thought him. He helped many slaves to earn their freedom, and performed anonymously many benefactions.

Land depreciation and legal squabbles ate into his estate, but there still remained for division between New Orleans and Baltimore $1,500,000.

In accordance with his own wish, he was buried in Green Mount Cemetery here, and it was long the custom for the students of McDonogh School to visit the grave yearly and place flowers. In 1945, his remains and his monument were alike moved to the campus of the school.

McElderry

By Henry C. Rauch

A man who had a hand in Baltimore's early development, who was a leader in civic improvements and who was finally elected as state senator left his name to McElderry Street — which on its path across Northeast Baltimore runs through land on which he lived.

The man was Thomas McElderry, or McEldery, as it was often spelled. About McElderry's origin and early life, no information seems to be available. He is already a landholder and a figure of consequence when he first appears in printed records in 1793.

For in that year he loaned the town commissioners of Baltimore £100 "free and clear of interest until paid" for the purpose of filling up and paving the lower end of Market Space.

This was obviously part of a much larger project of his own, for just three months later — at the beginning of 1794 — he and Cumberland Dugan applied for permission to construct neighboring wharves at the foot of Market Place. They got the permission, but in return the commissioners exacted another civic improvement; McElderry and Dugan had to extend Pratt Street across the head of their properties.

The wharves were duly built, and in 1800 McElderry asked to establish alongside his, a street bearing his name. Although

McElderry Street - 1941

this was granted, the name, if ever used, apparently did not stick, for so far as city records show, there was never any connection between that McElderry Street and the present one well to the northeast.

In 1804, McElderry was one of a group of men — John Eager Howard, Josias Pennington, Samuel Sterett were others — appointed by the State Assembly to purchase ground for a penitentiary and have it erected. The buildings that resulted were the nucleus about which the present penitentiary rose.

In 1805, McElderry got another job of this sort, being appointed to a body to build a new courthouse. The next year, he was elected to the State Senate.

Besides his waterfront property, city records show, McElderry owned land farther up in Baltimore, and a map dated 1801 locates his home, with extensive grounds, a bit to the northeast of the main part of the town.

It is through what was those grounds that the street bearing his name now runs. The first section of it was opened in 1810, the year of his death, and apparently at once named in his honor.

September 26, 1948

McHenry

By Karen Richards

With McHenry Street making an interrupted crossing of West Baltimore from Fremont Avenue through the Irvington section, and with Fort McHenry set out in the Patapsco, the name of James McHenry is spread over a wide swath of the city.

But the man covered a lot of territory himself while he was alive.

McHenry was born in Ireland, where he studied to become a lawyer, but ill health forced him to seek a less rigorous climate and in 1771, at the age of 18, he sailed for America. He went first to Philadelphia and to Newark and was so impressed with the colonies that he wrote to his parents to join him.

In 1772, the family settled in Baltimore, where James went into business with his father. He apparently gave up the idea of being a lawyer and prevailed on his father to send him to Philadelphia to study medicine. In the Revolutionary turmoil, he joined the Continentals as a surgeon.

During his service with the Army, McHenry made many friends among the early American leaders — George Washington, whom he served as a secretary; Tench Tilghman, who called him "Dear Mac"; Alexander Hamilton, who arranged his exchange when he was captured by the British; and Lafayette, for whom McHenry named his Baltimore home Fayetteville. (It was located in the vicinity of Baltimore and Fremont).

Independently wealthy after 1790, McHenry hoped for a diplomatic career. He became a member of the State Legislature and voted to allow the government to build a fort or arsenal at Whetstone Point. He lived to see the fort take his name.

He was appointed Secretary of War by his old friend, Washington, and while he was in the cabinet he drew up plans for the United States Military Academy and worked for the establishment of a Navy Department. It was McHenry who urged the construction of six frigates, including the Baltimore-built Constellation, to fight the Barbary pirates.

McHenry remained in the cabinet through Washington's administration and part of Adams'. He resigned in 1800 after a quarrel with John Adams, who accused him of taking Hamilton's side against him.

He retired to his Baltimore home and lived quietly till 1812. He was taken ill then, and his malady was aggravated by concern for his son, who was in the Army. He died in 1816.

May 28, 1950

Mercer

By William Stump

Mercer Street is small, but it poses a big problem: Does it preserve the name of Benjamin James Mercer, constable and innkeeper, or that of John Francis Mercer, landowner and governor? Or of someone else?

Neither Baltimore Town nor Baltimore City records indicate for whom or when the street was named. It is mentioned, however, in a document of 1793 as "Bank or Mercer" Street.

It seems logical, suggests James W. Foster, of the Maryland Historical Society, that it was named for — or by — Benjamin James Mercer. For the first Baltimore directory, that of 1796, lists Benjamin as both constable and innkeeper, with his address at 34 Light Street, near the west end of the narrow thoroughfare.

It does not list John Francis Mercer — for he was a wealthy Anne Arundel County gentleman with a seat in the House of Delegates, and not a Baltimorean.

In 1798, a year after the incorporation of Baltimore as a city, the City Council passed an ordinance calling for the appointment of a constable "whose duty it shall be to walk through the streets, lanes and alleys of the city daily with his mace in his hand, taking such rounds that within a reasonable length of time he shall visit all parts of the city."

Benjamin was the man appointed, and thus became the city's first policeman.

He was constable only until 1799, when the City Council, finding that the keeping of law and order in Baltimore was too big a task for one man, appointed eight more constables, one for each ward. Why Benjamin did not continue is a mystery.

The stint as constable was apparently the end of Benjamin Mercer's public life. After 1799, when he was assessed for two houses at 34 Light Street, his name appears only once more — in 1802, when his tavern license was renewed. There is no record to indicate the year of his death.

Sophia Sprigg Mercer's estate — Cedar Park – 1963

In 1802, John Francis Mercer was at the height of a political career which began in his native Virginia soon after service with the Continental Army, in which he was a lieutenant colonel. In 1782, while a member of the Virginia House of Delegates, he was elected to Congress.

In 1785, he married Sophia Sprigg, of Anne Arundel County, moved to Maryland and became master of Cedar Park, the Sprigg estate. In 1787, he was a Republican delegate to the Constitutional Convention, at which he spoke out against the document on the grounds that it tended to be aristocratic instead of democratic.

During the 1790s, he sat, without a great deal of fanfare, in Maryland's House of Delegates. In 1801, though, he was elected governor for the first of two one-year terms.

In later years, he worked to prevent the War of 1812. Then he retired to Cedar Park. In 1821, on a trip to the doctor's in Philadelphia, he died.

In 1822, the Fielding Lucas map of Baltimore referred to Bank Street as Mercer. However, there are no ordinances to explain the change. Perhaps the map-makers took up the name to avoid its confusion with another Bank Street. Perhaps, seeing the name in the records, they assumed that it had originally been named for the governor. Then they may have been thinking of someone else, although this is unlikely, for there were no other prominent Mercers at the time.

October 23, 1949

Merryman

By William Stump

In 1688, Lord Baltimore granted 210 acres of virgin timberland to Charles Merryman, a Virginia wheelwright who had become a wealthy Maryland planter. Today, that land includes a corner of Roland Park, Guilford and the Johns Hopkins University campus.

Merryman House – 1950

And although the Merrymans no longer live there, there are three streets in the area associated with the Merryman name.

They are Merryman Court, Merryman's Lane and Clover Hill Road. Merryman Court is believed to be a remnant of Merryman's Lane, now called University Parkway save for the block between Greenmount Avenue and 33rd Street, which retains the original name. Clover Hill Road, to the north, preserves the name of the original Merryman home, today the residence of the Rt. Rev. Noble C. Powell, Maryland's Protestant Episcopal bishop.

Although Charles Merryman accepted Lord Baltimore's gift of the 210-acre "Lott," as it is described in old documents, he probably never lived on the land. City records show him living farther south, near the Patapsco; the grant is not mentioned again in the county records until 1714.

In that year, "for the fatherly love and affection that I Bear Unto my Seed Son John Merryman for Divers

Merryman Court – 1949

good Causes and other Considerations," Charles gave to John half of Merryman's grant.

John cleared the land and built his house there — the same house, it is believed, that stands today as the bishop's residence.

Under John, and under his son, grandson and heirs, Clover Hill, as the estate was called, became a flourishing farm. "Scores of slaves," as a family letter discloses, took care of the acreage. Cattle, sheep and horses were raised; hogs, turkeys and

Merryman's Lane – 1949

chickens filled the farmyards. Fruit, grain and other crops thrived.

Merryman's Lane, running past the house, came into being in 1801 or 1802 when Joseph Merryman sold part of his land to Charles Carroll of Carrollton, who built Homewood as a wedding present for his son.

The lane was cut through, another family letter explains, in order to give the Carrolls access to their new property.

The estate remained in the Merryman family for 181 years. In 1869, a large part of its land having been sold off, it was purchased by Charles Reese, an "importer and dealer in wines, fine fruits and groceries."

It changed hands a number of times between that year and 1910, when the Episcopal Diocese of Maryland purchased the land for its proposed cathedral and the Merryman "home place" for the bishop's mansion.

Just about that time, Merryman court was developed; Howard Sill, one of the city's foremost architects of the time, designed the colonial type houses which front it today. Merryman's Lane, the long road over which the Merrymans and the Carrolls traveled for so many years, kept its name intact until about the time the Johns Hopkins University moved to Homewood; then, the section between St. Paul Street and Stony Run Road was renamed University Boulevard.

In 1927, the entire street, except for the one block, still called Merryman's Lane, was christened University Parkway.

February 28, 1954

Mondawmin Avenue

By William Stump

What would be a fitting name, a lasting name, for his vast new estate? George Brown could not find an answer, try as he might. So he asked his distinguished visitor.

The visitor looked out across the fields of corn rolling gently into the distance. "Why, I should say 'Mondamin,'" he said. "That was the beautiful Indian word for cornfield."

The distinguished visitor was Henry Wadsworth Longfellow, and George Brown gratefully accepted his suggestion. And for a century since that time, Mondawmin, its spelling altered by a city draftsman long ago, has been a name familiar to Baltimoreans, a name synonymous with wealth and substance and even mystery.

The estate is gone now. But its name will remain in the great shopping center rising where generations of Brown gardeners cared for the immaculate boxwood. And it will remain in Mondawmin Avenue.

Even so, the estate lasted a long time, a much longer time than most of its contemporaries — a monument to a family that has played an important role in the Baltimore drama since 1800, the year Alexander Brown, a merchant of Ballymena and Belfast, came to Baltimore and founded what is today the nation's oldest investment banking house.

Brown family's estate — Mondawmin – 1951

Alexander Brown started off selling imported linens; soon he was in the thick of the little city's financial life. In the next 34 years, he built the city's first water system. He built a fleet of sailing ships. He helped to organize America's first railroad. When he died in 1834, he was worth $2,000,000, and was one of the six richest men in the country.

His son George succeeded him, carrying on and expanding the house, which had come to be called Alexander Brown & Sons. In 1837, he saw to it that the resources of the firm saved the city from a financial panic. He created Mondawmin in 1840, buying up hundreds of acres northwest of the city.

But it was under his son and successor, George Stewart Brown, that Mondawmin came into full flower. In the years after the Civil War — like his father, George Stewart Brown helped avert a financial panic — the largest mansion became one of the first homes in Baltimore, a rendezvous for the city's foxhunting circle — and for the citizens who sought and got his leadership in local reform campaigns.

George Stewart Brown headed the banking firm for 31 years. Upon his death in 1890, he was succeeded by Alexander Brown, the man who consolidated the city's street railways and public utilities, who made fortunes in railroads and securities.

Like his forebears, Alexander Brown was an exceedingly vigorous man. At Princeton, he established an intercollegiate hurdle record that stood for years; later he became a sort of dean of Baltimore fox hunters. Indeed, he was a hard rider when he was in his 70s and 80s, and as late as 1945 Baltimoreans could see him trotting through the northwest section on a spirited horse.

Alexander Brown and his wife were the city's social leaders for a good many years; the parties they gave in the ballroom of their Cathedral Street home — since 1921 the property of the Knights of Columbus — were reported in detail in the press. That, however, was not true of the functions held at Mondawmin; the walls which surrounded the 45-acre estate made that place a land of mystery to the people of the city that grew up around it.

It was not until Alexander Brown died there in 1949 at the age of 90 that the public saw the fields and woods and boxwood gardens. And then it was rather too late. For the age in which Alexander Brown had cut such a figure had disappeared many years before, and Mondawmin was falling into decay.

February 12, 1950

Moore

By Ralph Reppert

There probably isn't a street in Baltimore with a more obscure namesake than Moore.

Unless, perhaps, it is Orchard.

The streets honor the name and property of a Baltimorean who, it was once advertised, completed successful experiments in perpetual motion.

The records would indicate that the man was also something of a genius in the business world. He was left only one shilling by his father, but he became a rich man with holdings in what is now the heart of the city.

Today Moore Street, running generally southwesterly from the 800 block of Madison Avenue to Tessier Street, is a narrow concrete thoroughfare wide enough for only one lane of traffic.

Orchard Street, running parallel to Moore, and extending from the 700 block of Madison Avenue to Pennsylvania Avenue, is of average width.

The streets honor the memory of David Moore, listed in a few records as a merchant, referred to occasionally as a gentleman, and listed, from 1781 to 1796, as the official flour inspector of Baltimore Town.

A haze of similarly confusing density hovers about David Moore's experiments in perpetual motion. Outside of the advertisement, carried in the Telegraphe in 1803, there is no mention of it in existing records.

David Moore was born in 1750, a son of William Moore, of Baltimore County. He married Mary Kelly, whose portrait Rembrandt Peale painted in later years.

One of his tracts known as Moore's Orchard (the site of Orchard and Moore streets) included in a general way the area now bounded by Biddle Street, Pennsylvania Avenue, Orchard and McCulloh streets.

Moore and Orchard, apparently small private byways, became municipal streets in 1833.

David Moore's family and scientific secrets apparently died with him in 1807. After his death a friend inserted a testimonial in the Federal Gazette & Daily Advertiser, "He resigned his breath with the most evincing proof of experiencing future happiness. By his death, society has lost one of its highest members, as he was a stranger to avarice and deception. . . ."

The friend published the testimonial anonymously.

June 6, 1948

Mosher

By Elizabeth H. Moberly

Considering Baltimore's penchant for memorializing its heroes — even adopted ones — it is not surprising that the name of a Revolutionary War soldier from Massachusetts who did the brickwork on the city's second courthouse was given to Mosher Street.

Col. James Mosher arrived in Baltimore in 1784, before the port town had been incorporated as a city, and he stayed to become a man of prominence.

It is not known where he acquired the rank of "colonel," for he served in the Continental Army as a private. He was a resident of Boston during the Revolution and served three years, taking part in the battle of Monmouth and the siege of Newport, R.I.

Mosher was a young man still in his 20s when he reached Baltimore Town, by way of Lancaster, Pa., where he had stopped for a short time. He went into the construction business and also served for some time as surveyor of the port of Baltimore. In 1797, he married Nancy Ridgely, of Baltimore.

He was not long in taking his place in the growing community. In the years that followed, he served as a director and incorporator for many of the new organizations formed in the city, including the Maryland Hospital, which was on the site of the present Johns Hopkins Hospital; the Baltimore Water Company; the National Mechanics Bank, of which he became president in 1811; and the Baltimore Gas Light Company.

When it was decided to build a new courthouse in the city, to replace the early one that was set on brick pilings, Mosher contracted to do the brickwork.

Colonel Mosher was a member of the Baltimore City Council from 1811 to 1818. When, in 1813, the City Council appropriated $20,000 for the defense of the city against the British, he was on the committee named to aid the mayor in directing the defense.

Not all of his efforts were directed toward business and politics, however. In a letter from Rembrandt Peale to Charles F. Mayer, Mosher is mentioned as being one of the committee which helped organize the Baltimore Museum, and he was chosen president of the society formed to lend "useful" books to the youth of Baltimore, the so-called apprentices library.

His death, on March 27, 1845, was noted in the daily paper as follows:

"Died. On Thursday evening last, in the eighty-fifth year of his age, Col. James Mosher, a soldier of the Revolution, formerly president of the Mechanics Bank, and for many years surveyor of the port of Baltimore. His friends and acquaintances are respectfully invited to attend the funeral tomorrow (Saturday) afternoon at 4.30 o'clock, from his late residence on Fayette Street."

March 14, 1954

Mount Royal Terrace

By William Stump

Unlike the majority of Baltimore's history-book mansions, Mount Royal still stands.

It is not falling to pieces. It has not been neglected. Indeed, standing atop its high hill at Park Avenue and Reservoir Street, it preserves much of the dignity it must have known when its terraced gardens marched down to Jones Falls.

Mount Royal dates back to 1792, local historians believe. It was built then by Dr. Solomon Birckhead, a well-to-do physician who was seeking a summer retreat far from the untidiness and odors that then characterized the growing port town of Baltimore.

Birckhead built his mansion in the Georgian style. But little has come down about its condition in the doctor's day, save that it stood on a tract bounded by Jones Falls, McCulloh Street, North Avenue and Druid Hill Park, and that the gardens in front of it stretched into Jones Falls Valley.

Birckhead died in 1836, leaving Mount Royal to his daughter Christiana. She was the wife of Dr. Thomas Emerson Bond, a physician and clergyman who at one time was editor of the Christian Advocate, and the family spent most of its time in New York.

Christiana Bond was the mother of 10 children, and one of them, Hugh Lennox Bond, chose Mount Royal as part of his inheritance when she died. At the time, he was a young lawyer who had spent most of his life in New York; in 1848 he had returned to Baltimore to read law, and in 1851 he was admitted to the bar.

He was an unusual man, who got into many a legal scrap during his long career. In the 1850s he was a leader of the American, or Know-Nothing, party in the city, and in 1860, Governor Thomas H. Hicks made him a judge of the Criminal Court. But unlike the rank and file of that short-lived party, Bond put law and order and respect for country first.

Not that this made him a popular figure; when the 6th Massachusetts was stoned on its way through Baltimore on April 19, 1861, he charged to the grand jury that those who had taken part in the riot were guilty of murder. Later he locked up Governor Swann's police commissioners and freed from jail 75 Union sympathizers who had flown the flag.

Yet when the government's military commissioners tried citizens for offenses against the United States when Maryland was not under military law, he had them indicted.

Bond was a supporter of emancipation with a warm interest in the progress of African-Americans. It was through his efforts that the first black schools were opened in the city.

In 1867, the new state constitution automatically retired Judge Bond, and he returned to private practice. In 1870, President Grant appointed him to the Fourth Circuit Court, which involved Maryland, Virginia, West Virginia and the Carolinas.

The post was in the nature of a hot potato, for almost immediately he was called upon to hear South Carolina Ku Klux cases. Bond imposed fines and, in spite of threats, sent men to prison — and broke the terror. Five years later, he rendered a legal decision removing an obstacle which had prevented Rutherford B. Hayes from taking office as president.

Bond served as circuit judge for 25 years after that, and when he died in 1893, he was one of the nation's most respected jurists. And by that time, Mount Royal Terrace had been named, for Judge Bond had given some of the land for it as well as for part of Druid Hill Park.

Mount Royal, the mansion, went to his son, also named Hugh Lennox Bond and also a lawyer of note. Family history says the son added a portico with its fluted Doric columns.

The lawyer died in 1922. Shortly after that, a bequest from Mr. and Mrs. Jonathan Taylor enabled the Baltimore Monthly Meeting of Friends to acquire the house as a home for its aged members.

O

October 3, 1948

O'Donnell

By Karen Richards

An Irish merchant who made two fortunes in the India trade and brought the first cargo of Chinese goods to Baltimore has given his name to O'Donnell Street, which runs eastward through Canton to the city line.

Like many another young man of the 18th century, John O'Donnell ran away to sea, shipping out on a vessel engaged in the East India trade. He was not long in seeing where there was money to be made, and he joined the British East India Company. His success came quickly, and in 1779, when he was 30, he thought himself wealthy enough to return to his native Ireland.

He left India by an overland route, through Arabia, but he and his traveling companion were captured by Arabs and held as slaves for two years. O'Donnell escaped and returned on foot to India, poorer than before.

He was able to build up a new fortune, and decided to engage in trade with the United States.

O'Donnell sailed for America by way of China and in 1785 arrived in Baltimore on the East Indiaman Pallas, with a cargo of teas, China silks, satins and nankeens, and a crew of Chinese, Malays and Moors whose native costumes aroused the curiosity of the populace. So much to his liking was Baltimore that O'Donnell, after selling his cargo at a profit, determined to settle here. He became engaged to Miss Sallie Elliott, of Fells Point.

About the same time, he purchased a plantation of 1,981 acres on the northwest branch of the Patapsco River, about 6 miles from the center of the city, and gave it the name of Canton — the name has lasted until the present.

There he erected a large house modeled after the British official residences he had seen in India, and, in the words of a contemporary, he "set out an orchard of great extent of red peaches for making peach brandy."

The Baltimorean by adoption made one last trip to the East in 1789 and on his return offered for sale his ship, the Chesapeake, and her cargo from India and China. He retired and spent the remainder of his life with his family at Canton and at Never Die, his estate in Howard County.

He died in 1805. His will was as unusual as he was. It provided that William Patterson and Robert and Charles Oliver, the executors, each be given a blooded horse for their services, and that his slaves be furnished with proper mourning attire.

March 28, 1948

Oliver

By Karen Richards

Robert Oliver, that legendary character of old Baltimore who is only dimly remembered along Oliver Street, was a Horatio Alger hero before Alger even began creating heroes.

Oliver arrived in Baltimore at the close of the Revolutionary War as a young immigrant from Belfast, Ireland. By the time of his death, he had amassed one of the city's largest fortunes. He had also become one of the colorful characters of his era.

Those were the days when the city honored men by naming streets for them, and Oliver Street was a tribute to Robert Oliver. It was first mentioned in the listing of city streets in 1837. Two other Baltimore landmarks are connected with Oliver

Oliver Street, Green Mount Cemetery Gate – 1948

— Greenmount Avenue and Green Mount Cemetery, which take their names from his vast country estate.

Like many another of Baltimore's outstanding citizens, Oliver was a merchant. The times were precarious for men whose fortunes were tied up in maritime commerce, but during the wars with France and England, Oliver displayed the kind of energy and initiative it took to make his business pay.

With European and African markets practically cut off from American shipping, he obtained licenses from the Spanish Government that enabled him to carry on a profitable trade with Vera Cruz.

In 1827, it was estimated he was worth $1,500,000, though part of this sum had been inherited from his brothers who were his business partners. His town house at Gay and Market (Baltimore) streets was the center of much lavish entertaining. It was a large double house of colonial architecture, made of brick which was said to have been imported from England, with doors of solid mahogany and mantels of carved Carrara marble. It was destroyed in the Baltimore fire. He erected a house adjoining for his daughter, Emily, who was married to Robert Morgan Gibbs, of Charleston, S.C.

Green Mount (as Oliver spelled it), where the present cemetery now stands, was made up of several tracts of land which Oliver purchased successively in 1815 and 1822.

At the age of 70, Oliver was described as being "a giant of a man" with thin white hair, keen eyes and erect carriage. He was a splendid horseman and still the leader of any hunt in which he participated.

He was one of the original board managers of the Baltimore and Ohio Railroad and, at 77, served as an honorary pallbearer in the funeral procession held by the city of Baltimore in July 1834, to commemorate the death of Marquis de Lafayette two months earlier. Oliver died in December of the same year.

The story of Robert Oliver is not without undertones of mystery, entirely in keeping with the traditions of 19th-century romanticism but not supported by fact. It was said that his wife was mad and Oliver kept her confined in the big house at Green Mount. It was said, too, that Oliver accidently killed his daughter and that, heartbroken, he vowed that Green Mount would henceforth be a home of the dead.

January 17, 1954

The Olmsteds

By William Stump

Frederick Law Olmsted's two careers were totally different in character — yet both of them made him a national figure.

The first career was that of a writer or, more accurately, a reporter. That really got under way in 1852 when Henry J. Raymond, editor of the New York Times, sent him into the South to write a series about slavery and its effects upon the people and their economy.

The articles, in which he cited the demoralizing effects of slavery, caused a tremendous stir. After they were gathered in a book, Olmsted made two more journeys into the Southland, and published two more books.

What makes these works notable today — and they were reissued in 1953 under the title "The Cotton Kingdom" — is not only the clarity of the writing and the incisiveness of observation, but Olmsted's plea for thoughtfulness and calm examination instead of violence.

American historians call the writings the classic work on the Old South. But then many a historian gives a good deal more attention to Olmsted's second career — that of landscape gardener. Indeed, they call him the American pioneer in that field and regard him as the father of the American park, the first articulate spokesman of the philosophy that parks are an integral part of urban living.

Olmsted's strong feelings for trees and lawns and shrubs and space were first evidenced when he was a child. Born of a prosperous family in Connecticut in 1822, he was taken on many a rural journey as a boy; after his graduation from Yale in 1847, his father bought him a farm on Staten Island where he opened a nursery and, on his own acres, experimented in landscaping.

His connections, studies abroad, and the fame he won with his Southern writings helped him win in 1859 a tremendously important job — the designing, laying out and construction of New York's Central Park. This imposing task was made even more difficult by the machinations of New York politicians. But Olmsted, working with an Englishman named Vaux, accomplished it.

During the Civil War, Olmsted was for a time chief of the United States Sanitary Commission, the parent of the American Red Cross. After the war he returned to landscaping. In the next 25 years he built Riverside Park in New York, Prospect Park in Brooklyn, a park for Buffalo, the Chicago South Park, Mount Royal Park in Montreal, Belle Isle Park in Detroit, and the parks of Boston.

He is responsible for the creation of Yosemite Park and the designing of the University of California and Stanford University. He helped save the Niagara Falls reservation and planned its improvement, and laid out George W. Vanderbilt's estate at Asheville, N.C., and the World's Fair grounds at Chicago.

Those are just highlights; Olmsted and his firm did many dozens of smaller jobs. One of them was the original plan for Sudbrook Park development near Pikesville; an old plat in the possession of a Baltimore surveying firm shows that the plan was made in 1889.

The plan was not followed in detail when the development was started some years later, but the curved streets that Olmsted loved so much were laid down much as he hoped they would be. One of those streets, indeed, preserves his name, mis-spelled — Olmstead Road.

And there is another local street bearing the Olmsted name. That is Olmsted Avenue, situated in Curtis Bay. It was named by the city in 1927 — for Frederick Law Olmsted Jr., a famous landscape man in his own right.

The junior Olmsted, trained by his father, has played an important role in Baltimore's city planning and park development. That began in the '90s, when he was called in as a consultant on the building of Roland Park, where the Olmsted philosophy of curving streets is followed.

He came to the city again in 1904, after the great fire; the widening of the old streets was a result. About that time, too, he was retained by the Park Board to create a master plan for park development. Although it was not fully carried through, Swann and Latrobe parks were created — and the theory that parks should contain unspoiled areas following river beds, a theory carried to fruition by Major Joseph Shirley, was born.

Olmsted, now 83, was a consultant in the laying out of the Johns Hopkins University campus. Moreover, he designed the parked section of Charles Street between 29th Street and University Parkway. He helped in the development of Gibson Island. He selected the Orleans-Bath street site for the cross-town viaduct. And he returned to the city shortly before World War II, persuading the city to acquire the Crimea estate for Leakin Park.

P

January 16, 1949

Paca

By Paul Fleming

The memory of William Paca, a leader in the American Revolution, signer of the Declaration of Independence and governor of Maryland for three terms, is honored by a street name in Baltimore which is mispronounced nine times out of 10.

The street branches off from Druid Hill Avenue, extends south to cross West Baltimore Street in the 500 block, and ends at Fremont Avenue.

Ordinarily, its name is pronounced "Packa." The correct pronunciation, according to various historians, is "Payca," employing a sharp "a," as in pay or say. Several years ago, when the subject had come up for one of its periodic discussions, one writer predicted that Baltimoreans would probably accept the correct pronunciation in time if reminded often enough — but he warned that the first 100 years would be the hardest.

William Paca played a quiet but important role in the early history of Maryland. He was born near Abingdon in Harford

Paca Street – 1945

103

County in 1740. After attending the College of Philadelphia, he studied law in Annapolis.

Paca was elected to the Provincial Legislature in 1768 and became a leader in the patriots' cause in the preliminary stages of the American Revolution. He served on the Maryland Committee of Correspondence, was elected to the first Continental Congress, was a representative in the Provincial Convention, and represented Maryland again in the Second Continental Congress. He was one of the four Marylanders to sign the Declaration of Independence. The other three were Samuel Chase, Thomas Stone and Charles Carroll of Carrollton.

From the time he entered politics until his death in 1799, William Paca was identified with practically every important political movement in Maryland. He was elected governor of the state in 1782 and re-elected unanimously in 1783 and 1784.

The statesman was a delegate to the state convention which adopted the Federal Constitution. He had given the document considerable study, and at the convention, he proposed 28 amendments. However, he voted for its adoption when the convention decided to accept or reject the Constitution as submitted.

President Washington appointed Paca federal district judge in 1789, and he held this position until his death, at Wye Hall, in Talbot County.

February 7, 1949

Patterson

By Megill Naylor

William Patterson himself, in his day, trod Patterson Park and the avenue that is named after it — and so after him. However, the scene was entirely different then. The 2 acres that were the nucleus of the park were the pasture of his country estate when he presented them.

A stretch of land is a fitting memorial to William Patterson, for, although he made his initial fortune in merchant shipping, he regarded "commerce in the shipping line as a hazardous and desperate game of chance" and made it a rule to put half of his profits into real estate.

Patterson Park Avenue – 1949

Patterson was born in Ireland in 1752. At the age of 14, he was sent to Philadelphia to work for an Irish shipping merchant. "This," he wrote many years later, "gave me an early knowledge and attachment to that business, a passion that has followed me through life."

An account of his first "desperate game of chance" has come down in his own words. "When the American Revolution commenced," he said, "it appeared to me that one of the greatest difficulties we should experience was the want of powder and arms. . . .

"This induced me in the year 1775 to embark all the property I then possessed in parts of two vessels and their cargoes, destined from Philadelphia to France, for the sole purpose of returning with powder and arms, and in one of which I embarked myself.

"Only one of these vessels got safe back to Philadelphia, where she arrived in the month of March 1776, with the cargo intended, and in a most critical time — when it was said that General Washington, then before Boston, had not powder sufficient to fire a salute."

For two years, operating from the West Indies, Patterson continued to send supply ships through the British blockade, and in this time amassed a fortune of more than $60,000. Half he lost through British captures, but the rest he brought to Baltimore in goods and gold.

Here Patterson continued his shipping business, and here he inaugurated his land-buying rule, and he prospered from the first.

He was one of the men who provided Lafayette with a large fund for supplies for the Yorktown campaign, and he himself went to the peninsula as a member of the 1st Baltimore Cavalry.

Patterson also figures in the story of Fort McHenry. He was active in raising money to complete its fortification in 1799; he gathered supplies for its defense in 1814, and he welcomed Lafayette there in 1824.

He figured in a variety of important ways in Baltimore's business affairs until his death in 1835. He was the first president of the Bank of Maryland, established in 1790. He was one of the organizers of the Merchants Exchange in 1815; one of the incorporators of the Baltimore and Ohio Railroad in 1827; and one of the incorporators of the Canton Company in 1828.

In 1803, meanwhile, one of his 13 children had made the Patterson name known over the world. For on Christmas Eve of that year, 18-year-old Elizabeth, or Betsy, married the 19-year-old Jerome Bonaparte, brother of Napoleon. The Pattersons foresaw Napoleon's opposition, which in little more than a year smashed the marriage, but they could not restrain their daughter.

Romantic figure though she appears today, she was far from that to her family. "The conduct of my daughter Betsy," said her father in his will, "has through life been so disobedient that in no instant has she ever consulted my opinions or feelings; indeed, she has caused me more anxiety and trouble than all my other children put together, and her folly and misconduct has occasioned me a train of expense that has cost me much money."

November 26, 1950

Payson

By Frances Kean

During Henry Payson's time, Baltimore changed from a hick town to an important city.

Henry Payson didn't sit back and watch it happen — he helped to make it happen. A merchant, a politician, a banker, an insurance executive, a churchman and a tireless civic worker, he had a finger in many pies, a say in almost everything that went on.

He was born in Massachusetts in 1762, and came to Baltimore

Payson Street – 1959

during the Revolution. By 1795, he was connected with a number of banks and insurance companies, and in 1803, he was elected to the City Council for the first of nine terms.

By 1805, he was prominent enough to be appointed to the commission which built the first city-owned courthouse; it was located on the site of the present one. In 1810, he was importing and exporting various goods on Baltimore vessels, was the owner of a paper mill on Gwynns Falls, was manufacturing gunpowder, and was the director of no less than seven insurance firms.

In 1813, when it became increasingly clear that Baltimore was going to be involved in a shooting war with the British, Payson became a member of the Committee of Safety. Along with other "merchant princes" who were members, he raised money to fortify Baltimore and to equip and train its troops.

That the British failed in their bombardment of Fort McHenry, failed at the battle of North Point and therefore failed to take the city was due in no small degree to the part played by Payson and his associates.

Payson's war activities — plus perhaps, his political activities and his prominence as a citizen — were remembered by the members of a state commission which drew up a map for the development of Baltimore soon after the war. Dozens of projected streets were drawn on the map and given names; Payson Street was one of these. Actually, it remained nothing but a mark on a map until the 1870s, when the city expanded westward. Today it begins at Ohio Avenue, south of Wilkens, and runs north to Elgin Avenue.

Helping Baltimore to arm may have been the most important single thing Payson ever did, but it was by no means the last. In 1815, he helped to plan and erect Battle Monument, and he helped to found the Baltimore Stock Exchange. In 1817 he took part in organizing the First Unitarian Church, and in planning the church building, which still stands at Charles and Franklin streets.

When he died, in 1845, he was an old man — and Baltimore was a wealthy, bustling city.

May 29, 1949

Potee

By William Stump

If John Edgar Potee hadn't been a space-time lamplighter in his native Brooklyn during the early years of the century, he probably would not have become a police magistrate, the sheriff of Anne Arundel County, the sheriff of Baltimore, the leader of Democrats in the southern district and one of the most colorful political figures in the state — and there would probably not be Potee Street today.

For John Potee's lamplighting duties, thanks to the quick wit and ready smile he displayed

Potee Street – 1951

on the job, made him the most popular young man in the neighborhood. This popularity, which gained him the magistrate's office, outlasted his lifetime; when the city decided to rebuild the southern section of Race Street, Brooklyn residents asked that the name be changed to Potee.

The City Council approved the request, and in October 1945, Potee Street was opened to traffic. A two-lane highway with a raised strip of concrete in the middle, it runs parallel to Hanover Street from the middle branch of the Patapsco to the beginning of Ritchie Highway at the south city line.

John Potee, the 15th of 16 children, was born and raised at 111 South First Street. His father was a prosperous well-digger, brick manufacturer and politician, so John received a good education. John joined the brick business when school days were over, but the work was not completely satisfying — there was not enough to do. That is why, he said years later, he took the after-hours lamplighting job.

His ladder under his arm, the young man tramped the familiar streets at dusk and again at dawn. Everyone got to know him well; adults and children looked forward to seeing him on his rounds. Like his father, he had a talent for winning friends, a feeling for politics. No one was surprised when Gov. Austin L. Crothers appointed him a Brooklyn police magistrate.

Soon people were calling him "Judge" Potee, a title which stayed with him for the rest of his life. He sat at the police bench for four years. In 1913, he ran for sheriff of Anne Arundel County, won, and served until Brooklyn became a part of Baltimore. Then he was appointed magistrate of the Southern Police District.

"Judge" Potee went about his new job with an ingenuity and individuality that won him a wide reputation and more friends. Once, a man was brought before him on the charge of driving a wagon while drunk. The magistrate dismissed the case. "If the man had been driving an automobile," he said, "it would have been a crime. But a horse has sense, even if a man does not."

In 1923, the voters of Baltimore chose John Potee as their sheriff. It was a landslide. On election night, thousands gathered in front of his Brooklyn home in the hope of shaking his hand.

John Potee brought his individuality to the sheriff's office, too. Its most famous manifestation was the force — the newspapers called it an "army" — of more than 600 deputy sheriffs that he formed. This force drew him a great deal of criticism from the public, but he got a diamond-studded gold badge from the deputies — and was re-elected in 1926.

Except for his leadership of the South Baltimore Democrats, the post of sheriff was the last that John Potee held. He ran again in 1930, but this time he was defeated. He spent the last three years of his life a sick man, sitting in the window of his Hanover Street home receiving the greetings of the friends and neighbors who passed by.

When "Judge" Potee died in 1933, Gov. Albert C. Ritchie, Mayor Howard W. Jackson and countless other political figures attended the funeral. So did hundreds of his old neighbors — who didn't really feel they had paid the full respects owed their friend until 12 years later.

September 9, 1951

Pratt

By William Stump

One of the city's busiest and most important streets is named for a man Baltimoreans had a good reason to idolize — although he lived in a country they had good reason to hate.

The street is Pratt Street; it preserves the name of Charles Pratt, Earl of Camden, who fought hard and well in Britain's House of Lords for the repeal of the Stamp Act, that despised bill which imposed a tax upon Colonial Americans.

In 1766, less than a year after its passage, his and his colleagues' efforts — plus a near mutiny upon the part of the angry colonials — caused Parliament to reverse itself and abandon the act.

Pratt Street – 1948

As a result, Pratt and his friends became tremendous heroes in the eyes of the American people. Maryland's Legislature, and the legislatures in most of the other colonies, passed resolutions of thanks; the Englishmen were praised in speeches and in the press.

In Baltimore, the city's principal waterfront street was renamed for Pratt. Camden Street is supposed to have been named in his honor, too — although some historians believe it could have been named in honor of the Revolutionary battle of Camden, S.C., where Maryland men fought and died.

It may have surprised Americans that Pratt, an English nobleman, would work so determinedly on their behalf. But it could not have been a surprise to anyone in England. For there, the Earl of Camden had long been a fighter for justice and the constitutional rights of His Majesty's subjects. His stand on the Stamp Act was merely in keeping with his character.

On the surface, curiously enough, there seemed to be little of the fighter about him; one would get the impression, rather, that he was interested in nothing save the pleasures of life.

He lived lavishly; he liked to eat, he liked to read romantic fiction and he liked to watch a turn at the music halls. He was, a British biographer says, "indolent . . . a dilettante . . . relaxed and languid."

Born in 1714 of wealthy parents who lived in the county of Kent, he studied at Eton where, significantly, one of his schoolmates was William Pitt, who was to become another champion of people's rights.

Later, he attended Cambridge and simultaneously read law in the Inner Temple. Upon graduations from the university, he was admitted to the bar.

He showed little promise at first. For three years, although he tried hard, he found no work to do. But just when things were at their darkest, a prominent lawyer took him on as a junior assistant — and then became sick, leaving the young man in charge of an important and celebrated case.

Pratt won it. That brought him to the attention of the Prince of Wales, who made him his counsel and attorney general. A few years later, William Pitt became the head of the government, and appointed him attorney general of the nation.

It soon became apparent that Pratt was a man of advanced ideas. Not long after his appointment, he introduced a bill to extend the right of habeas corpus to civil cases, a much-needed reform. Nevertheless, it was considered too radical — so radical that it was another 50 years before similar legislation passed.

In 1761, Pratt was his nation's Chief Justice and a knight as well — and soon afterward, a national hero to the non-privileged classes. This came about when one John Wilkes, regarded as an enemy of the government, was arrested and thrown into the Tower.

Pratt immediately ordered him released, on the grounds that the warrant on which he had been arrested was unconstitutional. A bitter struggle then took place in the government, with Pratt and the Constitution winning out in the long run.

The year the Stamp Act was passed, Lord Pratt was made Baron Camden, and as such assumed a seat in the House of Lords. Indeed, his maiden speech concerned the act — he raked it from stem to stern.

"A breach of the Constitution!" he yelled, after explaining that the colonials had nothing to say about it. "Sheer robbery!" he exclaimed, dwelling upon the fact that the colonials could not stand the expense.

England and her American colonies drifted further apart in the next few years. Pratt, with a few others in the government, tried to keep them together.

When the split finally came, he opposed the war. When England began to raise troops without an act of Parliament, he once again cited the Constitution.

In 1781, gout-ridden and wearied by constant struggle, the baron retired to his manor in Kent. It was for good, he said; but the next year he was back in London, speaking his mind on such heavy problems as independent rule for Ireland.

In 1786, he was made First Earl of Camden. From then on, he periodically retired, always to come back again. He died in 1794, still the "Watchdog of the Constitution."

October 11, 1953

Presstman

By William Stump

Although Presstman Street was named in 1822, it was not cut through until 1866. And at that time the City Council renamed it — officially renamed it to Presstman Street.

It seems that the council, when it ordered work on the street to begin, decided a new name would be necessary; the people of Baltimore, they reasoned, would confuse Presstman and Preston. And besides, who would remember the Presstman the street had originally been named for, anyway?

The councilmen pondered. Then one of their number — his name has long been forgotten — asked for the floor. Why not save time and trouble, he said, and simply rename the street in honor of Benjamin Cappel Presstman?

All agreed. For Benjamin Presstman was known and respected in Baltimore. He had been a councilman himself, and, after that, the city solicitor — or city counselor, as the office was then designated. And in 1866, he was judge of the Superior Court.

No important public dinner was complete without him — for Presstman had the reputation of being the wittiest after-dinner speaker in town. Indeed, years after his death, his wit was remembered by an English lady of title — who said that it was the one thing that had made a visit to Baltimore memorable.

But what of the Presstman for whom the street had originally been named? The councilman of 1866 may not have known it, but he too was well known and probably well respected in his time.

He was George Presstman — no relation at all of the judge. He settled in Baltimore in 1771, and three years later helped found the First Baptist Church. He also founded the Anti-Slavery Society of Baltimore and, like the later Presstman, he became a city councilman. In addition, he was the city's commissioner of health and later held the title of Trustee of the Poor.

George Presstman died in 1819.

September 10, 1950

Pulaski

By William Stump

Every schoolchild who studies American history learns that Gen. Casimir Pulaski was one of the heroes of the Revolution. But not all of them learn that the men he led into battle, the men who helped him win his place in history, were Baltimoreans.

"My legion, my Maryland legion!" the colorful Polish nobleman fondly exclaimed.

Like their leader, the Baltimoreans were rough, tough and hard-riding. Unlike their leader, few of them were of aristocratic birth; in fact, history indicates that a large percentage had quite dubious reputations in civil life.

True, many of Count Pulaski's officers were well-born Poles, Frenchmen and Americans. But the Baltimore troops were a counterpart of France's Foreign Legionnaires; for as long as they were fit and willing to fight, absolutely no questions were asked about their past.

The legion was organized in the spring of 1778, when Pulaski, who had been fighting nearly a year as Washington's chief of cavalry, was sent to Baltimore by the commander in chief. Upon his arrival, he rented rooms in the boarding house of a Mrs. Ross, on Baltimore Street between Light and Calvert.

The newspapers spread the word. The Maryland Journal and the Baltimore Advertiser urged "all those who desire to distinguish themselves" to join with Pulaski. It told of the opportunities for bounty, and suggested that the uniforms would

Pulaski Highway – 1953

be splendid but comfortable.

After three months of intense recruiting, which included a nightly searching of the streets for likely volunteers, the legion was assembled and trained. There were three companies of infantry and, to Pulaski's pride, three troops of cavalry, its members equipped with lances and a crimson banner — now in the possession of the Maryland Historical Society.

The new soldiers were impressed with the handsome 30-year-old general, who contributed to their morale by galloping at full speed on his horse, firing his pistol into the air, throwing the pistol ahead of the horse, swinging out of the saddle with one foot in the stirrup and picking up the pistol before it touched the ground.

The legion soon went into action. It fought bravely at Egg Harbor, N.J., though it lost many of its men in a British ambush. It pummeled the British, and was pummeled in turn, in South Carolina. It saw hard, exhausting service in the Georgia swamps, and went on from the swamps to fight at Savannah — where Pulaski secured his niche in American history by being mortally wounded. Paul Bentalou, who later settled in Baltimore, was wounded with him.

Pulaski was born in Poland in 1748, the scion of an old, wealthy family with a military tradition. Before he was 20, he was an officer in a fashionable cavalry regiment; when he was 20, he and his father, with other landowners, formed the Confederation of Bar, and pledged their fortunes and lives to liberating Poland from Russian domination.

They formed and equipped an army, and for a time waged a savage war against the Russians. While not successful, the war brought international attention to Pulaski, especially when he attempted to kidnap the Russian-backed Polish king.

Finally, his lands confiscated and a price on his head, Pulaski was forced to flee his country. He eventually went to Paris, and there Benjamin Franklin urged him to fight in America with Washington. Pulaski agreed.

Pulaski did so well at Brandywine that Washington made him a general and asked him to organize the Continental Army's cavalry. Then he saved the Army from a surprise attack near Philadelphia.

Pulaski was a strong-willed, single-minded man; because of this, many Americans hated him, and a great deal of his time was spent in argument.

Even after the Baltimore street was named, years later, he was the subject of a national controversy — caused by a veteran who claimed that Washington had been beaten at Germantown because Pulaski, who was supposed to be on patrol, was actually asleep in a barn.

But those charges did not stand up for very long, thanks to old Colonel Bentalou, who published two convincing pamphlets in his old commander's defense.

R

February 13, 1949

Redwood

By Henry C. Rauch

German Street is to become Redwood Street in honor of First Lieutenant George Buchanan Redwood, the first Baltimore officer to be killed in France. The ordinance wiping out the Hunnish appellation and giving to the street the name of a patriotic American and one that it can bear with honor and without apology finally passed both branches of the City Council last evening.

So exulted The Sun on the morning of September 17, 1918. And five weeks later, on October 25, it reported:

"German Street has at last been wiped out. The ordinance changing its name to Redwood Street was signed yesterday by Mayor Preston."

The "Hunnish appellation" that pained Baltimoreans during the first World War — when cities all over the country also stopped the teaching of German in schools, and banned German music and frowned on dachshunds — had itself, more than a century earlier, in some way displaced the original name of this street.

Redwood Street – 1948

In the early 1700s, the street had been called Lovely Lane. It still bore that name in 1774 when there was built on the site of the present Merchants Club the Lovely Lane Meeting House, in which ten years later the Methodist Church of the United States was organized.

By 1798, however, the section west of Charles Street seems to have acquired the name of German Lane, and in 1813 the whole street was given that designation. This change has been explained with a supposition that German merchants who settled in Baltimore more in its early days had established themselves along the thoroughfare — which later was promoted from "lane" to "street."

When World War I brought demands for a different name, "American Street" was proposed, and one branch of the City Council passed an ordinance adopting that. The other branch, however, held out for "Hollins Street." "State Street" was vainly offered as a compromise, then someone suggested Redwood and the idea behind the name won enthusiastic support.

George B. Redwood was a Baltimore newspaperman, born in 1888, the son of Francis T. Redwood, long a figure in the city's financial life. Always interested in military affairs, he attended the first Plattsburg camp before the United States got into the war, and once war had been declared was appointed to Officers Training Camp at Fort Myer, where he gained a lieutenancy.

Lieutenant Redwood was among the first Americans to go into France. He was assigned to the intelligence service, and made a record for bravery that won him the French Croix de Guerre and the American Distinguished Service Cross. Finally, in the battle of Cantigny, he was wounded and sent to a hospital. Because he had important papers, he eluded attendants and tried to get back to the front.

He was killed on the way.

Gen. George C. Marshall, who had twice encountered the young officer in France, later wrote to his mother:

"I was impressed with the intensity of his determination to do his duty to the full. . . . Many men, in fact most men, are brave; but few like your son, who so calmly and methodically sacrifice their lives in the line of duty."

September 18, 1949

Regester

By Ralph Reppert

Just north of the city line, from Rodgers Forge to Loch Raven Boulevard, there are people living on a thoroughfare named Regester Avenue — because long ago a young lady refused to live there.

It all began shortly after the close of the Civil War when Joshua Regester, a Baltimore industrialist of considerable means, offered a farm in that section to one of his five sons and his wife.

The farm was regarded as one of the most beautiful in this part of the state. Known as the Beulah Farm, it covered 400 acres, extending north to Stevenson's

Regester Avenue – 1949

Woods, south to what is now Walker Avenue, east to Hillen Road, and west to within a few blocks of York Road.

"Robert," the industrialist said to his son, "take Virginia out to the farm, and if the two of you like it I'll give it to you."

Virginia didn't like it, and she said so. The only approach to the farm was from the rear, by Hillen Road. She said the place was "too lonely looking."

Robert Regester and his wife went to live elsewhere. But the young lady's comment that the farm was "too lonely looking" set Joshua thinking.

He decided to build a new approach to the place from York Road. He bought a strip of ground from 60 to 80 feet wide, extending seven-eighths of a mile, through various intervening estates, from that road in to the farm. He had it graded with his own farm equipment, and later deeded it to the county.

The road — Regester Avenue — which was completed sometime between 1869 and 1874, at once made the farm less "lonesome looking." It did more; it joined Hillen and York roads, and soon was carrying quite a bit of public traffic. Much later, when Sherwood Road was cut through, Regester Avenue was continued on a comparatively straight line east to Loch Raven Boulevard.

But the young lady whose comment had initiated plans for the road never changed her mind; although she was a frequent summer visitor there in later years, she never lived there.

Harry Frank Regester, of Baltimore, a son of the late Robert and Virginia Regester, say these visits were principally for the benefit of the children.

Today Joshua Regester is better remembered as an industrialist than as the builder of the avenue to which he gave his name. His success story was of the Horatio Alger pattern; diligence reaped lasting rewards. He was born on the Eastern Shore, but came to Baltimore as a child to live with an uncle. When he was 16, he became an apprentice in a local brass and foundry business.

After 12 years there he struck out on his own and organized the firm of Clampit & Regester, a foundry specializing in brass articles and bells.

Eventually he purchased this entire enterprise, admitted his sons to it and finally left it to them.

There are two streets within the city limits which also bear the name of Regester — Regester Street, extending north and south from the 1700 block of East Baltimore Street, and Regester Avenue (also lane), extending eastward from Kenyon Avenue.

A part of what is now Regester Street was formerly Argyle alley; the name was changed to Register Street (note spelling with "I") in 1847. The street was identified by both spellings until 1908, when the name was standardized as Regester. Harry Frank Regester believes the street was named for an uncle of his grandfather's, John Regester, who once owned a great deal of property in East Baltimore.

Regester Avenue (or lane) was originally built as a private byway through a farm owned by Sebastian B. Regester, a cousin of Joshua Regester.

June 1, 1952

Ridgely

By William Stump

It is little wonder that Charles Ridgely Carnan consented to change his name to Charles Carnan Ridgely.

His uncle, Capt. Charles Ridgely, requested the change when he made Carnan his heir — which meant heir to Hampton, the great house he was building north of Towsontown, and heir to an immense fortune made originally by speculating in confiscated British properties during the Revolution.

The captain had his reasons. First and foremost, he had no children and did not want his name to disappear. Second, he had all but raised Carnan from childhood and was extremely fond of him. Third, uncle and nephew, despite many years difference in age, were brothers-in-law — the uncle having married Rebecca Dorsey, the nephew her sister, Priscilla.

Captain Ridgely died in 1790, and after some tense moments with a widow loath to part with the property, his 30-year-old nephew found himself one of the wealthiest men in the state, the lord and master of a six-month-old mansion, 400 slaves and 1,500 fertile acres on which were extensive iron ore deposits and a profitable furnace engaged in the manufacture of iron stoves and other iron products.

Life at Hampton, even then one of the showplaces of Maryland, was good. There were hunts and parties and balls; dinners for 50 were an everyday occurrence, and distinguished visitors called the food the best in America.

But Ridgely — who referred to himself as Charles Ridgely of Hampton — wanted a little more than the life of a country squire. A Federalist, he ran for the House of Delegates in 1790, was elected and served until 1795, when he ran for and was elected for the Senate. He was also appointed a brigadier general in the state militia.

Yet after 1800, the year he left the Senate, Ridgely dropped out of public life — because of his Federalist views, which made him extremely unpopular in the British-hating city of Baltimore. He went home to lay out the extensive gardens that visitors see today, to operate his furnace, to raise tobacco. It was not until 1815, the year after the war, that he re-entered public life.

Then he re-entered it in a big way — as governor of the state, and a Federalist governor at that. For even though that party was in people's minds as being against the war, inequitable representation gave the Federalist counties more representation than the more greatly populated, anti-Federalist city of Baltimore.

True, Ridgely became governor by a margin of two votes in the legislature, which in those days elected governors for one-year terms. But Ridgely was a popular governor nevertheless, because he succeeded in getting the federal government to partially reimburse the state for money that the state had spent in its defense during the war. Indeed, it pleased the legislature so much that he was re-elected in 1816 and 1817.

Today, there is a Ridgely Street in Baltimore, running from Fremont Avenue south and southwest to Atlantic Avenue. Because it first appears on a map of the period, it is thought to have been named for the governor — who in 1818 left public life for good.

He lived out the rest of his life at Hampton, dying in 1829 at the age of 69. Under a provision of his will, his 400 slaves were given their freedom.

Russell

By William Stump

When Marshall Field and Cornelius Vanderbilt erected their mansions in Chicago and New York before the turn of the century, they chose brick made by the Baltimore firm which Alexander Russell founded in 1790.

The bricks of the Flat Iron Building in New York came from the same source, as did those of Johns Hopkins Hospital and the Hotel Rennert in Baltimore.

In the 1820s Alexander Russell's brickyard was located at Spring Gardens on the Patapsco, at the site of rich deposits of good clay. His home was located on Lee Street, the extension of which led to the yard. And when the extension was given a name, the name was Russell. This, plus the fact that Alexander Russell was prominent as a founder of the Methodist Church and as a city councilman, resulted in what Alexander Russell 5th, president of the firm, calls "the strong family tradition" that the street preserves the manufacturer's name.

Russell Street — it extends south and southwest from Fremont Avenue all the way to Gwynn Falls — first appears in city directories in 1827. A year later, bricks from Alexander Russell's firm, Burns & Russell, went into the Shot Tower.

Alexander Russell was born in Ireland in 1765 and came to America in 1781. In 1788, he married Rachel Lane, a member of an early Maryland family. She had relatives, named Berry, in the brick business, and his marriage enabled Alexander Russell to secure a position with the Berry firm. Two years later, he established himself in business, and in 1818, he took Francis Burns into partnership.

The firm thrived. Alexander Russell became one of the biggest producers of brick in the country.

Alexander Russell apparently led a crowded life, for records show that he gave as much time to church affairs and to politics as he did to his business.

Rachel, Alexander's wife, died before 1810. He married twice again and was, all in all, the father of 20 children. Oddly enough, there are few direct descendants with the Russell name today — as far as Alexander Russell 5th knows, he and his daughters are the only ones.

S

October 3, 1954

San Martin

Our duty is to give comfort to South America, not to carry out conquests but rather to liberate peoples. The times of force and oppression have passed. I came to put an end to the period of humiliation. I am an instrument of justice, and the cause which I defend is the cause of mankind.

Gen. Jose de San Martin spoke these words, and they sum up his career — a spectacular career that saw him rally his people to overthrow Spanish rule in Argentina, Chile and Peru. The "George Washington of Argentina" he is called today.

San Martin was born to an aristocratic Argentine family in 1778. He was educated in Madrid for a military career and fought in the Spanish Army against the Moors and, later, against Napoleon. In 1812, when the government of Buenos Aires revolted against Spain, he offered his services and was put in command of a revolutionary army operating against the Spaniards in Peru.

But he soon resigned his command — because he believed that all of South America should go to war if it wanted freedom. So he put his enthusiasm and his spirit and his talents for organization to work, and raised a force of 4,000 Chileans and Argentines. Then after he had trained them and equipped them and whipped them up to a fighting frenzy he made a surprise march over the Andes and routed the Spaniards from northern Chile.

Next, with his army and with a fleet of ships the British helped him build, San Martin attacked Peru and won it, setting himself up as protector. Then trouble developed; jealousy broke out in the army, a royalist faction threatened a counter-revolution and Simon Bolivar, who had freed Colombia and Ecuador, marched into Peru.

Although the two great men then fought as allies, feeling between them became strained; Bolivar was the more ambitious man, and did not take kindly to rivalry. As a result, San Martin resigned his authority and eventually exiled himself to Europe.

The street bearing his name, San Martin Drive, was dedicated by Mayor D'Alesandro in August 1950, as a gesture of international friendship and goodwill. A short and pleasant thoroughfare, it runs from the northeast corner of the Marine Hospital grounds and Wyman Park Drive to University Parkway.

June 26, 1949

Sharpe

By William Stump

Any governors of Maryland who ever think they have had problems to deal with can find comfort by reviewing the term of Gov. Horatio Sharpe.

He had to cope with savage Indian raids on Frederick County, the possibility of an invasion by the French, riot and bloodshed over an unpopular tax, a dispute with Pennsylvania over the boundary line, and an Assembly so hostile that it considered his one secretary an unnecessary luxury.

Even those were only a few of the problems which Sharpe, one of Colonial Maryland's last governors, had to face during the 16 years of his administration. The job was the more difficult, too, because he was receiving little help from King George

II, who was more interested in politics than his subjects' welfare, or from Frederick Calvert, Lord Baltimore, the colony's proprietor, who thought of Maryland mainly in terms of the money it brought him.

That Sharpe nevertheless satisfied the king and Lord Baltimore and at the same time promoted the interests of the people seems evident from the following letter, written to him by the citizens of Annapolis upon his retirement in 1769. "Permit us, Sir," it says, "to express the Regrets we feel at the Apprehension of being deprived of a Governor and Chancellor, whose conduct . . . has for ever ensured to Your Excellency the Great Esteem and Respect of the People of Maryland."

And years after the Revolution, when reminders of Colonial rule still angered many Marylanders, the city fathers of Baltimore created a Sharp Street which historians conclude was intended to honor the governor even though the "e" was unaccountably dropped from the end of his name.

The oldest part of the street — it is a narrow alley — which dates to 1786 or earlier, connects Baltimore Street with Wyoming alley, just south of Lexington Street.

In the 19th century, Sharp Street was extended a number of times until it reached Ostend. However, one section of it is now called Hopkins Place.

Sharp Street – 1951

Horatio Sharpe's administration as Maryland's appointed governor was marked by crisis and action from the moment he arrived in Annapolis in 1753. Before he had had much opportunity to enjoy the life offered by the fashionable capital, King George appointed him commander in chief of all British military forces in America, for it appeared that a war with the French and their Indian allies was inevitable.

Sharpe, who although only 35 years old had seen extensive service in His Majesty's 20th Regiment, set out to inspect the defenses at Fort Cumberland and — with the aid of a young Virginian named George Washington — plan a campaign against the French at Fort Duquesne.

Before the attack could be made, however, word came that King George "desired the appointment" of General Braddock as commander in chief. A few months later, in 1755, Braddock was killed and his army defeated on the banks of the Monongahela — a defeat which might have been avoided had Sharpe, who understood Indian tactics, been kept in command.

During these years of conflict, problem followed problem. No sooner had the governor succeeded in persuading the balky Assembly to give him men, money and supplies for the war than he had to send the militia against the Indians who were ravaging and terrorizing Frederick County.

At one time, the people in Annapolis thought that the Indians, together with the French, would overrun the colony. After the Indians came within 30 miles of Baltimore on one attack, even the Assembly was more impressed with the danger. Yet Sharpe still had a job getting what he needed from the body.

More uncertain days developed when the Stamp Act for taxing the colonies was passed in England. Governor Sharpe, although officially required to support the measure, made no attempt to enforce it. Any such attempt, he informed Lord Baltimore, "would render us more obnoxious than ever to the people." When the act's potential danger was realized, after a considerable amount of violence, it was repealed. The people of Annapolis rejoiced — and drank toasts to their governor.

While these events were taking place, another vexing problem arose. This was the argument between Maryland and Pennsylvania concerning their proper boundary line. Sharpe and John Ridout — that hard-working secretary whom the Assembly regarded as unnecessary — journeyed to the disputed area, and nearly died of a fever contracted in swamps they visited. On their return to Annapolis, Sharpe advised Lord Baltimore that an impartial survey should be made. Finally, Lord Baltimore and the Penns appointed Charles Mason and Jeremiah Dixon to do the job.

After Robert Eden, Lord Baltimore's brother-in-law, replaced him as governor, Sharpe retired to White Hall, his mansion on the Chesapeake. There, surrounded by old friends, by fruit trees and by his extensive gardens, he lived the life of a country gentleman, free from official worries.

In 1773, though, family business called him back to England. For some reason — it may have been the confusion which resulted after the Revolution — he never returned, despite original intentions of doing so. He died in 1790, and, leaving no family, bequeathed White Hall to John Ridout, whose descendants owned it until the early part of this century.

December 13, 1953

Sisson

By Henry C. Rauch

In the 1880s Hugh Sisson was the marble king of Baltimore.

He was at that time, "the most extensive manufacturer of marble in Baltimore," the first dealer to import Italian marble into the city and the president of the Beaver Dam Marble Company, which provided marble for the completion of the Washington Monument in the nation's capital.

A biographer, writing in 1881, declared, "Mr. Sisson did the interior marble work of the new City Hall, the Peabody Institute, of all the banks, insurance companies' buildings, Post Office and Custom House of Baltimore."

Mr. Sisson was the most prominent marble man in town at a time when Baltimore had 41 marble establishments with an average capital of $426,701. The firms employed over 1,000 workmen and expended nearly $440,000 annually on material and $1,000,000 in production.

He was born in Baltimore on May 3, 1820, the son of Martin Sisson, of Virginia, and Mary Beard, a native of Ireland. After a few years of private-school instruction, he was apprenticed, at the age of 12, to learn the trade of marble cutting.

When he was 23, he started his own shop at Lombard and Paca streets. After his business increased, he moved his shop to Calvert and Mercer streets and then to North and Monument streets. On that site, he erected a steam marble mill to manufacture monuments, tombstones, mantels and "all character of marble work." When his Italian marble became popular, he began importing five and six cargoes a year.

In addition to running the marble cutting work, the Sisson firm operated Baltimore County quarries through the Beaver Dam Marble Company.

Mr. Sisson was married in 1848 to Sarah A. Lippincott, daughter of Samuel Lippincott, of Westmoreland County, Pa. They had 11 children and two of the sons, Hugh and John B., were associated with the father.

James M. Sisson, a surveyor, says that Sisson Street, which runs from 23rd Street, was named in honor of Hugh Sisson, who was his grandfather. A portion of the street, at one time called Mount Vernon Avenue, is on land once owned by Hugh Sisson. At several points, the street is adjacent to some old stone quarries — owned not by Sisson but by a man named Schwinn.

Mr. Sisson died at 73.

November 6, 1949

Slingluff

By William Stump

Jesse Slingluff, Baltimore merchant, banker and manufacturer, was too far along in years to join the Confederate Army. So he did the next best thing — equipped a Southern regiment.

The regiment was the 2d Maryland Cavalry. Jesse Slingluff bought its uniforms and its horses, and spent the rest of the war fretting that he was not, like his son, with it in the field.

The son, Fielder Slingluff, distinguished himself with the regiment. But before that, he raised the Confederate flag at its northernmost point in the Union.

At the outbreak of the war, Fielder was a student at Yale. Hearing that the shooting had started, he hoisted the Stars and Bars to the top of the Yale chapel flagpole. Then he locked the door leading to the flagpole, and headed home to join up.

His brother, C. Bohn Slingluff, a student at Heidelberg when the war began, hurried home, but too late to cross the

Potomac. His actions were not popular with the Union authorities and he found it advisable to return to Germany. So he stowed away on a ship, taking with him documents that the Confederates wanted delivered in Europe.

When the war ended, the brothers returned to Baltimore and settled down to the practice of law. Their father, until he died in 1882 at the age of 68, continued to live at Beech Hill, the handsome estate located in what today is Walbrook. It is from Jesse Slingluff's association with that estate that Slingluff Avenue derives its name.

Jesse Slingluff built the avenue around 1875, his heirs say, to gain access from Beech Hill to Liberty Heights Avenue. Eventually it was extended south to a point a little below Baker Street.

Until well into this century, Slingluff Avenue was a well-known thoroughfare. Now, however, Baltimoreans will have trouble finding it, for only 150 feet remain. This is the portion south of Baker Street; there are no houses on it. The part from Gwynns Falls Parkway to North Avenue was rerouted by the WPA in 1936; today it is called Dukeland Avenue.

The street is virtually gone. But there are still many Slingluffs living in Baltimore. The present Jesse Slingluff — son of C. Bohn Slingluff — has himself named two streets. They are Kathland and Ethland.

Kathland was named in the early part of the century for Mr. Slingluff's wife, Kathleen, and Ethland for Ethel Slingluff, the daughter of the first Jesse.

August 7, 1949

Smallwood

By William Stump

When Col. William Smallwood's Maryland troops arrived in New York in the spring of 1776, the town's Tories took one look at their elegant uniforms, and laughed. Such fancy young gentlemen, the New Yorkers exclaimed, would probably turn and run the first time they heard a British gun.

But the Maryland Line, as Smallwood's regiment was called, soon proved the New Yorkers wrong. At the battle of Long Island, by making repeated bayonet charges against the superior British force, it enabled a disorganized Continental Army to retreat successfully. The cost was high — 250 of the "400," as history calls them, were lost.

At the battle of White Plains, the regiment again helped save the Army. Later, its handsome uniforms tattered and its men sick, wounded and weary, it fought at Fort Washington, Princeton, Germantown and Camden, S.C.

As a result of his leadership, Smallwood, a huge and hot-tempered man, became one of Washington's most valued officers. After White Plains — where he was twice wounded — he was made a brigadier general, and subsequently a major general. When the war was over, he returned to politics and in 1785 was elected governor of Maryland.

Today, there is a Smallwood Street in Baltimore. Now extending from the Mount Clare yards north to the Western High School grounds on Windsor Road, it was named in 1818 by a special state commission which drew up a master plan for Baltimore's development. Smallwood was little more than a "paper street" until the 1870s, but now, except from Edmondson Avenue to Lorman Street, where it is interrupted by railroad yards, it is completely built up.

Smallwood was born in Kent County in 1732. As a child, he roamed his father's plantation, Mattawoman, in Charles County; as a youth, like many sons of wealthy Colonial families, he was sent to England to study at Eton. He came home in 1754 and settled down as a country gentleman.

This pursuit was interrupted by the French and Indian War. Like his friend George Washington, who visited the Charles County estate many times over the years, Smallwood served as an officer in the conflict. The war's end found him a mature and thoughtful man; like his father, he became interested in politics, and in 1762 was elected to the Assembly.

When it appeared that war with England was certain, Smallwood helped raise a military organization. The Maryland Convention of 1776 appointed him commander of the Maryland forces. Together with Mordecai Gist, the hero of Long Island, he set about training his men until, a historian says, they were the smartest looking and best drilled in Washington's army, and among the most determined.

Smallwood was apparently not content to settle down after the war. He was chosen a delegate to the Continental Congress in 1785. He declined the post, however, ran for governor, and was elected. He served three terms of one year each. In 1788, he finally retired to Retreat, a small mansion he had built at Mattawoman. There he died less than three years later.

He is buried there, his grave marked by a granite monument erected by Maryland's Sons of the American Revolution. Nearby stands a crumbling brick wall — all that remains of Retreat.

October 2, 1949

Sterrett

By William Stump

Col. Joseph Sterrett, who commanded the 5th Baltimore Regiment at the Battle of Bladensburg in 1814, must have had a red face when that battle came to its unglorious end.

For Sterrett's men, green and bewildered like most of the militiamen there, turned and ran when the British came face to face with them. Only Commodore Joshua Barney and his naval cannoneers stood and fought, and they were too few to stop

Sterrett Street – 1949

the beautifully trained Englishmen, who drove over them and on and burned Washington. The "Bladensburg Races," the battle was called in the newspapers.

Less than a month later, however, Joseph Sterrett and his men more than made up for that defeat when the same British force landed at North Point and marched on Baltimore. In the battle that followed, the American troops, most of whom were Marylanders, withstood the rocket attacks of the British and chased them to their ships.

The colonel was not the only Sterrett who took part in the important victory that rainy September day. There was James Sterrett, a bank cashier, who commanded the 1st Baltimore Hussars. There was Capt. Samuel Sterrett, of the Independent Company. William Sterrett and another James Sterrett served as privates in cavalry and infantry units, and Robert Sterrett was a private in Captain Bunbury's Sea Fencibles.

None of the clan was killed, none wounded; the only Sterrett casualty was the pantry in the colonel's country home, Surrey, on Philadelphia Road.

Sometime during the confusion of the invasion, three Britishers walked into Surrey and made themselves at home. Family legend says they ate and drank their fill. And they left behind them the following note:

"Captains Brown, Wilcox and McNamara, of the Light Brigade, Royal Hussars, met with everything they could wish for at this house. They return their thanks notwithstanding that it was received at the hands of the butler in the absence of the colonel."

Outside of his military exploits, little is known of Joseph Sterrett's life. He was born in 1771 and died in 1827, with the title of general. His ancestors were Scotch-Irish.

The first Sterrett in Baltimore — the family's name is often spelled Sterett in old records — came here from Pennsylvania in 1760. Joseph Sterrett married Mollie Harris, great-granddaughter of the founder of Harrisburg, Pa. They had two or three children, but all died in infancy. The Sterretts who fought with the colonel in the War of 1812 were cousins, listed as living on Gay and Eden streets in Baltimore.

City directories of the period say that Joseph was a merchant, and a descendant adds that he was also an auctioneer. He must have prospered, for Surrey is said to have been a handsome country home.

There is a Sterrett Street in Baltimore today. It is short and only 20 feet wide; it runs south from West Barre to West Street, just west of Paca. It is believed to have been created by the state commission which drew a map of Baltimore in 1822 and honored prominent citizens by naming projected streets in their honor.

July 25, 1954

Stevenson

By Henry C. Rauch

Charles Calvert, the third of the Lords Baltimore, dipped his quill into the inkpot and scratched his name on the charter

— and the Stevenson family came into possession of the land they then held for the next 200 years.

The first Stevenson named the land Fellowship Place; most of the southwestern part of Towson, from Towson High School to Eudowood to Hillen Road to Stoneleigh school, is located upon it. So is most of Stevenson Lane, one of the longest of all the streets in the county seat. No one knows today how old the lane is. But it has appeared on county maps for close to a century, and was probably once the farm lane.

The earliest Stevensons built a house there and cleared the woods — woods filled with game and clear streams, woods which, in 1690, were far away from any town. There was no Baltimore then; even the town of Joppa was some 30 years away.

Local lore contains little about the early Stevenson. The first member of the family it deals with in any detail is Josias Stevenson, who, born and raised on Fellowship Place, went to war in the Revolution and rose to be a paymaster in the Continental Army. When the war ended, he came home and married his second cousin, whose name was Urath Stevenson, and farmed 200-acre Fellowship Place until he died.

Joshua Stevenson was next; after him came Washington Stevenson, who got his name because he was born on Washington's birthday in 1830. Perhaps there are few Baltimore Countians who remember him, for he lived until 1895, working his land and taking pride in the fact that it was perhaps the oldest farm in the county.

When Joshua died, he left no male heirs and not many more years went by before pieces of Fellowship Place began to be broken off and sold to developers and seekers after the quiet country life.

June 10, 1951

Stricker

By William Stump

If any soldier ever served Maryland well, that soldier was Gen. John Stricker.

Born of Swiss ancestry in Frederick in 1758, he took up arms at the age of 18 when his father, a battle-wise old soldier who had been a colonel of the Colonial Guards, organized a company of volunteers to fight against the British.

The young man soon got his chance to fight — when he joined Col. William Smallwood's regiment of the famous Maryland Line and took part in the bloody battle of Long Island. After that, he won a commission and fought at Trenton, at Princeton, at Brandywine and at Monmouth. Once he was captured and released, later he campaigned against the Indians. When the war ended, he was a captain.

And, when the war ended, he was also a married man. Toward the close of the war, while in Philadelphia, he married a daughter of Gunning Bradford, a prominent citizen. Another daughter married Joshua Barney, the naval hero — and in 1783, the two men brought their wives to Baltimore and went into business together. Histories record that Stricker owned a mill on the Jones Falls and that he lived on Charles Street.

A few years later, Stricker organized the Maryland militia, which makes him the father of the Maryland National Guard. In 1794, when the Whisky Rebellion broke out in Pennsylvania, that militia — a brigade, which called itself the Independent Company — was ordered to Pittsburgh by President Washington. Stricker was then a colonel.

As the years went on, Stricker built and trained his militia, and by 1812, when America declared war on England, he was a general.

Two years later, the British invaded Maryland and marched on Baltimore. Under the orders of Gen. Samuel Smith, Stricker's brigade, 3,185 men strong, went out to meet them. The battle took place near North Point, and when it was over, the surprised invaders were retreating in complete frustration to their ships.

After the battle, which he had directed with a great deal of coolness and confidence, a grateful Baltimore elected Stricker a state senator, an office which he declined. Later still, he declined reappointment as general of the militia. He died in 1825, at the age of 67.

Baltimore found a way of honoring the hero even before his death, when, in 1822, it named Stricker Street. Located in West Baltimore, the street begins at Cole and runs north some 25 blocks to Baker Street.

T

February 26, 1950

Tessier And Deluol

By Francis E. Old Jr.

A city in miniature clusters about the walls of St. Mary's Seminary on Paca Street. Much as a medieval European town grew up beneath the sheltering walls of a castle, so have tiny houses on narrow ways crowded the neighborhood of this venerable institution.

On a winter's night, tiny, multipaned windows glow with soft lights of kerosene lamps, and the mica eyes of old Latrobe stoves wink cheerily. Gas street lamps cast just enough light to soften outlines.

But daylight reveals an area of huddled houses that lean wearily upon each other in the mutual dependence of desolate old age. Back yards are non-existent, or tiny, or as fantastically shaped as a gerrymander. There are open spaces only from casualties — where a house has sunk to the ground, where wooden fences have rotted away or been burned for firewood.

Strangely, the purposeful serenity within the walls of St. Mary's Seminary, and the aimless decadence without, alike owe their genesis to revolution — to three revolutions.

The American Revolution removed many religious restrictions, and when Father John Carroll of Maryland became bishop of all the United States in 1790, there was need for more priests in his vast diocese. He turned for help to the Society of St. Sulpice in France, an order devoted to the education of young men for the priesthood.

The aftermath of the French Revolution, on the other hand, had brought many religious restrictions. Father Emery, Sulpician superior general, fearing for the existence of his order, had begun inquiries about the possibility of re-establishing it in the New World.

The meeting of minds was perfect in timing and intention, and on July 10, 1791, Fathers Nagot, Tessier and Garnier landed in Baltimore, equipped with all that was necessary for the establishment of a theological seminary.

On the outskirts of the city stood the One Mile Tavern. The Sulpicians purchased it, and on October 3, with Father Nagot as superior, the seminary opened. At the same site today, the work of the Sulpicians is carried on — there, and in the magnificent new building on Roland Avenue.

With the tavern had come 4 acres. Later the seminary bought 10 acres more. But by 1802, financial difficulties led to a decision to develop the upper half of the tract for residential purposes. Streets were opened, ground rents created, speculators built houses.

Here another revolution plays its part. About the turn of the century, the French island of Santo Domingo was the scene of bloody slave uprisings. White settlers, loyal slaves, free blacks fled. Father Dubourg, a Sulpician, was among the refugees, and with him many of them came to Baltimore. French-speaking Catholics, they were naturally drawn to the neighborhood.

The poorer among them settled in the miniature houses about St. Mary's, and thus formed the nucleus of the black section which today spreads northward on both sides of Pennsylvania Avenue. On this land of the Sulpicians are streets named for them and their institutions.

Tessier Street honors Father Jean Marie Tessier, member of the pioneer band which established St. Mary's, and its second superior, from 1810 to 1829. In addition to his many duties at the seminary, he was vicar general to the first four archbishops of Baltimore.

His greatest memorial is his work among Baltimore's blacks. He devoted 31 years to them, and his work bore fruit when his protégé, Father Joubert, founded the Oblate Sisters of Providence, an order of black sisters, to take up teaching.

The name of Father Louis Regis Deluol, third superior of the seminary, from 1829 to 1849, was once given to what is now Moore Street. It remains today only in Deluol Court, an obscure backwash of Moore Street.

Elder Alley memorializes Father Alexius Joseph Elder, a native Marylander, whose devotion to the poor of the neighborhood was ended only by his death in 1871.

St. Mary's Street is, of course, named for the institution. St. Mary's Court, also called Seminary Court, is the approach to the great gate in the Pennsylvania Avenue wall.

July 23, 1950

Thames Street

By William Stump

One of the oldest streets in Baltimore is Thames Street — and so is one of the oldest in London.

Thames Street, Baltimore, is located just above Fells Point, and dates back to the days when Baltimore was nothing more than a village; historians think that William Fell or one of his relatives named it after the Thames River of London.

Thames Street, London, was named for the river, too. Exactly when is unknown — but it was hundreds of years before Englishmen had ever heard of Baltimore, or even America. The street may have been used as a road by the Romans, for they are supposed to have built a bridge near it, on the site of London Bridge.

Chaucer lived on Thames Street between 1379 and 1385, during which time he was Comptroller of Petty Customs in the Port of London, as well as poet and writer. Christopher Wren knew the street well — he built four churches along it, one of which, St. Magnus the Martyr, is considered to be among the finest examples of his work.

In addition to St. Magnus the Martyr, another famous landmark on London's Thames Street is Vintners Hall, built by Wren in 1671, the headquarters of the Vintners Company. One of the 12 great London "companies," it was organized in 1436

Thames Street – 1950

as a sort of early trade union. Over its members and their work it had great authority; at one time it even tried to regulate their marriages.

On Lower Thames Street is the Billingsgate Fish Market, the "narrow and congested thoroughfare redolent of fish from one end to the other." The fish markets gave England the expression "billingsgate," which is synonymous with coarse language and, incidentally, an insult to a fishmonger.

Baltimore's Thames Street may not be as old, but like its namesake, it has seen its colorful days. In the last century, sailing vessels, including the famous Baltimore clippers, tied up to the wharves along it, and seafaring men in striped shirts and long pigtails drank and sang in its bars.

Today, Baltimore's Thames Street is largely industrial, with warehouses and garages and plants dwarfing the old buildings. But near Broadway the ships from distant lands still tie up, and their sailors still drink in the bars — bars where the Greek, Spanish, Italian, Danish, Norwegian and French languages are every bit as common as English.

November 25, 1951

Towson

By William Stump

It was not only on Maryland soil that Maryland men helped win the War of 1812.

Take, for example, the bitter campaign along the Niagara frontier, which began two years before the battle of North Point and the bombardment of Fort McHenry. In it, an amazing young Maryland captain named Nathan Towson played a decisive role in a number of important engagements with his blazing Maryland-manned artillery.

"I cannot refrain from advertising to the manner in which Captain Towson's artillery was served," wrote an American general after the Marylander's guns had repulsed the British efforts to recapture Fort Erie. "I have never seen it equaled."

"This officer has so distinguished himself that to say simply he is in action is a volume of eulogium. I have no idea that there is an artillery officer in any service superior to him in the knowledge and performance of his duty."

In that battle, the officer's battery fired so rapidly and constantly that the British, impressed with the glare of the gun flashes against the sky, respectfully named it "Towson's Lighthouse."

At Chippewa, its accuracy silenced the main enemy battery and, in ruining the major charge of the enemy infantry, won the battle.

At Niagara — which some historians call the bloodiest battle of the entire war — it fired from dawn to midnight without letup, and helped win the day even though Towson's two lieutenants were killed, and 27 of his 36 men killed or wounded.

Towson was one of the campaign's most celebrated soldiers. His coolness and his willingness to expose himself to enemy fire were legendary. During a battle it was not unusual, according to his biographers, to find him offering advice to the generals. In fact, when it came to choosing the sites for the guns, the generals deferred to his judgment — and were never sorry.

And his fighting was not confined only to artillery. As a voluntary reconnaissance man, he liked to draw enemy fire so that he could determine its location.

When Towson came home to Baltimore after the war as a lieutenant colonel, the citizens offered to make him sheriff of Baltimore. He refused, choosing to remain in the Army. But the citizens honored him anyway — by giving him a gold sword and, a few years later, by naming a street in his honor. This is Towson Street; located just west of Fort McHenry, it today extends northeast from Fort Avenue past Marriott Street.

The citizens who offered him the sheriff's job should not have been surprised that Towson chose to remain in the Army, for it had been his big interest in life even as a boy. Born in 1784, in Towson, a village named for his family, he was the youngest of 12 children. Although he was an avid reader, his education was slim; his early years were spent on the family farm.

In 1801, his father sent him to Kentucky to claim and work some land which supposedly was owned by the family. Upon his arrival, he found that the land actually belonged to someone else. So he went to Natchez and happily enrolled in a company of volunteers bound for New Orleans to guard the governor of the newly acquired Louisiana Territory.

The trouble the Americans expected from the French of New Orleans, who were rumored to be opposed to the selling of their city, did not materialize. But Towson found an opportunity to prove himself anyway — when he talked the poorly treated, unhappy volunteers out of deserting.

For this he was appointed first lieutenant of his company, and then captain of the Natchez Volunteer Artillery. After spending a few years at this post, he returned to Towson in 1805 and resumed farming; two years later, he was adjutant of the 7th Maryland.

In 1812, when it became certain that war was coming, Towson was made a captain of artillery and in the next months he recruited and trained a company of Baltimore County boys. He must have done this job well, for Lt. Col. Winfield Scott, who was to be his commanding officer during much of the war, soon sent his outfit off to Lake Erie, considered the place where most of the war would be fought.

After the war, Towson served for a time in Boston, and married there. In 1819, he was appointed Paymaster General of the Army and he held this post until he died, a major general, in 1854.

July 31, 1949

Tyson

By Henry C. Rauch

Tyson Street, running its narrow, interrupted course north from Saratoga Street to Franklin, and then from Monument north and northeast to Park Avenue, keeps fresh the name of Elisha Tyson, dead now a century and a quarter.

When he was alive, and for years afterward, any Baltimorean could have given some account of Tyson, for an unending fight that he waged against slavery kept him much in the public eye.

Nowadays, it is necessary to turn to a little "Life" that was written by "A Citizen of Baltimore" and published in this city in 1825.

The Tyson family, this volume relates, was originally German, but Elisha's great-

Tyson Street – 1957

grandfather heard William Penn preach in Germany, was converted by him to Quakerism, and followed him to England and then to Philadelphia. There he married, there his descendants stayed, and there Elisha was born.

At an early age, however, the son came to Baltimore. His biographer thinks he did so because there were greater opportunities in Maryland than in Pennsylvania for righting injustice.

For Elisha's chief interest in life became the abolition of slavery, and all the while that he was amassing a fortune "by industry and temperance" he was also campaigning against that.

Since Maryland was not only a slave-holding state but a slave-breeding one as well, Tyson encountered no little opposition. But he was as determined as his foes.

Now and then he also showed concern for the treatment that was being accorded the Indians, but for the most part it was the lot of the slaves that engaged his sympathy and attention.

Up almost to the day he died, he was working furiously to obtain the freedom of one group of slaves that had been captured by a Baltimore privateer, impressed into service as members of the ship's crew and ultimately brought to this city. His legal battle brought victory; 11 of the slaves were set free and repatriated in Liberia.

When Tyson died, in 1824, it is related, 10,000 blacks — nearly the whole black population of the city — attended his funeral.

In recent years the street that was named for him has undergone a rebirth in part. The southern section is still a mere alley. That part between Read Street and Park Avenue, however, is lined with little brick houses.

After having fallen into an almost slumlike state, this part of the street became the subject of determined renovation about 1946, and has been colorfully and effectively reclaimed.

V

December 17, 1950

Venable

By William Stump

The mere mention of Major Richard M. Venable to those Baltimoreans who knew him is enough to bring forth exclamations of pleasure and outbursts of reminiscence.

"What a man the major was!" exclaims Harry N. Baetjer, who practiced law with him. "Physically, he was immense, with a big white beard that made him look like Santa Claus; he was one of the most striking figures in Baltimore 45 years ago.

"He was tremendously good-natured, and it was an unforgettable experience to spend an evening with him, because he was a delightful storyteller, a brilliant mind.

"I have never met anyone who had read as much as the major. He was the best read man on religion in the city, perhaps save for a few clergymen.

"As for the law, I can best sum up his achievements in it by saying that his book on real estate law — 'The Syllabus on the Law of Real Property,' he titled it — is still the standard work on the subject."

Major Venable did much for Baltimore, Mr. Baetjer declares. In 1899, he was elected to the City Council, having been moved to run for office by what he termed the corruption of the municipal government.

But his serious purposes did not prevent him from having his characteristic good time: "Although the major's constant jokes upon his fellow councilmen interfered at times with the dignity of the branch," a Sun editorialist later wrote, "he assisted in accomplishing needed civic improvements."

In 1904, after he left the Council, Major Venable was appointed president of the Park Board. He has been praised as one of the men "responsible for the Baltimore park system," for through his efforts, the area of Patterson Park was almost tripled, Carroll Park had many acres added to it, and Wyman, Gwynns Falls and a number for other parks were created.

Shortly before World War I, the city opened another park and named it for the major. It is gone now — Eastern High School and Memorial Stadium stand on its site. But Major Venable's name is preserved nearby in Venable Avenue, which extends east from Barclay Street to Ellerslie Avenue, one block above 33rd Street. Edward J. Gallagher Sr. named it in 1916 as part of a real estate development.

Mr. Baetjer's enthusiasm for Major Venable is equaled by that of J. V. Kelly, who was secretary of the Park Board when the major was its president.

"We spent a lot of time together," Mr. Kelly says, "inspecting the parks. At first we used a buggy, and later, a blue automobile that he bought. The Blue Goose, he called it. He bought it because he didn't want to be seen in the city-owned vehicle — said that it was disgraceful the way politicians rode around on the taxpayers' money.

"The major often said that he never outgrew his boyhood. That was true; he loved to tease people and play tricks on them. And then, he was terrible shy about some things. I remember when he gave me a wedding present — some fine silver spoons. He presented them to me without a word and hurriedly walked away.

"We spent hours talking. He would talk about everything from death — he claimed no one really feared it, because it was as natural as being born — to religion. He certainly knew that subject. And because of his knowledge, or in spite of it, I don't know, he was an agnostic.

"Yes, the major was head and shoulders above most of the men in Baltimore in the old days."

Major Venable was not a Baltimorean; he was born in Charlotte County, Va., in 1839. His earliest ambition was to be a mathematician and an engineer, and he studied these subjects at Hampden-Sydney College and the University of Virginia.

He was just finishing his schooling when the Civil War began, so he enlisted as a private in the Richmond Howitzers.

Eventually, after serving as an engineer in the Army of Northern Virginia and in Mississippi, he became a major. But little is known about his war experiences in Baltimore; he seldom spoke of them. Sometimes, though, he would tell about the time he was awakened, while sleeping on the ground, by a heavy foot stepping across his chest. The foot, he said with pride, belonged to Gen. Robert E. Lee.

After the war, Venable returned to Charlotte County, only to find his family's home and fortune in ruins. He then became a teacher, first in Texas and later, under General Lee himself, at Washington and Lee. It was while he himself was teaching mathematics and engineering that he studied law. In 1871, he came to Baltimore.

Major Venable never married. In fact, one of his favorite topics was bachelorhood and its joys. At his home at 930 North Calvert Street, he expounded on that and countless other topics to the friends he brought home to eat at his sumptuous table.

His closest companion was Dr. William H. Welch, one of the famous men of Johns Hopkins. Once, these men, who loved to pit their brains against each other, read an entire encyclopedia and spent months quizzing each other on its contents.

The accomplishment of which Major Venable was proudest was his work in building up Baltimore's parks. He often said that he wanted his ashes strewn over Druid Hill Park, and when he died in 1910, this was done.

W

April 10, 1949

Walker

By Charles Purcell Jr.

Walker Avenue was christened with a bottle of extra dry champagne on a spring day in 1896.

The Avenue, an asphalt road that runs along the northern boundary of Baltimore City from the east side of York Road to Sherwood Avenue, crossing Banbury and Southwood, was formerly part of Drumquehazel, the country estate of Henry M. Walker.

Mr. Walker, for whom the road is named and who now lives at 2927 North Calvert Street, says that if it hadn't been for Albert A. Blakeney, chairman of the Board of Commissioners at the time, the road might have been designated part of Gittings Avenue.

Gittings Avenue, which had been named after John S. Gittings, stopped at the west side of the York Road, a half block below Walker Avenue.

Mr. Walker relates that during the christening ceremonies which consisted of passing the champagne around to a group of friends — Harrison Rider, Will Burns, George Lamb and Mr. Gittings — Mr. Blakeney raised the empty champagne bottle and said:

"Is there anyone here who wants to suggest a name for this new road?"

Mr. Gittings stepped forward and stated, "I think this road should be named Gittings Avenue, as the two nearly join on the York Road."

Mr. Blakeney, with the bottle still raised, turned to Mr. Gittings and asked, "Who donated the land and contributed money to build this road?"

"Why, Henry Walker, of course," said Mr. Gittings.

"Well, that's the name of this road — Walker Avenue," Mr. Blakeney said, and he broke the bottle over a culvert.

Mr. Walker, who is now retired, was born in 1868 at Dumbarton Mansion in Pikesville. He bought Drumquehazel in 1891 for $18,000. The reason he was anxious to have a road cut through the property, he says, was to provide a short cut between York and Hillen roads, saving about two miles of travel over Regester Avenue.

"Two miles doesn't sound like much to a motorist today," he says, "but when you're driving horses it means a great deal."

Mr. Walker started Walker Avenue in 1895. He donated a 20-foot strip from York Road east to the rear of Drumquehazel, and the owner of the property behind his donated the rest. It was partly graded by a Democratic administration, but the Republicans gained office and appropriated no money to finish it.

Mr. Walker was persuaded by Mr. Blakeney to finish the road at his own expense, which proved to be nearly $1,000.

January 24, 1954

Wallis

By James C. Bertram

The leader of the Baltimore bar for half a century. A lawyer unsurpassed in the city's history. A speaker without peer anywhere. The man who reformed a rotten city government and who himself could have won any office within the gift of the people of Maryland. A brilliant writer and linguist, a scintillating wit, a celebrated gentleman.

That, according to his contemporaries, was Severn Teackle Wallis — whose likeness is preserved in three statues, for whom two streets have been named, and who, 61 years after his death, is still a hero to the lawyers of Baltimore.

Wallis' career was as long as it was notable. Born in Baltimore of an old aristocratic family, he graduated from St. Mary's College at the age of 16. Immediately he entered the office of William Wirt to study the law; three years later, at 19, he was admitted to the bar.

At the same time, he began writing articles and poems for local newspapers and periodicals — and commenced a study of the Spanish language and Spanish literature. By 1844 — in which year he helped found the Maryland Historical Society — he had become one of the few foreigners invited to be a member in Madrid's Royal Academy of History. Shortly after that, he made a journey to Spain, which resulted in a travel book that received acclaim in both England and America.

In 1849, the government interrupted his practice and sent him to Spain on a mission connected with old Florida land titles. That enabled him to meet the country's important men and to become thoroughly acquainted with its government; the result was another widely hailed book.

Years later, one of its readers asked the Spanish consul in Baltimore if Wallis really spoke good Spanish. "He speaks Spanish better than any Spaniard I know," the consul replied.

In the 1850s Wallis firmly established himself as the city's leading lawyer — and writer, too. His articles on local government and politics had tremendous influence. In fact, they spurred a reform movement which, with Wallis as a guiding light, brought the city police under state control, established new election laws, and cleaned out the Know-Nothing city government, said by historians to have been the most corrupt and tyrannous in Baltimore history.

And Wallis played a vital role in the dangerous days of 1861. When the 6th Massachusetts Infantry was stoned in the streets in April, it was Wallis who cooled down the mobs with a speech in Monument Square. And it was Wallis who went with a committee to Washington and pleaded with Lincoln to stop routing troops through the city.

Wallis' sympathies were with the South — but he considered the preservation of the Union more important. When Gov. Thomas Holiday Hicks refused to convene the existing Legislature, special elections were held to form a new one; because Annapolis was occupied by federal troops, it met in Frederick. Wallis, against his will, was elected to the House and appointed head of the key committee on federal relations.

It was a ticklish position; upon the handling of it depended the fate of Maryland. A bill to secede had been put forward; Wallis threw it out, saying the House had no power to pass it. And at the same time, he killed a plan to call a convention to vote on succession.

But Wallis took a strong stand against the war, too — and in spite of his role in saving the state for the Union, the federal government clapped him in jail, along with a number of other prominent Marylanders. No charges were made — nevertheless the prisoners were locked up in Fort McHenry, then Fort Monroe, Fort Lafayette and Fort Warren in Boston. The imprisonment lasted 14 months — and ended because Wallis insisted that the Marylanders be brought to trial or released.

After that, Wallis returned to the law. In the reconstruction era, he argued thousands of cases before local, state and federal courts, and before the Supreme Court. His very appearance in the courtroom brought out his colleagues in droves.

One of them, William Cabell Bruce, later United States senator from Maryland, later wrote some of his recollections of Wallis. He speaks of the "tall, bent figure, dressed with scrupulous elegance, but thin almost to tenuity, the bold classical profile, the high narrow brow indicating a perceptive intellect . . . the certain refinement which seemed to pervade the entire personality of the man."

He speaks of his command of language — of his fluency, his references to the classics, his ability to hold and enrapture any audience. "In my opinion," Bruce says, "Wallis was the most captivating speaker I have ever heard — including Henry Ward Beecher, Bourke Cochran, Woodrow Wilson and the most celebrated British orators."

He speaks of Wallis' knowledge of the law — how an obscure point of law, brought up in court, could be discussed by Wallis as though he had made a lifelong study of it; how in any case, whether it involved charwoman or magnate, received painstaking study and preparation; how Wallis' mind — "the most highly cultivated ever brought to my knowledge" — could see through any legal tangle; how his wit could captivate a courtroom.

And Senator Bruce discusses the Wallis paradox — that Wallis' fame was purely local. Like many others, Bruce says the lawyer could have gone on to become governor, senator or cabinet officer, and perhaps an important man in American history. But Wallis was for some reason content to remain a local figure, running for office only when a local situation demanded it, as in 1875, when another corrupt city government was in power.

Wallis — the Duchess of Windsor, Wallis Warfield, bears his name, her grandfather having been a close friend and her father named Teackle Wallis Warfield — died in 1894. He had never married. Shortly after that, his writings were collected, running into four fat volumes. In later years, statues were erected in his honor in the Courthouse, in Mount Vernon Place and in the Peabody Institute, one of the many organizations of which he was an official.

And some years after his death, the city named the block in which he lived, the 200 block of St. Paul Street, Wallis Place. That name is no longer in use. But there is a Wallis Avenue in the Bancroft Park section in the northwest corner of the city; that street is one of a group honoring famous Baltimore lawyers, and was named early in the century, presumably by George Williamson and B. S. Woolston, property owners in the area who broke up two large estates for development.

June 5, 1949

The Walterses

By William Stump

After 40 years, a Baltimore street bearing an internationally famous name is emerging from its status as a country lane.

The street — located in northeast Govans between Beauregard and Abner, south of and parallel to Belvedere — is Walters Avenue, named for the family which gave Baltimore the Walters Art Gallery. The land the street crosses was once part of the vast Walters estate.

But although a developer planned the street in the 1890s, it never amounted to more than a lane until just six months ago, when a building firm began fronting it with apartments.

The Walters family could well afford a large estate and the finest European art.

Walters Art Gallery – 1950

William T. Walters, who amassed a fortune from railroads, steamship lines and coal mining, was one of the wealthiest men in Baltimore; his son Henry, who doubled the fortune, was the wealthiest man south of the Mason-Dixon Line, a 1920 survey showed.

William Walters was born in Pennsylvania in 1820. His parents were pioneers in the development of the nation's coal mining industry, and consequently he was training as a mining engineer. When his schooling was completed, he took to the wilds of the Allegheny Mountains in search of new sources of coal. By the time he was 21, he was managing the first smelting mill in America to produce iron in coal-fueled furnaces.

But William Walters decided that commerce, not engineering, was the way to make a living. In the 1840s already well to do, he settled in Baltimore and established himself as a commission merchant. He prospered quickly and was soon operating a number of other businesses. He established a steamship line; he began building railroads; he made money at banking. In another 20 years, he was one of the richest men in the city — and one of the greatest patrons of the arts in the country.

In spite of his varied business interests, William Walters found time to make numerous journeys to Europe in the quest of art masterpieces. While he traveled and lived on the Continent, he met the major French, German, Belgian and English artists and he brought their works home in huge quantities. In 1870, he opened his home at 5 Mount Vernon Place to the public, collecting a small admission fee which went to charity.

Henry Walters — born in Baltimore in 1848 — followed in his father's footsteps. He became, through the extension of his own and his family's enterprises, a man who ranked in importance with such financial giants as Morgan and Rockefeller. He controlled 10,000 miles of railroad, countless banks and other enterprises; he owned houses and other property in Europe and the South as well as in Maryland.

His appreciation of art was matched only by his ability to pay for it. Whenever a great painting or statue was placed on the market in Europe, the name of Henry Walters came up as a possible purchaser. In 1902, he purchased the Maseranti collection of early Italian art at a cost of $1,000,000, chartering a ship to bring it to Baltimore.

The collection which the Walterses were accumulating became too big for their home, and in 1909 the present gallery at the corner of Charles and Centre streets was opened. But William Walters, although he had helped his son plan the gallery, never saw it; he died, at age 84, in 1904.

Although Henry Walters' name was famous in Baltimore — and in the art centers of the world — he remained a man of mystery, avoiding publicity. He maintained his legal residence in this city and his name came into the papers in connection with new art acquisitions and his building of racing yachts to defend the America's Cup.

But he lived in New York. Visits to Baltimore were infrequent; most people believed he had forgotten his birthplace.

At heart, however, Henry Walters was more of a Baltimorean than anyone realized. When he died in 1931, he left his gallery to the city, with more than 2 million dollars to maintain it.

November 5, 1950

Warren

By William Stump

Although his name is seldom mentioned in history books, Joseph Warren, physician and major-general, was one of the major figures of the Revolution.

One of the major heroes, too. The reason that so little is written about him today is that his major contributions were made prior to the actual fighting; when the fighting began, he was one of the first to fall.

He died bravely in the trenches of Bunker Hill. His death made a deep impression on every oppressed colonist: he was eulogized and honored in every village, town and city. The Warren Avenue on Baltimore's Federal Hill is supposed to have been named for him at the time.

Actually, Americans were moved by his death for more reasons than the death itself. They remembered that the Bostonian was one of the first to stand up against the British, one of the most articulate voices of protest, and one of the men who, seeing there was no way out, made it possible for the colonists to go into the fight with some semblance of organization.

Joseph Warren was born in Roxbury, Mass., in 1741. He entered Harvard at the age of 14 and graduated with honors at 18. He became a schoolteacher and an active Mason. Then he decided to become a doctor.

Warren Avenue – 1940

That was not difficult in Colonial times; Warren simply apprenticed himself to an established physician. At 23, he was able to set up a practice.

By specializing in the treatment of smallpox, so rampant in America then, he soon made a name for himself. One of his patients was Samuel Adams, one of the colony's foremost political figures. The two became close friends and it was not long until medicine became secondary to political activity in Warren's life.

Warren threw himself into the budding struggle against the British. He joined political clubs and made speeches that whipped up public sentiment.

As events raced to a climax, he became a member of the Committee of Safety and a delegate to the Massachusetts Provincial Congress. On the eve of war, he was the man who dispatched Paul Revere on his historic ride. He fought at the

Battle of Lexington, then became president of the Provincial Congress and helped to equip and train an army. His impressed colleagues made him a major-general.

Just before the battle at Bunker Hill, he presented himself to Israel Putnam, the commanding officer; Putnam, who held a lesser rank, asked him to direct the battle. Warren replied that he came as a volunteer, and asked to be placed where the fighting would be thickest.

The request was granted. He took a place in the redoubt on Breeds Hill, where again he refused to assume command. But when the fighting got heavy, the men turned to him for leadership. This time he gave it; he was trying to rally the patriots, who were just about out of ammunition, when the British overran the trench. A British officer recognized him and shot him.

As Warren Street appears on maps not long after Bunker Hill, and as Warren received numerous letters from Baltimore patriots praising him to the skies, Wilbur H. Hunter, director of the Peale Museum, feels sure that it was named for this patriot.

Originally, Warren Avenue was Warren Street. It begins at Light Street, extends east along Federal Hill Park and dead-ends short of Covington Street.

February 22, 1953

Washington

By William Stump

Probably every American city has one or two streets named for the nation's first president. Baltimore has four — Washington Place, Washington Street, Washington Avenue and, stretching a point, Washington Boulevard.

And this is especially fitting, for George Washington knew Baltimore well. Indeed, it is recorded that he passed through the city three dozen times — and slept here on many of the visits.

Once he stayed with James McHenry, later secretary of war in his Cabinet and the man for whom Fort McHenry was named. Another time he stopped with Charles Carroll of Carrollton. But he really

Washington Boulevard – 1949

preferred to stay at the Fountain Inn, which stood where the Southern Hotel now stands at Light and Redwood streets.

And no wonder. The Fountain, owned by Daniel Grant, was one of the fine hostelries of its time, celebrated for its kitchen, its bar and its accommodations. And George Washington, in spite of some notions, was a man upon whom the pleasures of the table and the barroom were not lost.

Many of his visits to Baltimore took place at times that were landmarks in his life — and in the life of the young nation. For example, he stopped in 1775, on his way to attend the Continental Congress in Philadelphia — where Maryland's Thomas Johnson was to nominate him as commander in chief.

On that Baltimore visit, he reviewed the militia and was entertained at the new courthouse; the citizens, the fires of freedom burning in their hearts, went wild over him. They gave him a similar reception in 1781, when he passed through with a number of French and American officers to accept the surrender of Cornwallis at Yorktown. Apparently, Washington felt that he could at last relax, for on that occasion he ran up a phenomenally high bill for punch, wine and grog.

Washington stopped at the Fountain Inn two years later, on his way to Annapolis, then the new nation's capital, to surrender his commission. He was a guest in 1787 on his way to attend the Constitutional Convention in Philadelphia. And

Washington Street – 1923

he came through in 1789 en route to New York to take the oath as first president.

That time he was met in Howard County by a large committee of handsomely uniformed mounted men who escorted him into the city as cannon boomed and citizens shouted themselves hoarse. As usual, there was a dinner and reception. As usual, there was a written message from a welcoming committee.

And, as usual, Washington sat down with a quill pen and wrote an answer to the committee.

"I cannot now," he said, after disclaiming his own worth, "resist my feelings so much as to withhold the communication of my ideas respecting the actual situation and the prospect of our national affairs.

"It appears to me that little more than common sense and common honesty in the transactions of the community at large would be necessary to make us a great and happy nation. For if the Government, lately adopted, shall be arranged and administrated in such a manner as to acquire the full confidence of the American people, I sincerely believe, they will have greater advantages, from their natural, moral and political circumstances, than any other people ever possessed."

Washington came through after that, too — with Mrs. Washington on the way home to Mount Vernon, and on various business trips, including one in 1798, the year before his death, to Trenton for the purpose of reorganizing the Army.

But Baltimore was not the only place in Maryland that was well known to Washington. When he was 21 years old, the governor of his native Virginia sent him to what is now the northwest corner of the state to check up on the movements of the French. Later he served at Fort Cumberland, and marched through the surrounding country with the ill-fated Braddock in the French and Indian War.

He knew Annapolis, Frederick, Williamsport, Hagerstown — in fact, save for the lower Eastern Shore, there was hardly a part of the state that Washington did not visit during his long career. And, of course, he had to pass through it every time he went north, whether in war or in peace.

Sometimes he passed through the city and up to Havre de Grace — and there are records of his having taken a boat from the city to Elkton, then called Head of Elk. Occasionally he went north through Frederick. But most often he took a boat at Annapolis to Rock Hall, in Kent County, going north from there through Chestertown.

December 25, 1949

Water Street

By William Stump

Baltimore's Water Street and London's Water Street have two things in common besides their names — both are near important bodies of water and both are centuries old.

Early records of Baltimore Town reveal that the street here, a little north of the Upper Basin of the Patapsco, was laid out in 1747 when Nicholas Ruxton Gay (Gay Street is named for him) made a survey for the town officials. London's Water Street, on the banks of the Thames River, is said to have been in existence hundreds of years before our city had even been thought of.

Water Street – 1949

One theory has been advanced that the Baltimore street was named for the London one, which in turn, supposedly got its name through its use by water carriers centuries ago. Another theory is that both streets derive their names from their proximity to their cities' principal rivers.

The Baltimore street today runs a broken course from Light Street to Market Place. Originally, it extended from South Street to the market space one block west of Jones Falls; later that part of Second Street which ran east from South to Light was renamed Water. The London Street originally led from the Thames to the Strand, one of the best-known streets in the Empire. But the block closest to the river disappeared when buildings were erected over its bed.

Water Street, London, is a narrow thoroughfare, similar to Baltimore's Clay Street. It twists and turns; many of the buildings along it were reduced to rubble during the Blitz.

Water Street, Baltimore, presents no Blitzed appearance now, although it did in 1926, when workmen excavated a portion on the south side between Holliday and Gay streets. A few inches below the surface of the street, the workmen found a series of brick and granite vaults, connected by narrow doors.

Many persons believe the vaults were the wine cellars of the Exchange Hotel. Others say they housed the slaves of the hotel's guests. Some conjecture that officials of the Custom House, still the most famous structure on the street, stored records and money there. There is also a theory that the vaults served as bulwarks against the seepage of the marshes which covered the area when Water Street was young.

February 19, 1950

Watson

By William Stump

William H. Watson didn't have to go to war.

He was a middle-aged civilian with three children. He was comfortably established as one of Baltimore's most prominent and wealthiest lawyers. He had been a city councilman and was speaker of the House of Delegates. But his interest in military matters, his love of adventure and his patriotic zeal were greater.

So, when the government asked Maryland to furnish volunteers for the Mexican War, Watson, who had often paraded as an officer with the fashionable Independent Blues, volunteered immediately. The governor made him a lieutenant colonel and put him in command of "Baltimore's Own" — an infantry battalion made up of four Baltimore and two Washington companies.

John Kelly, commander of one of the Baltimore companies and a close friend of Watson's, tells in his memoirs how the battalion suffered weeks of misery aboard the Massachusetts on the voyage to Mexico. He tells how pleasant that country appeared when the men landed — how they enjoyed the warm Mexican sunshine and the bounty of the seemingly peaceful countryside. He describes the colorful uniforms, the friskiness and the high morale of the Baltimoreans. And he tells how many of them died with their colonel at Monterey.

Monterey was a well-fortified city, situated on a hill; the Mexican Army was able to pick its targets with ease. Even so, the Americans were well on their way to taking the city when the point of attack was abruptly changed by an untalented brigade commander. Consequently, the Mexicans gained the upper hand, forcing the Americans to retreat with heavy losses. But Watson rallied "Baltimore's Own," attacked again — and was shot dead by a Mexican rifleman.

After the battle had been won, Colonel Watson's body was shipped to Baltimore and interred with much ceremony in Green Mount Cemetery. That was in 1846; a few months later, in 1847, the city councilmen honored their former colleague by passing an ordinance which changed the name of Salisbury Street to Watson Street. It is located one block south of Baltimore Street, and extends east from High to Central Avenue.

March 5, 1950

Webster

By William Stump

If it had not been for the sharp ears and accomplished gunnery of Lt. John Adams Webster, the British might have established a beachhead to the west of Fort McHenry during the bombardment of 1814, and the fort might have fallen.

For it was Webster, the young man in command of the "exposed six-gun battery" between McHenry and Fort Covington, who heard the British barges approaching to make an attempt to land troops.

It was midnight, September 13, 1814; Webster was taking a cat nap at the time. The sound of the barges awakened him, giving him the opportunity to alert his men. Then the battery poured 18-pound balls and grapeshot in the direction of the noise, and routed the invaders.

Not that the action was cut and dried. Webster, a naval officer who had been detached from the battered American flotilla, had a lot to do besides aiming his guns.

Finding that he was short of men at the height of the engagement and fearing that the enemy would succeed in landing some soldiers, he sent a midshipman named Andrews to a nearby battery to fetch some men that he had loaned the day before. The midshipman ran all the way to town, telling everyone that Webster had run from the battery, letting the British land.

On top of this, to use Webster's own words:

"I had my right shoulder broken by a handspike, and subsequently broken again, which rendered me a complete invalid. During the fight, one of my seamen, an obstinate Englishman, attempted to lay a trail of powder to the magazine; without thought, I laid him out for dead with a handspike."

"He, however, came to and crawled off before the fight ended, and he and Andrews were ever after among the missing."

Though in pain, Webster directed his guns against the retreating barges. The next morning, while preparing for another possible attack, he and his men found "upwards of 20" enemy cannon balls in the area. Webster loaded his guns with them, "having a wish to return the enemy their own property."

After a few more days, Webster contracted bilious fever, which in combination with his broken shoulder, forced him to leave his battery. Later, he received a pension of $20 a month for his injuries, a gold sword from the city of Baltimore and another gold sword from the state. Both of these swords are now in the possession of the Maryland Historical Society.

Webster apparently received another honor a few years later, when a state commission published a map which was to serve as the plan for Baltimore's development. The map showed a great number of projected streets; these were named for prominent Marylanders.

According to the records, Webster Street was named for John Adams Webster. It is in South Baltimore, in the vicinity of other streets named for war heroes of the same war, and extends from a point north of Key Highway south to Wells Street.

The incident in the defense of Baltimore was only one chapter in the adventurous life of John Adams Webster. Born in Harford County in 1789 — his mother was related to President John Adams — he left home at the age of 14 and went to sea.

When the War of 1812 began he promptly volunteered, joining Commodore Joshua Barney on the privateer Rossie. He took part in all of Barney's actions up and down the Chesapeake and was present when the illustrious man's gunboats were scuttled at Pig Point.

Not long after, Barney's men served as artillerymen at the Battle of Bladensburg, and were about the only troops which stood and fought. Barney was wounded and captured; the men, Webster included, finally had to retreat.

Webster later wrote that he scurried through Washington, picking up as many horses and cannon as he could. But his effort was in vain, for retreating militiamen stole the horses, forcing him and a handful of men to walk back to Baltimore. He was in time to take command of the battery on the Patapsco.

After the war, Webster joined the Revenue Cutter Service, the forerunner of the Coast Guard, and served on a number of ships in Chesapeake Bay. When the Mexican War came, he went into action again, commanding a small flotilla of gunboats on the Rio Grande. A newspaper obituary shows that he took part in the battle of Vera Cruz.

Webster eventually became a captain and the senior officer of the revenue service. He retired to Harford County when the Civil War was in progress and lived out the rest of his life at the Mount, a mansion now owned by his descendants. He died at the age of 88 in 1877.

November 19, 1950

Wells, McComas

By James C. Bertram

There was nothing particularly outstanding about Daniel Wells and Henry McComas.

They were just apprentice boys who spent their days hard at work in two smelly Baltimore saddle factories. Good, decent boys, yes. But not the sort that anyone, back in 1814, gave much mind. Not the sort of boys anyone would expect to become heroes.

Yet Wells and McComas did become heroes — two of the best loved and most celebrated in Baltimore history. They did not expect the designation, and they did not know of it, for in the process of becoming heroes they were killed.

It happened at the Battle of North Point, the battle in which a bunch of Baltimore bankers, lawyers, merchants and printers saved their city by trouncing some of England's finest troops. That the battle resulted in such a victory for American (or more properly, Baltimore) arms was due in no small way, according to legend, to 19-year-old Dan Wells and 18-year-old Henry McComas.

The boys were credited with shooting the British commander, Maj. Gen. Robert Ross, shortly after the bat-

Wells & McComas Monument – 1947

tle began, thereby robbing the British of a great deal of effectiveness. That they actually did shoot him, however, is strongly believed or strongly questioned or strongly doubted; the boys could not say, for they died in the battle. But that they came to be regarded as heroes is something over which there is no argument at all.

There is a Wells and McComas monument in Baltimore's Ashland Square; the boys are buried beneath it. There is a Wells Street and a McComas Street, located on Locust Point, a section that abounds in streets named for heroes of the War of 1812.

McComas Street extends east from Hanover Street to Key Highway. Wells parallels a railroad track a little to the north; it is a cindered alley that is a far cry from the handsome thoroughfare envisaged by the state commission that named it in 1820.

Wells and McComas became Baltimore heroes shortly after the battle. No one in the city doubted that they shot General Ross, for Dr. Samuel Martin, a respected medical man, said he had seen them do it and had then seen them fall.

The apprentices were riflemen in Captain Aisquith's company of sharpshooters, which on the first day of the battle was sent forward, along with a number of other companies of Major Heath's battalion, 5th Maryland, to feel out the enemy and fight a holding action with him. Dr. Martin, surgeon of Major Heath's battalion, went along.

In the deep woods east of Boulden's Farm, the Baltimoreans discovered the scarlet-coated British soldiers. There was sporadic firing; the Baltimore men advanced a little through the thick forest. There was more firing, a great deal of confusion and running around. The men moved back a little, became more confused and moved back some more, this time with a great deal of haste.

Riding toward the noise of the firing was Major General Ross, a professional soldier who had fought in Egypt, Portugal, Italy and France. The general was not terribly concerned about the success of the battle; his men had routed the civilians-playing-at-soldiers at Bladensburg, and could certainly do it again.

Besides, he had just enjoyed a good breakfast at the Gorsuch Farm, not far behind him. There, when Gorsuch had asked him if he would return for supper that night, he replied, "I'll sup tonight in Baltimore or in hell!"

In the American front line — if little groups of men among the trees could be called a line — were Wells and McComas. The legend has it that they saw Ross approaching with his staff and recognized his white horse.

"Dan, I see a mark," Henry McComas is supposed to have said.

"So do I," his friend replied.

They fired. The figure on the white horse leaned forward, dropping the reins from his hands; a colonel caught him as he began to fall. As this was happening, the British skirmishers saw Wells and McComas and fired, killing them instantly.

There are other versions. Wells family tradition holds that the boys hid near a spring and shot the general when he stopped for water. The McComas family says the shooting was no chance thing; that Henry, having had the plume of his hat shot off at Bladensburg, vowed to kill the general. "Here goes for a golden epaulet or a wooden leg," he told his family as he left for North Point.

Many historians say that someone in Captain Howard's Mechanical Volunteers killed Ross, that Aisquith's men were elsewhere. A British account written by the general's courier says the men who fired were three in number; that one was in a tree, the others laden down with canteens, giving the appearance of a water party. Then there is a dispute as to what type of bullet killed the general.

Who, though, can really say whether or not the apprentice boys killed Ross? A battle is a confused thing; troops get mixed up, and each man who took part remembers the fighting differently, in his own way. Can anyone prove it beyond a doubt?

But what matter? On future Defenders' Days, as on past ones, Baltimore schoolchildren will hear the story of Wells and McComas.

And they will believe, because they want to believe, that young Dan Wells and young Henry McComas shot the British general and helped save the city.

July 1, 1951

Whittier, Bryant and Ruskin

By William Stump

William Morris Orem, the master of a famous and handsome Baltimore estate called Auchentoroly, must have loved poetry. Evidence that he did can be seen in the names of a number of streets.

These streets are Whittier, Bryant and Ruskin avenues. Orem is believed to have created them around the turn of the century when he broke up Auchentoroly, situated at the southwest corner of Druid Hill Park, for real estate development.

"From everything, I've heard about Mr. Orem, it would have been characteristic of him to choose the names of poets for his streets," says Mrs. William Chase Orem, his daughter-in-law.

"I've never heard him spoken of as anything but an unusually cultured and brilliant man — one of the most brilliant in Baltimore in the latter years of the Nineteenth Century."

He named Auchentoroly Terrace after the estate on which, Mrs. Orem says, he spent most of his life, living as a country squire; his father, John Morris Orem, was an extremely wealthy man. "It was the kind of living that doesn't exist anymore," says Mrs. Orem wistfully.

The house, Mrs. Orem remembers her husband saying, was large and magnificent; it was surrounded by ancient trees, smooth lawns, well-kept gardens and color-laden greenhouses. Along the handsome lane that led to its front door — an almost equally handsome lane that led to the back door is now Orem Avenue — Baltimore's wealthiest families came for parties and balls, and Baltimore's intellectuals for good talk.

Perhaps that good talk took place on the wide, shaded verandas, or in the big library of the house, among the works of John Greenleaf Whittier, William Cullen Bryant and John Ruskin; perhaps the talk concerned these men and their poetry.

There is no telling, of course, why Orem chose to name streets for those particular men; certainly, he must have been impressed with their genius. But the three had one thing in common that may have appealed to him — they wrote rather extensively of the glories of nature. Orem, among his trees and gardens in an area that was almost entirely unspoiled, may have felt a kinship with them for that reason.

Then too, Orem would have felt closer to those poets than most readers of today. For Whittier, Bryant and Ruskin, at the time the Orems were living at Auchentoroly, were alive and enjoying a respect that few, if any, poets enjoy today.

Bryant, for example, who wrote "Thanatopsis" when he was 19, was as respected as any man in the nation. Not only his poetry, but his editorship of the New York Evening Post, a paper which raised the level of American journalism to a respected station through his editorials and policies, won him admiration.

Whittier was also a national figure, and had been since long before the Civil War; the New England Quaker's volumes of nature poetry, his ballads, many of them directed against slavery, and his spiritual verse were in thousands of American homes.

Ruskin, the Englishman, through his articles and essays on natural beauty and the arts, plus his verse, epitomized culture and intelligence.

Bryant died in 1878, Whittier in 1892 and Ruskin in 1900. Soon after, Auchentoroly and the man who lived the good life there had also gone.

February 8, 1948

Wilkens

By Karen Richards

William Wilkens was a man with a vision.

When he deeded 33 acres of his estate to the city of Baltimore in 1870, he foresaw the development of a neighborhood of comfortable homes set on streets that would (the story goes) bear the names of members of his family — among them his wife, Catherine, and three of his sons, Wilhelm, Christian and Charles.

But Baltimore already had one Charles Street, the familiar thoroughfare running north and south, and the city officials saw no reason to repeat the name, even though Wilkens' new street running east and west with a wide area of green park down the center would possibly rival the original in elegance.

The settled the problem by calling the new thoroughfare Wilkens Avenue, and so it stands today. Nearby, in comfortable family proximity, are Catherine, Wilhelm and Christian streets.

As streets go, Wilkens Avenue is not old. Though it has grown from an initial length of a few blocks to a heavily traveled boulevard that stretches more than two miles before it ends at Rolling Road, beyond the city limits, there are people who remember the man for whom it was named.

He came to Baltimore in 1843 and established a hair-processing factory that grew into one of the largest industries in the city during the last century.

Wilkens was German-born. When he arrived in the United States he had 18 cents in his pocket — but a plan for making a fortune. Those were the days when ladies wore hats and chignons and false curls, and Wilkens saw the opportunities in the business of manufacturing hair products. After he had obtained capital for his enterprise by working as a trader between New Orleans and Texas, he decided that Baltimore would be the best place for his plant.

Renting a part of Colson's glue factory he commenced the business that was to make him wealthy. As his firm outgrew its original plant, he leased a 100-foot lot on Frederick Road, near the Carroll estate, and moved his factory there.

The building was located in a shallow valley called Snake Hollow and the uninitiated said it was fortunate the factory

Wilkens Avenue – 1930

was set in a hollow because that kept down the aroma which hovered over the place, the odor of scalded hair laid out to dry.

Subsequently the factory was expanded to cover 15 acres, and there were 150 acres about it to accommodate the workmen's homes. It was part of this land that Wilkens gave to the city, taking in the beds of such present-day streets and McHenry, Monroe and Bentalou, as well as Wilkens Avenue.

The plant at one time employed 700 people. There were branches in New York, Chicago and St. Louis. The first telephone in Baltimore was set up between the Wilkens factory and its warehouses on Pratt Street. Wilkens was the founder of the railroad that used to run between Baltimore and Catonsville.

Wilkens liked to share the benefits of his money. He patronized musical events in the city and was one of the supporters of the old Concordia Opera House. He built homes for his employees and at Christmas time presented gifts to each.

He personally saw to the development of the park area down the original seven blocks of Wilkens Avenue. With the widening of the traffic lanes on Wilkens Avenue, the park was cut to the size of a safety island.

He once erected a monument to a horse on the lot across the street from the Wilkens home.

Wilkens was married three times and had seven children. He died in 1879.

Twice efforts have been made to change the name of Wilkens Avenue; each time the attempt has been thwarted. In 1932, someone thought it would be a good idea to call the street Sunset Boulevard, but the idea was so coldly received that it was never more than a thought. In March 1941, the City Council took action to change the name to Crozier Boulevard, honoring one of the former engineers of Baltimore City, and the measure was signed by the mayor.

Overnight, the citizens of Wilkens Avenue, many of them descendants of the men and women who had worked in the hair factory, rose to the defense of their street. The vigor of their protests moved the City Council to act promptly to change Crozier Boulevard back to Wilkens Avenue. It seems likely to stay that way.

Wilkens Avenue – 1948

March 20, 1949

Winans

By Henry C. Rauch

The story of a fortune made from engineering projects in Russia a century ago lies behind the name of Winans Way, which runs north through Hunting Ridge from Edmondson Avenue to Leakin Park, and then on in the park to Franklintown Road.

The street gets its name from Thomas Winans, for the park to which it leads was once that man's country place — named Crimea in memory of his Russian experiences, just as his city estate was Alexandroffsky.

Thomas Winans was a son of Ross Winans, the inventor and engineer who played a big part in the Baltimore and Ohio Railroad's early history. Thomas was born in New Jersey, on December 6, 1820, but was brought to Baltimore when 10 years old.

Proving to inherit his father's mechanical bent, he was apprenticed to a machinist after only a common-school education. He showed such skill that at the age of 18 he was entrusted with the delivery of some locomotives to a New England railroad, and before he was 21 was made head of a department in his father's engine works.

His New England trip proved momentous, for on it he is said to have first met George W. Whistler, who was later called to Russia as a consulting engineer of a projected St. Petersburg-Moscow railroad. And Whistler accepted Thomas and his brother William as substitutes when in 1843 Ross Winans declined an invitation to head the mechanical department of the

Thomas Winans' estate — Alexandroffsky – 1925

Russian line.

With two Philadelphia men, Thomas Winans obtained a contract to equip the Russian line with rolling stock. Shops were established near Alexandroffsky, near St. Petersburg.

Other contracts followed, netting huge profits, and Winans' Russian stay stretched to five years. In 1847, he married a Russian woman. In 1851, he finally returned to America, leaving his brother to wind up their work.

Here he purchased the country estate of a couple hundred acres that he named Crimea, and the city place he called Alexandroffsky — it occupied the block bounded by Fremont Avenue, and Hollins, Callender and Baltimore streets.

In 1866, Winans again went to Russia on an eight-year contract, but after only two years the czar's government took over the work and released his firm, with the payment of a large bonus.

Thenceforth, except for some visits to Europe, and to Newport, R.I., where he also had a villa, Winans spent his time in Baltimore, devoting himself to invention as a pastime. The most noteworthy of his products was a cigar-shaped hull that he and his father devised for high-speed ocean vessels — the prototype of modern hulls.

Less significant among his diverse inventions were a mode of increasing the volume of sound of a piano; a method of ventilation that he installed at Alexandroffsky; and glass feeding vessels for fish, which were adopted by the Maryland Fish Commission.

Winans died, at Newport, on June 10, 1878. His brother William never got back from Russia; his health broke there, and he died on the way.

Former site of Thomas Winans' estate – 1947

April 9, 1950

The Winders

By William Stump

Winder Street, a wide thoroughfare in conception, but a cindered alley in reality, is named for one of Maryland's prominent men in the War of 1812.

Just which one, city records fail to reveal.

Located in an area where nearly every street bears the name of a hero of that war, Winder Street may be named for Levin Winder, Maryland's governor during the war, or for his cousin, Gen. William Henry Winder, the man who led Maryland's troops to the worst defeat of the war.

The governor, who armed the state when President Madison refused to do so, aroused the fighting spirit of the citizens and helped plan the successful battle of North Point, was regarded as a hero; the general, whose failure at Bladensburg led to the burning of Washington, was not.

It seems logical, therefore, that the state commission that named Winder Street — sometime between 1818 and 1823 — intended to honor the governor.

There is irony in Levin Winder's reputation as a hero of the war, for originally he was opposed to fighting the British. This was not surprising — he was a spokesman for the Federalist party, which was very much against the war.

For their stand, the Federalists were decidedly unpopular, especially in Baltimore. In fact, the Republicans — as the Democrats were called in those days — went so far as to burn the offices of a Federalist newspaper.

That act had a strange effect, though, for instead of hurting the Federalists, it turned public sentiment, especially in the counties, in their favor. As a result, Winder, the Federalist majority leader in the House of Delegates, was elected governor in 1812.

In spite of his feeling against the war, Winder was aroused by subsequent British raids on Maryland soil, and appealed to the president to arm the state. The president would not, on the grounds that Maryland was Federalist-controlled. So Winder called a special session of the General Assembly and demanded that the members give him enough money to buy arms.

Those arms, under Levin Winder, who as governor was commander in chief, defeated the British at North Point. As far as most Marylanders felt, the victory made up for the earlier defeat of Gen. William Henry Winder at Bladensburg.

General Winder was in complete command at Bladensburg. The fault for the defeat, in the final analysis, was his. Most historians believe that he was incompetent, and had no business leading the militia.

After the war, General Winder returned to his prosperous law practice in Baltimore. He lived as a respected citizen, and when he died, the citizens, forgetting or not blaming him for Bladensburg, buried him with a great deal of ceremony.

That was in 1824, a year after a map showing many proposed streets, among them Winder, was published. The street was envisaged as a fine thoroughfare, running west from the Middle Branch of the Patapsco to a point near Fort McHenry.

Today, though, no signs mark Winder Street, for it is a dirty unpaved alley extending from Light Street on the east to a trash heap near Hanover Street. Lost in the wilderness under the Hanover Street bridge, it takes up again at Race Street, and extends through the plant of a chemical company to the B.&O. property. Few people who work in the area have ever heard of Winder Street.

In many ways, the lives of the governor — he died in 1819 — and the general were similar. Both men were born in Somerset County, of well-to-do parents. Both were educated as lawyers. Both saw active and bloody military service — Levin at Long Island and Camden in the Revolution, William Henry at Stony Point and Bladensburg in the War of 1812. Both were prominent men. But Levin Winder was the luckier one.

May 8, 1949

Wolfe

By Henry C. Rauch

A reminder of the Colonial days when British heroes were Baltimore heroes lies in the name of Wolfe Street. For although documents as late as 1799 and 1801 sometimes also spell the name "Woolf" and "Wolf," antiquarians say that General James Wolfe, the conqueror of Montcalm and Quebec, is the man after whom it was called when the first part of it was laid out.

That first part, from which the street gradually thrust northward across East Baltimore all the way to Clifton Park, was the part on Fells Point that almost touches the harbor. That was laid out, Thomas Bond states in a legal document dated near the end of 1782, by his father John Bond, "above nineteen years ago" — around 1763.

In 1763, the great victory that Wolfe achieved at Quebec had just borne its final fruit. In February of that year, by the Treaty of Paris that closed their Seven Years' War, France had yielded up all of Canada to Britain.

James Wolfe was born in Kent on January 2, 1727, the son of a soldier who himself reached the rank of lieutenant general. From his earliest years, the son, too, was determined to be a soldier, and in 1741 — when only 14 years of age — received a commission in the marines. The next year, he transferred to the line, was sent to Flanders as an ensign, and then throughout the War of the Austrian Succession was on active service.

Wolfe's intelligence and zeal won him steady advancement until at the age of 22 he was a major in acting command of a regiment. In another year, he was a lieutenant colonel. Then in 1757, after Britain had begun the Seven Years' War against

Wolfe Street – 1956

France, he was made quartermaster general of an expedition against Rochefort.

That expedition failed, but again Wolfe won attention; there was a strong belief that if its commanders had adopted plans that he suggested, it would have succeeded. As a result, Wolfe was made a brigadier in the force sent to capture Cape Breton and Quebec in 1758.

Soon after his return to Britain from that campaign — a full colonel, now — he was raised again to the rank of major general and given command of the expedition that was to assail Quebec anew.

Leaving England early in 1759, Wolfe mustered his 9,000-odd troops at Louisburg, and the force arrived before Quebec in the last week of June. Heights across the St. Lawrence River from Quebec were captured, and the city shelled from there. Also a camp was established at the mouth of the Montgomery River, between which and the city Gen. Louis Joseph Montcalm, the French commander in Canada, had entrenched nearly his entire army.

To the puzzlement of the British, Montcalm made no attack on that camp, and so finally at the end of July, Wolfe himself attacked. This time his strategy failed and he suffered a costly repulse, but shortly afterward he and his brigadiers devised a plan that succeeded.

A British force was sent well upriver beyond Quebec, and then part of it was secretly brought down again and landed by night at a spot only a mile and a half from the city. Montcalm was forced to attack without real preparation, and although there were five days of fighting before the city's capture was completed, the issue was never in doubt.

Ironically, both Wolfe and Montcalm were mortally wounded in the first day's fighting. Wolfe died that same day, September 13, 1759, and Montcalm the next day.

INDEX
(In alphabetic order)

Street Names

Photographs

With grateful acknowledgment to the staff and
pages of The Baltimore Sun and The Sunday Sun.

Special thanks to The Sun's librarian, Paul McCardell

THE BOOK STAFF

Article and Photographic Researcher: Zachary J. Dixon

Arranged By: Zachary J. Dixon

Newsroom Editor: Jennifer Badie

Book and Cover Design: Marsha Miller

Project Manager: Zachary J. Dixon